AMERICAN PISTOL SHOOTING

AMERICAN PISTOL SHOOTING

Major William D. Frazer

Skyhorse Publishing

First published in 1929
First Skyhorse Publishing edition 2015

Skyhorse Publishing books may be purchased in bulk at special discounts for sales promotion, corporate gifts, fund-raising, or educational purposes. Special editions can also be created to specifications. For details, contact the Special Sales Department, Skyhorse Publishing, 307 West 36th Street, 11th Floor, New York, NY 10018 or info@skyhorsepublishing.com.

www.skyhorsepublishing.com

10 9 8 7 6 5 4 3 2 1

Library of Congress Cataloging-in-Publication Data is available on file

Cover design by Owen Corrigan
Cover photo credit: Thinkstock

Print ISBN: 978-1-62914-386-6
Ebook ISBN: 978-1-62914-856-4

Printed in the United States of America

CONTENTS

The use of the finger joints. Side pressure. Rapid
squeezing. Trigger squeeze exercises. Value of
smooth clean triggers.

The solutions of aiming problems. Principles and
methods. The sight picture. Binocular aiming. The
master eye. The normal method of aiming. Other
methods. The effects of the grip on sight settings.
How to "sight in" a pistol. Rules for adjustment.
Sights. Advantages of large sights. Bead and blade
sights. Sporting sights. Eyesight and shooting
glasses. Light effects. Artificial light problems. A
solution. Effects of light changes. Calling the shot
and its value in aiming.

The advantages of accurate rapid shooting. The development of co-ordination. "Freezing." Practicability of rapid fire. A demonstration. Revolvers or
automatics for rapid fire. Basic principles of shooting
against time. Starting positions. Time wasting movements. The line of sight. Catching the aim. Revolver manipulation. Double action. Volume of fire.
Three methods of cocking. Rapid fire exercises.
Firing intervals. Automatic pistol exercises.

Origin of the game. The International Shooting
Union. Rules for practice. The main objective.
Time limits. Targets and ranges. Free pistols de-
scribed. The technique of their use. Set triggers.
Holding and gripping. Touching or squeezing. Ap-
plication of American methods. Customs at compe-
titions. Attractions of the game. Its advantages.
Popularity in America.

How to get speed out of a single-action revolver. How to attain skill in gun pointing. The personal equation in defensive shooting.

A few points of especial interest to police officers. What is practical police practice? How should it be taught? Pistols versus fists. The trend of police thought. Evidences of greater interest in police marksmanship. Instructors for the police. Desirable practice. Encouragement of police teams. The National Police Team match. Police ranges. Police tactics. How to fire from kneeling, sitting and prone positions. Taking cover. Guarding the flanks and rear. Covering a crook. Firing at running criminals. Hints on disarming. Firing with both hands. Three methods. Poor tactics when under fire. Remedies. Double action work. Methods of carrying guns. The best holster for police work.

Why exhibition shooting? Amateur and professional work. What the crowd likes. Faking and legitimate shooting. The average stage exhibition. The showman's viewpoint. The average person's knowledge of shooting. Difficulties of shooting before a crowd. How to please an audience. Alibis. Necessity for rehearsals. Working out a program. The set-up. Suitable targets. How to prepare one's self. Lights and distances. Single shots. Firing with both hands. Breaking moving and stationary targets simultaneously. Splitting cards. The most satisfactory bullets. Hitting without sights. Mirror shots. William Tell stunts. Their dangers. Aerial stunts. Outlining designs. Toy balloon shooting. The ignorant critic.

Overweight triggers. Preparation of equipment. Checking sights. Inspecting ammunition. Blackening sights. Familiarity with rules and conduct of matches. Behavior on the firing line. Marking and scoring. Challenges. Safety regulations. Last-minute advice. Check list of equipment for firing line.

The coaching instinct. What are the qualifications of a good coach? The necessity for studying individual shots. Dividing marksmen according to temperament. The characteristics of each group. How should individuals in each group be handled? How to treat the pessimist, the optimist and the ornery types. Temperament not to be tolerated on a team. The organization and training of a team. The Team Captain. The Coach. Duties of each. The Supply Officer. The undesirable team official. A training plan outlined. The selection of a team. How not to select a team. Coaching on the line. Checking up on equipment. Precautions for a coach. Discipline on the line. The technique of a good coach. Influence of the voice in coaching. The power of suggestion. Studying a shooter's technique.

A woman's inherent dread of firearms. Its cause and remedy. Confidence the first essential for a woman learning to shoot. Problems in instructing women. Can girls learn to shoot quicker than boys? A few experiences in handling girls' classes in rifle and pistol shooting. How to overcome the fear of pistols. Why a woman should learn to shoot. Target practice and shooting for personal protection. Small bore and large caliber work. Hints on selecting pistols. For target work. For self-defense. Recommendations. Is pistol shooting a suitable sport for ladies? Places to shoot. Out-of-doors. Indoors. The reward for a good shot.

Opportunities for shooting game with the pistol. Emergency game shooting. A State hunter's success. The game pistol as a supplementary arm. For trappers. Coyote shooting. Should heavy caliber pistols be carried when on a big game hunt with the rifle. The real reasons for game shooting with a pistol. Ruffed grouse shooting. The big rifle versus the pistol for small game shooting. Game shooting as a sporting proposition. Difficulties of hitting camouflaged game. The necessity for stalking. Squirrel shooting. The difference between animate and inanimate targets. How to sight a pistol for game shooting. The proper sights. The reason for overshooting. Suitable pistols and ammunition. Crippling game. Blue grouse shooting. Which type of hand gun is best for game shooting? The advantages of the revolver and automatic. Advantages of large calibers. A few recommendations. Shot pistols for game shooting. Targets for game shooting practice.

Long range controversies. Is the pistol an effective long range weapon? What are its possibilities? A comparison with long range rifle practice. "The Long-Shooters." Captain Hardy's demonstration. Other examples of long range work. A discouraging experience. The effects of poor ammunition. A satisfactory experiment in California. The value of a good coach in "doping" the wind. When not to shoot. The fall of a bullet at three hundred yards. A practical method of determining it. Small bore long range pistol work. Most pistol cartridges unsuitable for long range firing. Aiming errors. Advantages of a long sight radius. The best pistols for long shooting. The most accurate cartridges to use. A few recommendations. The question of long barrels. Sights for long range shooting.

The "Service" pistol. Its popularity today. Safety precautions for its use. Tests of its safety devices. Should it be carried with a cartridge in the chamber? Accidental discharges. The original and the improved models. How to grip this pistol. Wrist strain. How to eliminate it. An instructive experience. The position of the thumb. How to get a uniform grip. Mechanical defects and their remedy. Issue and match barrels. Jamming and its cause. The old and new sights. Heat waves and their effect on the sights. A study of the trigger action. The weight of trigger pull. The dangers of light pulls. The minimum weight for matches. Spongy trigger pulls. The reason for creep. Instructions in adjusting triggers. Emergency adjustments. Burnishing the sear. A safe procedure in working on a service pistol trigger. "Be sure you're right, then go ahead." Desirable tools for trigger work. Trigger weights. Leaving well enough alone. A summary of instructions.

The most important accessory to practical pistol work. Poorly constructed holsters an abomination. Holsters on the market today. Pistol cranks and holsters. Change in the design of military holsters. Most

proper way of cleaning pistols. Pistol cases, their
value, purpose and construction. A specially designed
carrying case. Pistol cabinets. How they should be
designed. The work bench. Spotting telescopes.
Binoculars. The stop watch. Cartridge blocks.
Medal cabinets. Pistol shooting literature. The
"Dope Book."

They speak for themselves.

FOREWORD

The main objective in mind in writing American Pistol Shooting was to provide a means of instruction in all forms of pistol practice in vogue in America today. Discussions of historical incidents and developments in arms have been reduced to a minimum and the text was planned so as to give progressive lessons in the fundamentals of shooting and in the more advanced steps of all-around practice. It should be of assistance to police officers and to military men in their professional training and of particular value to the young pistol enthusiast who lives in the country or the small community where instructors are not available.

When the Author took up the sport more than twenty years ago he had to learn it much as he did swimming and skating as a small boy, without instructors or the aid of books of any kind, and this handicap was keenly felt at times. It resulted in slow progress and many discouraging hours because of the necessity for correcting bad habits formed by lack of proper coaching. These difficulties are indelibly impressed on his mind and they, more than anything else, are responsible for this effort of a pistol shot to write a book about shooting for shooters.

Throughout the text the term "pistol" is applied indiscriminately to hand guns except where it is necessary to mention a particular arm, in which case, that arm has been accurately designated in accordance with modern practice.

The Author feels very grateful to all those who have assisted him in the preparation of this manual by suggestions, information and material and to that splendid body of sportsmen with whom he has spent many pleasant hours in friendly competition with the attendant benefits of valuable experience and. healthful recreation. To those pistol marksmen of an older generation who gave so willingly of their time and knowledge to him, a novice, he is doubly appreciative.

Thanks are also due to the publishers of "Field and Stream" for the use of material originally written for that magazine.

LIST OF ILLUSTRATIONS

AMERICAN
PISTOL SHOOTING

Chapter I

WHAT IT'S ALL ABOUT

PISTOL shooting was originally confined to the military and naval services, to that necessary for personal protection, and to the long countenanced practice of duelling.

The first weapons that rightly belong in the category of pistols were the crude cumbersome muzzle-loading matchlocks invented about the beginning of the sixteenth century, and their improved and immediate successors, the more efficient wheellocks. The wheellock dispensed with the inconvenient glowing match for igniting the priming charge and substituted therefor a lock so constructed that, by releasing a tightly wound spring, a notched steel disc or wheel was revolved at high speed against a stationary flint thereby producing a stream of sparks in the flashpan. Because of their size, these weapons were convenient only for mounted men and soon became generally known as horse or holster pistols.

Authorities differ as to the birthplace of the pistol and the origin of the name given the weapon. It is claimed to be so-called because its caliber was that of the coin known as the "Pistole." Some maintain that it was named after Pistoja, Italy, and others that it derives its name from the word "pistallo" which means pommel. Caminellio Vitelli is generally credited with having made the first model at Pistoja in 1540, but this

3

is disputed on the grounds that there were weapons of this type made previous to that date at Perugia, Italy, and elsewhere.

The value of the pistol for military purposes was appreciated soon after its invention. As early as 1550 the pistol was adopted for the French cavalry. It has always been well adapted to mounted service.

The invention of the flintlock about 1630 increased the dependability of small arms and made practicable the manufacture of pocket pistols in addition to increasing the output of the heavier Horse and Navy pistols. Weapons with this type of lock remained in use for over two centuries, and long after the invention of the percussion cap system of ignition in 1807.

In the last quarter of the eighteenth century when the small sword gave place to the pistol as a more equitable means of settling affairs of honor, the dueling pistol was perfected. This marked the first real strides in pistol shooting. During this period great impetus was given to gunsmithing by the demand for suitable pistols for this form of practice. This resulted in the manufacture of more accurate weapons and the development of better shooting. Pistol dueling became so firmly established in continental Europe that when it finally met with public disapproval and was largely discontinued, substitutes in the form of target practice at silhouette targets and duelling with wax bullets, was adopted by men interested in the sport of pistol shooting. These forms of practice are still followed to some extent in France today.

To the pistol enthusiasts of Europe we are also indebted for that highly refined form of practice known as "free pistol" shooting which is much in vogue today among pistol men of many nations, who are organized under the International Shooting Union. The International style of shooting is rapidly gaining favor in our country, increased no doubt by the several defeats administered to our teams in International Matches in recent years.

American pistol shooting began in colonial days with the introduction of European hand guns into the several colonies and the developments in the practice of dueling. Since that historic day on Lexington Green when the first shot of the Revolutionary War was fired from a Highland pistol by Major Pitcairn of the British Regulars, the pistol, and its contemporary arm, the rifle, have played an important rôle in the history, growth and development of our country. The pistol and revolver have also played a most unfortunate part in our national affairs and has been the cause of many ineffectual laws to control its unlawful use, and even its manufacture, sale and possession. The famous pistol duel that was the cause of the death of Alexander Hamilton at a time when the services of that brilliant statesman could ill be spared by his country, as well as the assassinations of Presidents Lincoln, Garfield and McKinley were deplorable examples of the misuse of pistols. When events of this nature are combined with the ruthless and despicable murders by gangs of bandits and gunmen in our large centers of population, it is not surprising that pistol shooting as a sport is condemned by many unthinking persons who do not appreciate that it has some benefits.

American literature is interwoven with innumerable

thrilling tales of travel, romance and adventure, in which the skillful use of pistols is exploited, and while much is fiction based on ignorance of the capabilities and limitations of weapons, these exciting stories are the results of the tremendous sale and use of pistols and revolvers during the expansion of our frontiers, the waging of Indian wars, the settlement of our western territories and the establishment of our social code in what was popularly known as the "Wild West." In addition to the use of pistols by our pioneers, our Army and Navy has always believed in the use of these weapons as side arms for our armed forces. The advantages of having a weapon that is instantly available for sudden emergencies has always been appreciated by our mounted services and they have always been equipped with the best available revolvers and pistols. These were especially useful during the Mexican, Civil, Indian and Philippine Wars because of the kind of warfare, the nature of the terrain, and the large proportion of mounted troops employed. Even today our Infantry divisions and field armies have a much greater preponderance of pistols than rifles in their tables of organization, and considerable emphasis has been placed on Pistol Marksmanship by the War Department. Our Navy and Marine Corps both use the same excellent automatic pistol that has been adopted by the Army as the official side arm. From 1799 to 1828 over fifty thousand flintlock Horse and Navy pistols were made for our Army and Navy by Simeon North of Berlin, Conn., first official pistol maker for our government. To North's has been added the famous names of Colt, Remington, Browning, and Smith and Wesson as the inventors or manufacturers of the celebrated pistols and revolvers with which our military and naval forces have been armed.

The use of the pistol and revolver by police and constabulary officers is of importance second only to that of their use by military personnel. The revolver has long been the chief arm of reliance of law enforcement officers. The automatic pistol is now being adopted for the same purpose. United States Marshals, County Sheriffs, State Constabularies and municipal police officers have been armed with hand guns since they became practical. Skill in their use by such officials has always been in accordance with the demand and necessity for marksmanship, good, poor or indifferent.

Within the last ten years there has been a decided increase in pistol practices on the part of municipal and other police forces. Whether or not this is due to the increased activities of gunmen, bandits, hijackers and bootleggers, or to the realization that a straight shooting police force which shoots to kill is much more efficient than one composed of poor pistol marksmen cannot be definitely stated. It is apparent in some places, however, that the necessity of checking the increasing "hold-ups," robberies and homicides by more drastic methods than those that have failed in the past, has resulted in many of our large city governments installing pistol ranges, appointing competent instructors, and requiring of their police a certain standard of marksmanship with the pistol. New York, Philadelphia, Seattle, Los Angeles, Toledo, and Portland, Oregon, have made great headway in properly arming, instructing and training their police forces, and the moral effect of this intensive work on the criminal element has been quite noticeable and well worth the efforts and expense involved.

Aside from its use in self defense, home defense, for the enforcement of laws, or for military purposes, the pistol has been the means of providing a beneficial form of recreation. Pistol target shooting has been practiced with much profit and pleasure for many years and interest in it has always been retained by those, who as the result of the development of skill in the art, have become pistol enthusiasts. Once a pistol shot, always a pistol shot, is a familiar slogan among devotees of the art of pistol shooting.

State laws, passed for the avowed purpose of reducing crime, often restrict the manufacture and sale of pistols suitable for home and personal defense and even those adapted to recreation or military shooting. These laws are generally ineffectual and more harmful to our country and to Americans than their advocates realize. The criminal will never be without suitable weapons for the commission of crime, whether they be knives, pistols, blackjacks, machine guns, or what not, no matter how drastic the laws forbidding their possession. Unreasonable, poorly conceived laws which may prevent law-abiding citizens from possessing suitable weapons with which to protect themselves, their homes, and their property from highwaymen, burglars and reckless hoodlums not only work injustice to good citizens but indirectly aid and abet the criminal. Any sensible law which tends to put all possible obstacles in the way of undesirable gentry securing and carrying pistols and at the same time makes it possible for reputable persons to possess and use these weapons for proper personal or property protection, for training for national defense, and in the pursuit of happiness in healthful recreation will always receive the support of right thinking people and particularly those who follow pistol shooting as a sport and pastime.

The popularity of target shooting has increased with the improvements in the accuracy of pistols. Whereas fifty years ago certain favorite frontier models were most popular, nowadays the civilian pistol shot's fancy turns to the more accurate small caliber revolvers, "automatics," and single shot pistols. The methods of firing have also changed and the skill of the practical frontiersman in quick drawing, gun pointing and snap shooting has given way very largely to modern super accurate deliberate fire and to well coördinated rapid and timed fire. This shooting now consists of firing a group of shots within short time limits at disappearing or bobbing targets.

A certain group of enthusiasts still prefer the practice of bygone days and they get much pleasure and very practical training out of practicing quick drawing and snap shooting, at moving targets. Regardless of a tendency to overrate skill of our pioneer pistol shots, credit must be given to the experts of that period for the cleverness they developed with the ammunition and arms then available. They deserve a place in the hall of fame for their mastery of the art of pistol shooting as practiced at that time, for they pointed the way to a new sport, in which we as followers thereof now derive much pleasure and profit. The names of Travers, Cody, Hickok, Paine and others will always be to pistol shots as inspiring as the names of Boone and Crockett are to riflemen.

Chapter II

PISTOL SHOOTING CLASSIFIED

WHEN a person takes up a new sport or hobby in earnest it is usually with a definite object in view. Though his ultimate achievement may be different from his original purpose, he does have, nevertheless, something in mind when his enthusiasm is really aroused or he probably will not go beyond the stage of casual interest.

If we study the art of pistol shooting with the purpose of mastering the theory and practice as part of our professional education, as an army or police officer might do, we are then apt to solve its problems as we would any others that are incidental to our profession. If we learn to shoot a pistol because we have reasonable knowledge or assurance that our life may depend on our ability to draw quickly and fire rapidly and accurately at a time of great personal danger, this responsibility will cause us to put forth a maximum effort in learning the game, much as the pioneers did during the settling of our western frontier. If we have as our object the winning of a national championship, or the making of a national team we will approach the subject from an entirely different viewpoint than we would were we considering personal safety or professional efficiency as our chief objective. Likewise, if we follow the game mainly for pleasure and recreation we will probably solve its problems, enjoy its fascinations, and reap its rewards in a much different frame of mind than when more responsibility rests on the outcome of our efforts.

With the foregoing in mind we may divide present day pistol shooting into three classes:

(a) Military practice.
(b) Police and Defensive shooting.
(c) Recreational target practice.

A knowledge of the characteristics of each style of shooting, including the targets, weapons and methods of firing used, will aid a novice in deciding which kind of practice to take up and the proper pistols to select for the purpose.

Military shooting is practiced by the personnel of the Regular, Reserve, and National Guard components of the Army and Navy and in addition by many civilians who either acquired some skill and training in this class of shooting during the World War, or to whom big bore pistol shooting appeals much in the same way as do the fascinations and complications of heavy artillery to the Coast Artilleryman. To the man interested in National preparedness or military work of any kind, or to the one who likes to play with the highest powered weapons of the hand-gun game, or to those who feel that small bore shooting is a child's game, then, to them the military game with its variety, action and thrills opens a field of endeavor in which they can indulge with much profit and pleasure.

With all its fascinations however, military shooting would be very expensive were it not for the interest taken by the War Department in its encouragement. This department through the Director of Civilian Marksmanship sells pistol ammunition to members of the National Rifle Association at the Government price. As an incentive to attendance at the National Rifle and Pistol Matches, the War Department also issues without charge, selected match ammunition for practice and record shooting for all who participate in these matches thus permitting one to shoot as much as desired as long as he uses a pistol that is designed for the service ammunition.

In American pistol competitions a military pistol or revolver is defined as one of .38 or larger caliber that has been adopted by any civilized government for the armament of its Army and Navy, without modification or additions, with a minimum trigger pull of four pounds, and with substantial fixed front and rear sights of the general type made for military service.

Practice and pistol qualifications in the army consists of mounted and dismounted firing at various targets. At present, dismounted practice is limited to 25 yards although in the past some firing was done at 50 yards. Cavalrymen fire the dismounted course in the first year of their enlistment only, and thereafter the mounted course, while other branches of the service fire only the dismounted course.

The targets used are:

Target "E"; for quick fire in the dismounted course.
Target "M"; for the mounted course.
Target "L"; for the dismounted course.

They are shown herein.

The target used for general pistol practice in this country is the Standard American Target. It is required in pistol competitions conducted by the National Rifle Association, the United States Revolver Associa-

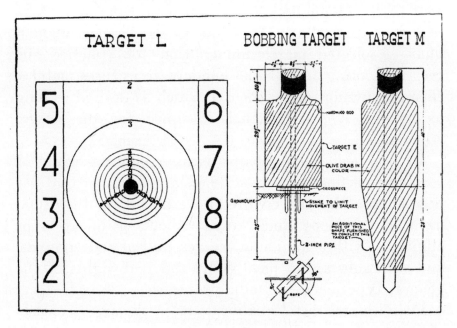

ARMY TARGET "L"

Ring		
10	5	inches
9	8.5	"
8	12.00	"
7	15.5	"
6	19.0	"
5	22.5	"
4	26.0	"
3	46.0	"
2	Remainder of 4' x6' target	

tion, and the United States Army and is an excellent practical target for slow or rapid fire. This target reduced in size is used for twenty yard indoor practice and competition.

The character of shooting is varied in military practice. In fact all military qualifications require skill in slow, timed, rapid and quick firing and it is this variety that makes it interesting, for it encourages the development of all-around pistol shooting. Many men can shoot well if they have plenty of time, but when they are limited to 10 or even 20 seconds for a string of five shots they lose their control and in their anxiety to get the required number of shots fired are very apt to jerk, flinch and otherwise shoot badly. Excellent military shooting is more difficult than it appears to be, not because of the targets used or the range at which it is done, but because of the heavier pistols with their greater recoil and the effects of both these factors on the muscles and nerves. After one has fired ten or more shots rapidly with the .45 caliber Service Automatic pistol or its contemporary a .45 military revolver, he may find that the repeated shock of the heavy recoil on his pistol hand has caused tremors in it, and this, exclusive of any nervousness due to mental agitation, makes steady holding more difficult and is conducive to flinching. If one uses a .38 caliber military revolver of reputable make designed for the .38 Special cartridge it will be found to be much more pleasant to shoot and will give most excellent results. It must be borne in mind however, that if one expects to compete against military automatics in rapid fire it will be necessary to develop great skill in manipulating the revolver as a single action gun, in order not to be put at a decided disadvantage in this kind of firing.

The rewards for military pistol shooting in addition

to the satisfaction that comes with the accomplishment of a worthy purpose are the ratings and badges given by the Government for qualification as Marksman, Sharpshooter, Pistol Expert and Distinguished Pistol Shot. These can be obtained by members of the military or naval services and by civilians who attend the National Rifle and Pistol Matches conducted by the War Department.

A practice pistol range at Camp Perry, Ohio.

Persons who qualify as pistol marksmen, sharpshooters and experts receive a silver badge indicating their qualification, while those who gain the coveted rating of Distinguished Pistol Shot receive a very handsome gold badge, the possession of which places them in an enviable position among marksmen.

Pistol practice for police officers, unlike that for the military personnel of the country, lacks uniformity.

The municipalities with well organized practice in pistol marksmanship are endeavoring to prescribe courses of fire that will simulate as far as possible the kind of firing that might be expected of officers on duty.   This may

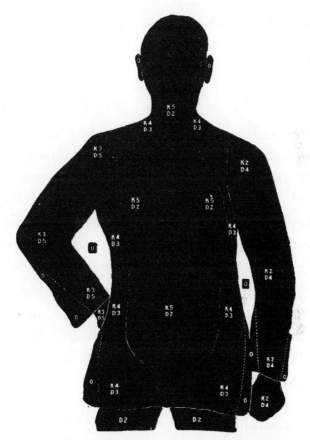

Colt's Police Silhouette Target.

consist of very close work in sudden emergencies in which quick drawing and shooting by instinctive pointing rather than by aiming may be necessary.   It may be more often at fleeing criminals concealed by darkness, at gangs of speeding automobile bandits, at mad dogs running amuck in crowded thoroughfares, and occasionally in riots to disperse mobs. Firing may be done from afoot, from a rapidly moving automobile, from a motorcycle or horseback but seldom from a position conducive to accurate shooting. Obviously the practical kind of training would be that similar to military practice, with emphasis placed on quick and rapid fire at silhouette targets either bobbing or moving. As in military shooting it is very essential that the novice police shot be trained first in slow fire and then in rapid shooting in order that the idea of accuracy be firmly instilled in his mind, after which he should practice at moving targets and should be taught certain tactics of police fire.

The main difference between police and military shooting is in the weapons used. The great majority of police departments arm their officers with .38 caliber revolvers or automatic pistols and these are usually of the pocket type with a barrel of four inches or less in length. Many police departments do not prescribe any particular type of weapon and consequently officers of such forces carry anything from .32 to .45 caliber. In certain sections of the country police officers are now arming themselves, or their municipalities are doing it for them, with .45 caliber pistols and revolvers which take the service ammunition. By purchasing ammunition through the government practice can be held with reasonable cost. It insures uniformity as well as efficiency in equipment as there are only a few weapons that take this cartridge at present and they are of reputable manufacture. The adoption of this heavier weapon really takes the police gun out of the pocket pistol class and necessitates, for quick work at least, that the pistol be carried in a belt or shoulder holster, and in addition makes the carrying of such weapons somewhat of an inconvenience except for the mounted patrolman. A well made .38 caliber pocket revolver designed for the .38 Special cartridge, with a good grip, four inch barrel and military sights is a fine shooting gun and accurate enough for target work up to fifty yards especially that kind of work in which police officers should be proficient. Defensive shooting in the protection of lives and property should be anticipated and prepared for in much the same manner as that for the police, and with similar weapons.

When one enters the field of recreational shooting there is spread before him many attractive phases of a sport incomparable for its variety, its fascinations and its liberal rewards. At once one finds himself in an environment of good fellowship with real sportsmen, with men of good habits and reputation, who follow the game because it is worth while. Here one finds an attractive and intriguing assortment of interesting hand guns with which to develop skill and gain healthful recreation. Let one who is interested in arms gaze upon and handle an assortment of beautifully polished pistols of superior workmanship, with their alluring and mysterious fascinations and suggestions of pleasure, sport and adventure, and he cannot help but feel his blood tingle, his enthusiasm kindle and his ambition whisper of skill to be acquired and worlds to be conquered.

At once the novice is struck with the fact that he must make a decision before he can get action in this broad field of pleasure shooting, and he must determine for himself whether he wants to do any of the standardized forms of target work or merely improve his skill and shoot for fun at miscellaneous targets. He must first decide between small bore and big bore work, or expressed differently, between twenty-two caliber shooting and that of the larger calibers. This should be an easy decision and one that is natural and logical, for, as the artillery gunner gains skill and accuracy in firing big guns by first firing Sub-caliber weapons, so should the pistol man first become proficient with an accurate, easy shooting, neat handling twenty-two pistol or revolver of good make such as are now available on the American market.

While it is by no means impracticable to become a good shot by starting with a thirty-eight or larger caliber pistol it is nevertheless more satisfactory, if good progress is desired, for the beginner to start with the smaller weapon and gradually work up to the heavier calibers.

The twenty-two weapon in addition to being much cheaper to shoot is more accurate and much more convenient and pleasant to fire. It is important to know in this connection that in many indoor ranges anything above twenty-two caliber is barred because of the noise, fumes and other disturbing features of the heavy weapons, to say nothing of the wear and tear on the backstops and adjacent fixtures. These objections apply out-of-doors to a less degree but one may avoid many embarrassing moments, caused by nervous neighbors or by overzealous police officials, if he uses a twenty-two target weapon and confines his big bore shooting to a properly equipped and operated range or to the open prairies, the mountains, or the heavily wooded country.

In addition to grouping pistol shooting under the three general heads just described, Standardized Pistol Practice might be divided into three classes:

(a) Target pistol shooting.
(b) Revolver shooting.
(c) Automatic pistol practice.

The first class is intended for single shot target pistols and deliberate firing. The second and third classes are frequently combined, in that matches are open to either revolvers or automatics, and the shooting is either slow, timed or rapid fire.

Target practice with single shot pistols is the most accurate kind of pistol shooting. In the United States today two methods are being followed. The majority of deliberate fire shots are practicing, as they have been for many years, under rules which restrict target pistols to ten inch barrels, to trigger pulls of not less than two pounds, and open sights located between the hammer and muzzle. Firing is done on the Standard American Target and must not be slower than fifty shots an hour. These rules practically leave the game open to American pistols only. The other style which is rapidly gaining favor, is the International or "Free Pistol" shooting of Europe, in which the only restriction as to weapons is that the sights must be open. The International target with a five centimeter center (less than two inches) is used at fifty meters (about 55 yards) and no time limit is fixed for completing a score. This class of practice demands the finest kind of shooting equipment and has been followed in Europe for many years though it is comparatively new to Americans. For its practice a special target pistol superior to any other type for the purpose, has been designed by the gunsmiths of Europe. Being hand made they are more expensive than American arms and the import duty adds considerably to

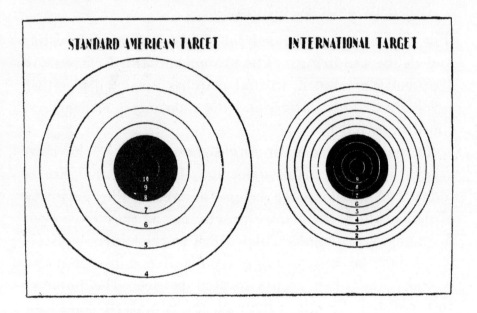

their cost. In either American or International target pistol shooting it is evident that only single shot target pistols are suitable or advisable for use if the best results are to be obtained, consequently a novice desiring to become strictly a target pistol shot should start with such a weapon.

For revolver or automatic pistol practice the novice will find matches for all models of these types of hand guns. There are matches for "Military revolvers or automatic pistols," for "Any revolver or automatic pistol" and for "Pocket revolvers or pocket magazine pistols." If one prefers either type of hand gun he can find plenty of opportunity to use it, especially in the heavier or military calibers.

The following tables give a comparison of the standard pistol targets in use today.

Ring	S. A. (50 yd. target)	International (50 meter (54.68 yds.) target)		S. A. (20 yd. target)
10	3.39 inches	5 centimeters = 1.9685 inches		1.15 inches
9	5.54 "	10 " = 3.937 "		1.88 "
8	8.00 "	15 " = 5.905 "		2.72 "
7	11.00 "	20 " = 7.874 "		3.74 "
6	14.80 "	25 " = 9.842 "		5.03 "
5	19.68 "	30 " = 11.811 "		6.69 "
4	26.83 "	35 " = 13.779 "		9.12 "
3		40 " = 15.748 "		
2		45 " = 17.716 "		
1		50 " = 19.685 "		

The Standard American 20 yard target is not reduced in proportion to the range at which it is used. The U.S.R.A. and the N.R.A. have, however, reduced the International target for 20 yard shooting indoors, in proportion to the range and this makes it out of proportion with the S.A. indoor 20 yard target.

The U.S.R.A. also issues a combination target with both the S.A. and the International rings on it, the former being printed in heavy circles and the latter in light circles.

The latest improvement in pistol targets is to change the old 50 yard Standard American target with its eight inch black aiming bull's-eye, which was always quite satisfactory for fifty yard shooting, to one more suitable for short range rapid firing. This has been accomplished by reducing the black so as to include only the

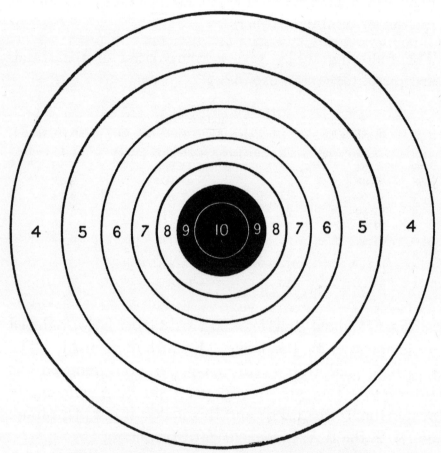

FIFTY YARD STANDARD AMERICAN PISTOL TARGET
FOR TWENTY-FIVE YARD RAPID AND TIMED FIRE

nine and ten rings with a total diameter of 5.54 inches. The new target has proven very satisfactory for the purpose intended and is now used in the timed and rapid fire matches held at Camp Perry each year. The diameter of all scoring rings remains the same as formerly.

A great many enthusiasts follow pistol shooting principally for fun. They see little sport in firing at paper targets once they have learned to shoot. They like the thrill of seeing something break or show some active sign of being hit, much as the trap shooter likes to see his targets fly into dust when he hits them. There is a thrill that comes from hitting miscellaneous targets of varying difficulty. The bottle or tin can bobbing on the water or rolling on the ground, growing acorns, walnuts or the round buttons of the sycamore tree all make fascinating targets at which to shoot. The man who lives in the cattle country of the West can show his skill by hitting the elusive prairie dog chattering over his burrow or the running jack rabbit or coyote scurrying through the underbrush, or in bringing to bag the wonderfully camouflaged sage chicken squatting under the bush from which it gets its name. Some fishermen like to carry an accurate revolver or automatic target gun with them on their trips to put the finishing touches to a fighting muskallunge or to cut off the annoying branch that has ensnared a trout fly in the overhead brush of a favorite mountain stream or to afford profitable recreation in camp on rainy days when time hangs heavily and the reading material is exhausted. There is a great deal of pleasure to be obtained from mastering the art of aerial shooting, that is, to hit objects thrown in the air. A novice wishing to excel in this kind of shooting will find it not so difficult to learn, but a game that requires good co-ordination, constant practice and the use of plenty of ammunition. It is most fascinating and to the layman the most spectacular and marvellous of all forms of pistol shooting. And incidentally it is the game to be avoided while one is training for any other forms of competition.

Chapter III

ON SELECTING PISTOLS

THE preceding chapter should furnish the necessary information to enable the novice to decide, if he has not already done so, on the form of pistol practice he desires to pursue, for until he has done this he cannot logically select his shooting equipment. Even with this decision made, there is such a variety of arms from which to choose that he can profitably give considerable study to the subject. There is no essential of the game in which one can go wrong more easily than that of selecting suitable pistols for the different classes of shooting. There is no one detail that will cause deeper regret to a novice than to buy the wrong kind of arm, especially if his funds are limited, and there is no greater pleasure to be experienced than that of having the most suitable equipment for the work to be done.

While proper ambition is always commendable, there are two things a novice must not expect or attempt to accomplish. He must not expect to become an all-around pistol shot in a month or a year and he must not attempt to find an all-around pistol, for it is not made. There are occasionally, however, several suitable pistols or revolvers for each class of practice and not infrequently we find several which are satisfactory for more than one kind of work. But, for example, there is no military hand gun at present manufactured that is suitable for free pistol shooting, and vice versa, free pistols are not suitable for military work, if the requisites of both kinds of practice are carefully considered.

Having decided on the character of shooting to be practiced, pistols should be selected with due regard to their mechanical efficiency and accuracy, their cost and that of the ammunition for which they are designed, as well as the availability of the latter, and finally with regard to their fit and balance. The best advice that anyone can follow in buying hand guns is to purchase the very best, from the standpoint of mechanical efficiency, reliability and accuracy, that one's funds will permit. The best is none too good for certain classes of work, whereas the low grade products made of poor materials and with inferior workmanship are a source of constant annoyance, discouragement and danger. Since the World War the American market has been flooded with cheap foreign revolvers and magazine pistols made to imitate, in appearance only however, the arms of our most reputable small arms manufacturers. They should be avoided in spite of their attractive prices. If one's funds are limited and his interest and desire to own a gun so keen that he feels he must buy a pistol, then by all means curb that enthusiasm until enough money is available to buy a weapon of at least reputable make.

The purchase of used or second hand pistols is not to be recommended unless one possesses reliable information concerning the actual condition of the action and of the barrel of the gun whose purchase is contemplated. A well worn bore carefully polished with emery dust may present a creditable appearance to a novice but

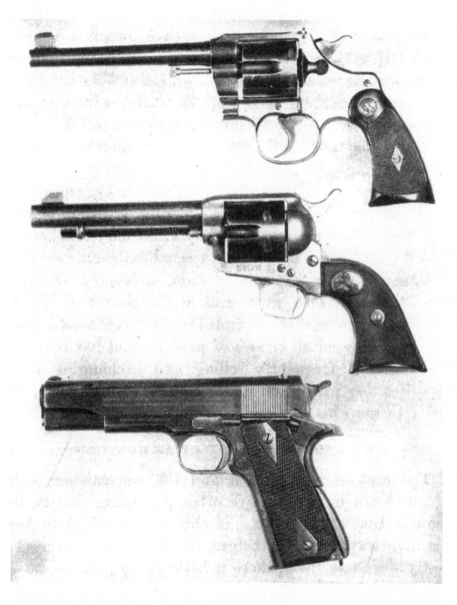

A Colt trio suitable for all-around big bore shooting. The Officers' Model, the Single Action Army and the Government Model automatic.

appearances are of minor importance compared to accuracy and reliability. A knowledge of the care and attention given a gun by the previous owner is a good guide but a thorough try-out of the pistol by an experienced shot is always preferable and desirable before a decision to purchase is made. It is also advisable for the prospective owner to try the pistol to see if it fits his hand, balances well, and has a satisfactory trigger pull.

While one's funds may be limited at times, especially when the initial purchases of a shooting outfit are made, it has been the experience of many who follow this hobby that it is not long before one's arsenal expands, perhaps sometimes at the expense of more necessary articles. Nevertheless it does grow and in the course of a few years the pistol enthusiast finds that he has the necessary arms to carry on all classes of practice and has reached the stage of frequently selling and exchanging first favorites for pistols of more modern manufacture, in order to keep his equipment up to date.

COST AND AVAILABILITY OF AMMUNITION

The cost of ammunition and the convenience with which it can be secured are often governing factors in the selection of any gun. If one cannot afford to fire the more expensive cartridges, or if he cannot conveniently purchase them, there is little or no point in buying a weapon designed for such ammunition, unless one does it merely for the sake of collecting rather than shooting. When we jump from the inexpensive small bore, rim fire ammunition, to the large caliber center fire cartridges with jacketed bullets, we at once increase the cost of our pleasure very materially and at the same time make more difficult the securing of ammunition, especially if we live in the more thinly populated parts of the world. Small town and country stores carry only the more popular cartridges and usually a very limited supply of these. In the days of the settlement of our Western Frontier, the difficulties of securing ammunition caused the most popular revolvers to be designed for the 44-40 or 44 Winchester rifle cartridge used so extensively in the rifles of that period. A glance through the catalog of an ammunition manufacturer will reveal the fact that there is a great variety of cartridges designed for an equally varied assortment of pistols and revolvers. The latter, like many other articles, have been designed to serve certain purposes, and the ammunition adapted to them has been made accordingly. Hence we find many pistol cartridges of the same caliber yet possessing decidedly different ballistics.

The popular .22 Short and .22 Long Rifle ammunition can be obtained nowadays wherever 12 gauge shotgun shells can be bought. In certain localities, the old favorite .44 Winchester and .45 Colt cartridge can still be readily obtained, and since the World War it is becoming much easier to buy the .45 Colt Automatic pistol cartridge for use in the official sidearm of the military Service, which has now become so popular. Aside from the ease of securing these cartridges, it is problematical if one can get his favorite .32 or .38 cartridge from the average small town hardware or sporting goods store and he must depend for his supply on a mail order house, or on the factory, which involves additional expense. The local situation in regard to the cost and supply of ammunition should be investigated as a pertinent item bearing on the choice of calibers.

FIT AND BALANCE

Shotgun experts continually harp on the necessity of fit and balance in a shotgun, especially in one for field shooting. They maintain that a gun with a good balance handles rapidly, and if it fits the shooter in such details as length of stock, thickness and shape of the comb, the length, shape, size of grip, the slant and shape of the butt plate and similar particulars, it can be shot with much better results, especially when it comes to quick shooting in thick cover, where aiming is the exception and gun pointing the rule. If it is desirable to have fit in a shotgun that throws several hundred shot at a target and makes a killing pattern thirty inches in diameter at forty yards, then it is extremely desirable to have a pistol that fits the hand and balances well if we wish to do accurate shooting, especially rapid shooting, with a weapon that fires only single bullets.

Fortunately for the wing shot, he can have a stock made for his shotgun that will fit his physique without interfering with the mechanism of his gun, whereas almost without exception the pistol shot must accept the product of the pistol maker as issued, inasmuch as the model or shape of the frame governs the size, shape and length of the grip and its distance from the trigger. The length and size of the barrel determines to a great extent the balance of the gun and its suitability for certain kinds of shooting. A pistol that is not well balanced when held in the hand in the normal shooting position, requires muscular effort to keep the muzzle up while aiming and when the hammer falls.   On the other hand, one that balances well does not require this effort and

The Author's favorite pocket battery. A specially made Colt Police Positive Special and a Remington Model 51 automatic.

consequently steadiness is maintained and sights kept in alignment more easily.   The weight of a pistol, while not exactly affecting its balance, does have an important bearing on the steadiness with which it can be held on a target, for very light long barrelled pistols are more affected by wind currents and nerve tremors than are those of greater weight and better balance. To test the balance, hold the pistol loosely in the shooting hand and with arm extended point the gun at a target. In the case of revolvers, support the gun mainly by the index finger held inside of the trigger guard, and when testing pistols of the automatic or European target type support the gun by the second finger under the guard. If the barrel remains horizontal without the necessity of gripping the stocks, the gun can be considered as well balanced. To fully appreciate this test however, it is necessary to try it on several guns of different model and length of barrels. This can be accomplished best by visiting a gun shop or inspecting the arsenal of a real pistol crank.

The balance and fit of a gun are very closely related. If a well balanced pistol fits an individual, it is capable of being pointed easily and accurately. A gun may be balanced well and yet not fit a shooter at all satisfactorily and as a consequence he is handicapped in his work. To obtain the very best results, especially for rapid firing, for shooting in the dark or at aerial targets it is very essential that a pistol fit the hand of the marksman. If the grip is too large, or if the distance to the trigger is too great for the trigger finger, or if the shape of the stocks is uncomfortable the gun cannot be handled most efficiently. A man with a large hand and long fingers needs a grip of corresponding size, while one with a small hand or stubby fingers cannot handle effectively a large sized hand gun.

On some single shot target pistols, it is possible to substitute specially made grips to fit any person's hand,

An unbeatable pair for miscellaneous small bore shooting. The Colt Woodsman automatic and the 22-32 Heavy Frame S. & W. target revolver.

and to so construct them as to provide finger and thumb rests and even a support for the fleshy part of the hand nearest the butt. Trigger guards shaped in conjunction with the stock sometimes furnish finger holds for the second and third fingers of the pistol hand. On other target weapons, the metal frame of the butt prevents any but makeshift improvements of the grip. On military revolvers and magazine pistols, alterations of the grips are not generally practicable, even if they were advisable, for usually rapid fire competitions are limited to military pistols as defined in the preceding chapter. To obtain a military pistol of good fit and balance and one eligible for competitions, it is necessary to select one from among those models now on the market, and this should be done only after testing them for balance and the way they fit the hand of the prospective buyer. Those who prefer revolvers for military shooting will have no great difficulty in finding one to fit the hand fairly well except in the matter of shape, and in this particular it will be necessary to accept the maker's ideas of a well shaped grip, which are usually based on convenience of manufacture rather than on sound principles of marksmanship. For balance, facility in handling, and general utility, a revolver with a barrel of not to exceed six inches in length is the best six shooter for military work, especially for rapid and quick fire.

Those who prefer magazine pistols for military practice will find their choice more limited if they desire American made guns, and the man with a small hand may have difficulty in getting a satisfactory fit. It was with the idea of improving the balance and pointing qualities and of making the grip more suitable and comfortable for men with average sized hands that the Service automatic pistol, caliber .45, Model 1911, was modified by shortening the trigger reach, knurling and raising the mainspring housing, extending the tang of the grip safety, and cutting away the receiver on each side of the trigger. The pistol as first issued had a tendency to point slightly downward when held naturally in the firing position, due to the angle between the grip and the barrel. In calibers less than .45, the grips of automatics are smaller and a fairly good fit can

The old and new in S. & W. target pistols. The Perfected Model and the 22 Straight Line.

be obtained for a small hand unless one is too fussy. It is well to state at this point that if one desires to practice rapid fire exercises in connection with military or police shooting it is desirable to have a pistol with an outside hammer in order to cock it conveniently for snapping practice.

MILITARY PISTOLS

For military shooting, a choice must be made between revolvers and magazine or automatic pistols. The former are rapidly becoming obsolete for military purposes, and matches open to Army and Navy weapons are favoring automatic hand guns more and more, because rapid and quick fire is being given greater emphasis. In this the automatic pistol has considerable advantage, as it cocks itself after each shot. These modern weapons have the advantages of greater rapidity of fire, of quicker reloading when using extra magazines, of a greater number of shots without reloading, of no escape of gas between the chamber and barrel resulting in loss of velocity and corrosion of adjacent parts. They are of greater compactness with generally higher velocity and lighter recoil in proportion to the caliber, as some of the recoil is absorbed by the auto-loading mechanism.

The revolver is still a favorite among many older shots, who through years of experience have become accustomed to its grip and balance and have learned to manipulate it with speed and facility to the extent of competing favorably against men armed with automatic pistols. As to the relative accuracy of military revolvers and automatic pistols, there is some advantage in favor of the former. As to reliability in functioning, they are about on a par except in a windy, sandy country such as along our Mexican border where excessive dust and sand in the air make it difficult to keep the service automatic functioning perfectly without careful and frequent attention especially during active military operations. There is greater possibility of jamming in automatics than in revolvers, due to defective magazines, variation in ammunition and lack of cleaning. A misfire with an automatic means a stoppage until the faulty cartridge has been ejected and this generally requires the use of both hands. Revolvers if closely fitted are subject to jams, due to primers which bulge on firing and prevent the rotation of the cylinder. It must be remembered in this connection that automatic pistols are comparatively new and are still subject to improvements, which necessity is rapidly providing, and which time will soon perfect.

My advice to a novice who contemplates following military pistol shooting would be to select an automatic pistol in preference to a revolver though the latter is the safer weapon to handle. Of the military automatics in use today, there are few the equal and none superior to the present side arm of our Army and Navy.

The following pistols and revolvers are recommended for military shooting:

.38 Colt Super Automatic.
.45 Colt Automatic Pistol Government Model.
.45 S. & W. Revolver (U.S. Model 1917).
.45 Colt Revolver (U.S. Model 1917).
.44 S. & W. Revolver (.44 Military Model).
.45 Colt Revolver, New Service.

PISTOLS FOR POLICE OFFICERS

The primary requisites of a pistol for police officers are: Safety, reliability, handiness, medium weight and stopping power.

Outside of the field of recreational shooting it is

doubtful if one can find a subject on which there is greater difference of opinion than on the question of the best type of pistol for police use. Several years ago

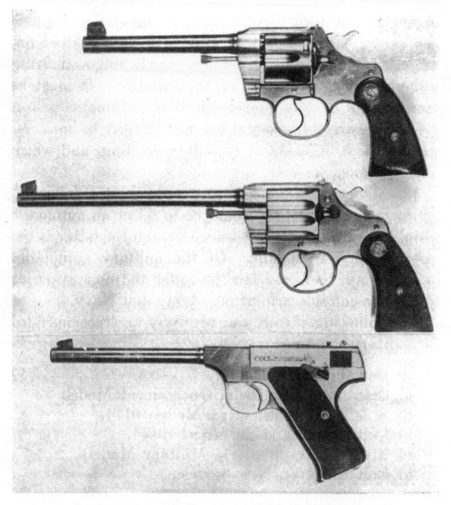

A Colt combination suitable for any kind of target practice. The Officers' Model, Camp Perry Model and "Woodsman."

while instructing the police force of one of our large cities, the author was asked so many questions regarding the relative merits of revolvers and automatic pistols for police purposes that it was very evident that this was a question of considerable discussion among those officers who really used their weapons in the performance of duty and the enforcement of laws. At that time magazine pistols and their ammunition were not as reliable as they are now, and the revolver was the favorite weapon among pistol men.

A pair of S. & W. Pistols with specially fitted grips. The Perfected S. & W. Target pistol and the 22-32 H. F. Target revolver.

For many years hand gun makers have specialized in police revolvers and have developed a characteristic design for these weapons. The popular police gun for the dismounted patrolman is of the pocket type, with caliber from .32 to .45, barrels about four inches in length, and weigh about 1½ pounds. For semi-military organizations such as State Constabularies, Texas Rangers and other mounted forces, military weapons are generally used. It has been quite noticeable, however, that when there is an increase in crime and in the activity of gunmen and auto bandits, there is a decided trend toward more powerful hand guns among police officers. Whereas the .38 caliber weapons were considered of ample size in the past, the .45 caliber guns and especially military automatics have been gaining in favor in certain localities. Motorcycle patrolmen, mounted officers, plain clothes men and special officers who feel the need for suitable life insurance from their weapons are depending only on those with maximum stopping power.

To the patrolman, who at most has only occasional need for his weapon, the lighter caliber and more convenient pocket pistol appeals and this type of police gun still remains the great favorite. A .38 caliber revolver with a barrel of from 2 to 4 inches, designed for the .38 Special cartridge and using full factory loaded ammunition, with preferably the square-shoulder or wadcutter bullet, makes an excellent weapon for general police use. It is safe, convenient, easily concealed, comparatively light, and if made by a reputable firm, has sufficient accuracy for ordinary police purposes.

If, on the other hand, a police officer's duty requires the enforcement of laws and the protection of property in localities where quick, accurate shooting is essential to self protection, and where it is a case of stopping the criminal before he gets the officer, then a weapon of large caliber should by all means be used. A Texas Ranger once stated that he wanted a pistol big enough that when he put a bullet through a "bad man" and he didn't drop, it would be necessary to go behind him to see what was supporting him.

The choice between revolvers and magazine pistols can be made on the same basis as for military shooting, that is by weighing the pros and cons and then selecting the weapon preferred.

To get away from generalities and be more specific the following arms and cartridges are recommended for police work:

In selecting pistols for self-defense, the rules which govern in choosing a suitable weapon for police work are equally applicable. If pocket weapons are adequate for the purpose, the police type of pistol with barrel not to exceed four inches is suitable. If belt or shoulder holsters can be worn and personal danger is great, heavier caliber weapons with barrels not to exceed six inches in length may be carried and used to advantage.

Weapons carried unconcealed have been known to have a deterrent effect on offensively inclined individuals, but carefully concealed pocket weapons give one a comfortable feeling of confidence and protection without attracting attention and creating comment. If they are carried in a position to be put into action quickly, they possess an element of surprise that may give the user the drop on a slow thinking thug and be the means of preventing assault and robbery.

For recreational shooting there are many pistols available, and when one decides which kind of shooting he intends to follow, the selection of a pistol suitable for its practice is greatly simplified. Opinions based on sentiment, prejudice, and advertising propaganda frequently cause us to make decisions and selections which

		Arm			Cartridges
Cal.	Make	Model	Type	Length of barrel	
.38	Colt	Police Positive Special	Revolver	2 to 4 inch	.38 Colt Spl .38 S & W Spl .38 Spl Mid Range Wad Cutter
.38	Smith & Wesson	Military & Police	Revolver	4 inch	Same
.38	Colt	Official Police	Revolver	4 inch	Same
.38	Colt	Pocket Hammerless	Automatic Pistol	3¾ inch	.380 Auto
*.38	Remington	Model 51	Automatic Pistol	3¼ inch	.380 Auto
.38	Colt	Super	Automatic	5 inch	.38 A. C. P.
.44	S & W	Military	Revolver	5 inch	.44 S & W Spl
.45	S & W	1917 Army	Revolver	5½ inch	.45 Auto Rim Lead (Peters) .45 Auto (With Clips)
.45	Colt	U. S. Model 1917	Revolver	5½ inch	Same
.45	Colt	New Service	Revolver	5½ inch	.45 Colt
.45	Colt	Govt Model	Automatic Pistol	5 inch	.45 Auto

*Not manufactured at present.

experience eventually teaches us are erroneous. The recommendations made herein are based on actual experience in the use of pistols and are made without partiality or favor. They are listed in the author's order of preference.

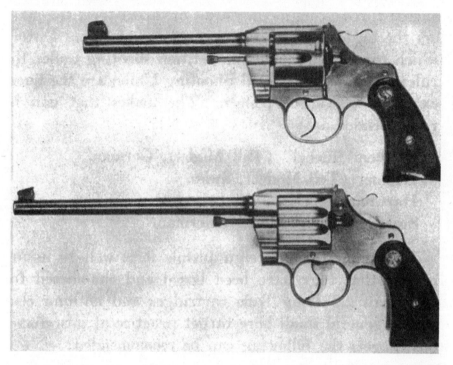

A matched pair of Colt Target pistols both made on the same frame and with similar grips. An ideal battery for target shooting. The .38 Officers' Model and the .22 Camp Perry Model.

For small bore deliberate fire target practice there are on the market at the time this is written the following American made pistols that can be recommended for this form of shooting:

Colt .22 Caliber Single Shot Pistol. (Camp Perry Model.)

S & W .22 Straight Line Pistol.

Colt .22 Automatic Target Pistol. "Woodsman" Model.)

No. 10 Stevens Target Pistol.

No. 35 Stevens "Off Hand" Pistol.

In addition to these target pistols, there can be purchased through importing firms or direct from the makers the highly refined European type of "Free Pistol" which for International competition shooting under the rules of the International Shooting Union are the finest examples of target pistols. The makes that can be recommended are:

"System Buchel" (Tell Model), German.

Widmer (Tell Model), Swiss.

Hartmann, Swiss.

Stotzer (Perfect Model), German.

In buying these foreign pistols it is well to assure oneself that they have been bored and chambered for American .22 Long Rifle cartridges and nothing else.

For general small bore target practice at miscellaneous targets the following can be recommended:

Colt Automatic Pistol Caliber .22 "Woodsman" Model.

Smith and Wesson 22-32 Heavy Frame Target Revolver.

Colt .22 Caliber Police Positive Target (New Heavy Frame Model).

For general target practice with pistols of larger caliber any of the following hand guns will give excellent service and satisfaction:

Colt Officers' Model Target.

Smith & Wesson Military and Police Target.

Smith & Wesson .44 Target.

Colt New Service Target .44 S & W Special Cartridge.

Colt Auto Pistol, Govt. Model Cal. 45.

Colt Single Action Army, chambered for .44 S & W
Special, .45 Colt or .45 Automatic Cartridge.

For fit, balance, weight, accuracy and workmanship
the first two named revolvers are the finest models of
target weapons made today. They are adapted to the
.38 S & W Special, and the .38 Colt Special cartridges
in full and mid range loads all of which are very pleasant to shoot, free from excessive noise and recoil and
with sufficient accuracy to suit the most particular gun
crank. The last named revolver is included, not because
it is a special target gun, for it is not, but because it is
the most famous of all Colt guns and though it has been
out since 1872 is still used extensively. It has the finest
grip of any of the hand guns made in America and is
chambered for at least eight different cartridges, the
latest of these being the .45 automatic cartridge. It is
made with either 4¾, 5½ or 7½ inch barrels. With a
5½ inch barrel it is a well balanced gun. Many tales
have been told of using this gun without a trigger and
of firing by "fanning" or "slipping" the hammer. By
using a special hammer with short spur, slip shooting
has been done and is still being done by a few specialists
with quite remarkable results in speed and accuracy.
"Burro Puncher" John Newman, of Seattle, is the leading exponent of this form of shooting and it has been

the author's privilege to witness his skill on many occasions.   At either military or aerial targets Newman's
work is quite astonishing.

The Newman Slip Hammer Colt.   Showing the Single Action
Army Colt made over by J. D. O'Meara from specifications by John
Newman, the cleverest exponent of slip shooting in America.   The
cylinders shown are interchangeable, making it possible to use either
the .45 Colt or the .45 Automatic cartridge.   The pistol may be fired
with the trigger or by tying the latter back and slipping the hammer
from under the thumb.

Chapter IV

THE ESSENTIALS OF PISTOL SHOOTING

To MASTER an art one must be endowed by nature with certain talents and the ambition and perseverance to apply these inherent advantages to the attainment of super skill by practice, study and experience. Comparatively few of us possess the qualifications of a master artist but on the other hand we can by reasonable study and practice acquire a skill that will classify us as experts in many of the arts unless we are handicapped by some mental or physical deficiency. The art of pistol shooting is more difficult to excel in than that of rifle or shotgun shooting and yet there is nothing about the game that is mysterious or that requires special aptitude. It can be learned readily by a beginner who is properly instructed providing he will carefully and diligently practice the principles taught.

There are many cases on record of men qualifying as "Pistol Experts" who have little real knowledge of the weapon they used, but nevertheless they were able to win the expert rating because they were well coached and trained in the technique of shooting and their pistols were properly adjusted for them. The term expert is a comparative one and may mean little or much. Though a man may have qualified as a Marksman, Sharpshooter, or Pistol Expert over a military course using military weapons he may be a novice at the more highly refined deliberate target shooting game practiced with special single shot pistols against more difficult targets. Likewise the deliberate fire specialist would probably be rated "poor" should he attempt to compete with a skillful, quick drawing snapshot in a match fired at rapidly moving aerial targets and, carrying the comparison still further, the snapshot usually makes a fizzle of firing at fifty yards on the Standard American target. So one may become an expert in one of several forms of pistol shooting and make a reputation for himself which is creditable and enviable, or if he is not satisfied and inclined to look for greater accomplishments he can in due time take up each style of shooting and work for the distinction of being known as an expert all-around pistol shot.

To master the art of pistol shooting one must excel in all its essentials. These may be grouped under three headings:

(a) Knowledge.

A thorough knowledge of the pistol must be acquired. Its capabilities and limitations must be known. Its care, all necessary adjustments for its efficient use, and familiarity with the ammunition for which it was designed must be understood and observed.

(b) Skill.

One must gain superior skill and accuracy in the technique of firing by learning and applying to practice those principles of shooting known as aiming, holding, squeezing the trigger and calling the shot.

(c) Co-ordination.

One must, through training and experience, develop a high degree of co-ordination of mind, nerves and muscles to the end that he may eventually shoot mechanically.

A comprehensive knowledge of pistols is an excellent foundation to a thorough course in shooting and while very desirable is not so important to the novice as an accurate, practical acquaintance with the pistols with which he wishes to become proficient. Information tracing the development of the hand gun from its origin, through the various steps in its alteration and improvement to the period of its present perfection is of value, chiefly to the collector. An intimate knowledge of the mechanism of the pistol with which one practices so that he can quickly dismount it for purposes of adjustment, repair or alteration of trigger pull is of infinitely more value to the shooter than to know who made the first matchlock.

The lack of practical skill in the adjustment of one's pistol is very much appreciated when, through ignorance, one is forced to send it to the factory for repairs because that rarest of all mechanics, the good gunsmith, is not to be found, or if he is located it is found that he has so much work ahead that one must wait indefinitely to have his particular job finished. The old adage "Know your gun" has great significance to the pistol marksman.

While stationed in the Philippine Islands the author had the misfortune to have the hammer break on a fine hand made European target pistol. The rupture passed through the sear notch in such a manner as to make welding impracticable and the nearest good gunsmith was seven thousand miles away. Realizing, at the time the pistol was purchased, that it was hand made and that spare parts were not available the precaution had been taken to make a study of the mechanism of this so called "free pistol" and this knowledge now came to be very useful.

With the assistance of a Filipino machinist a new hammer was made and I then had the satisfaction of being able to accurately fit this into the action and to cut the delicate sear notch so that the trigger mechanism functioned perfectly on the first atempt. No doubt there was some luck in this, but fifteen years' experience in filing and stoning various kinds of trigger mechanisms had given me some skill in this one detail.

Of equal importance with those mentioned in the foregoing paragraphs is that of sight adjustment. This must be not only understood but skill in actually adjusting sights must be acquired. This is especially true when it becomes necessary to change the elevation or windage of a pistol with fixed sights. Sight adjustment is covered more in detail in the chapter on Aiming.

Pistols and revolvers are essentially short range weapons and rifle accuracy cannot be expected from them. It does give one confidence to know that his target pistol or revolver will shoot closer than he can hold, and all good pistols will do this. The best single shot pistols will group their shots in an inch circle at fifty yards when fired from a machine rest. A knowledge of the capabilities and limitations of the pistols now available for our use makes it possible for us to quickly decide on which weapon to use for a particular kind of shooting and lack of this information puts us at a distinct disadvantage should we attempt to use a pistol in a match for which it is entirely unsuited. Familiarity with pistol ammunition is absolutely necessary nowadays when one considers how many different cartridges there are available for each of the different calibers of hand guns. Every gun is designed to do its best work with a particular cartridge and we should be sure that we know which cartridge that is. If we attempt loading our own ammunition, then as a safety precaution, if for no other reason, we must know the powder suitable to use and the maximum load it is safe to put in our cartridges, otherwise our shooting career may end abruptly. A study of·the ballistic tables of pistol cartridges as issued by our leading cartridge manufacturers will be found very helpful in the study of questions of ammunition.

Assuming that one has absorbed the necessary general knowledge prerequisite to intelligent practice and has decided on a particular kind of pistol with which he desires to become proficient his mission then becomes one of developing skill in the technique of firing. This resolves itself into acquiring further knowledge, but of a more specific nature and the intensive application of his knowledge to practice.

As the golfer, the fencer, and the batter must learn to take positions most suitable to the games they play, so must the pistol novice learn the proper shooting position. As the bowler or billiard expert learns to align his sight with the pin or ball he desires to hit, so must the shooter learn to point or aim his pistol correctly and accurately on the target he desires his bullet to strike. As the sculptor, the painter and the surgeon learn to hold their instruments with firmness that is at once positive and yet so delicate as to be responsive to the slightest impulse of mind and muscles, so must one learn to be steady without tenseness, to use sufficient strength to grip his pistol firmly but without rigidity and to squeeze the trigger so gradually that the movement borders on the imperceptible. All this means that he must learn and practice the essentials of technique which are aiming and holding the pistol, squeezing the trigger, and calling the shot. Each of these important factors will be covered thoroughly in other chapters.

Co-ordination in pistol shooting may be defined as the harmonious action of brain, nerves and muscles which results in automatic shooting with mechanical precision. All forms of shooting demand co-ordination but none so much as the pistol game. The good clay bird shot gives an excellent example of mechanical shooting showing co-ordination in which the time element is intimately associated with a moving shotgun and a rapidly moving target. The expert rapid fire rifle shot also exhibits good muscular and mental co-ordination when he makes a ten shot possible in a minute. Both of these marksmen however have their sights held in alignment with the eye by the support given their weapons by the shoulder, cheek, arms and hands and with them co-ordination consists largely in squeezing the trigger decisively when the target comes in the line of sight or, in the case of the bird shot, when the point at which he shoots passes the sights of his moving gun. The pistol shot has the problem of co-ordinating his aim, hold, and squeeze with nothing to aid him in maintaining the alignment of his sights except the nervous and muscular control of his shooting arm.

The beginner has his lack of co-ordination impressed upon him when he finds that he has difficulty in aligning his sights with his eye and when he gets them aligned that he cannot hold this alignment and finally, when he tries to bring the target into the line of aim he meets with increasing difficulty. If he does get eye, sights, and target aligned he discovers that he cannot maintain his aim and that he cannot co-ordinate his trigger squeeze with his aim, with the result that his pistol fires when his aim is off the target. It is during this trying period that one realizes what the lack of co-ordination means and the necessity for developing it.

With intelligent practice and greater experience there comes a time when the aim is caught instantly, is maintained by a steady hold, the trigger squeezing muscles function without hesitation, the shot is fired and the call is "good." Due to acquired bad habits experienced shots frequently develop a condition such that while they are able to aim accurately and hold steadily they are unable to squeeze the trigger. This condition is known among shooters as being "frozen" but it is nothing more or less than a lack of co-ordination. The cause, effects and remedies for this phenomenon are discussed in a later chapter.

Chapter V

SHOOTING FORM

GOOD form or a correct position is as essential in pistol shooting as in any kind of athletics. If it is necessary for a golfer to take a good stance while driving or putting, or a tennis player to co-ordinate his service by a proper position of body, arm and racket, it is equally important for a shooter to learn to assume a correct position in order to develop with minimum effort the high degree of co-ordination necessary for successful pistol shooting.

There are certain governing principles that determine a correct shooting position. These may be summed up under two main headings, namely, steadiness and comfort. By steadiness is meant such a position of the entire body that at the instant the pistol is to be fired there is an equilibrium of body and gun approaching immobility. By comfort is meant entire freedom from muscular strain, discomfort or fatigue. Keeping constantly in mind that you are striving for steadiness with a minimum of muscular strain and fatigue, or expressed differently, for absolute steadiness with comfort, you must study shooting positions from this point of view.

It will seem to a beginner, if he studies the positions of many of the best pistol shots, that there is an apparent marked difference of opinion as to just what constitutes a correct position. A careful analysis of these apparent variations in form however, will show that while the positions assumed look different they are based on the principles above stated, and do give steadiness and comfort while firing. Unless one assumes a steady, comfortable, well balanced position, one unnecessarily handicaps himself by straining or tiring more muscles than is necessary. Nervousness and consequent unsteadiness always result from tired muscles. For this reason extreme, unnatural and grand-stand poses should be strictly avoided.

The application of the above principles to practice at once reveals certain factors that tend to prevent the acquirement of steadiness and comfort in one's position. These are wind, the effects of recoil when using heavy weapons, and the inherent untrained nerves and muscles of a novice which soon become tired and shaky.

Your position must be suited to the particular style or kind of shooting you are to practice. Obviously if you intend to limit yourself chiefly to indoor shooting with small caliber target pistols you might adopt a position that would be comfortable and steady and yet poorly suited to rapid fire with a heavy large caliber pistol out-of-doors, under varying weather conditions. If you intend to practice outside with these last mentioned weapons, you will find that in addition to the ever present tendency of the body to sway, you must combat the effects of wind, which greatly increases the swaying. Again if you practice rapid fire to any extent with weapons such as the .45 caliber service automatic pistol or its equivalent, the .45 caliber revolver, you will find that the rapidly repeated shock of recoil has a tendency further to decrease your steadiness and equilibrium.

Considering all these factors, it is desirable to adopt

a position suitable to any form of shooting; in other words what might be termed an all-around shooting

A STUDY IN SHOOTING POSITIONS.

The 1924 American Olympic Team practicing at Versailles, France.

This Team won First Place for the United States. From left to right they are: First Lieutenant W. J. Whaling, U.S.M.C., First Lieutenant E. Andino, Inf., Gunnery Sergeant H. M. Bailey, U.S. M.C., Gunnery Sergeant B. G. Betke, U.S.M.C., and Major W. D. Frazer, C.A.C. Sergeant Bailey won the Individual Olympic Championship, with a run of fifty-four consecutive hits on the French Silhouette Target. Sweden took Second Place and Finland, Third. The similarity in the individual shooting positions of the members of this team should be noted.

position, and use it in preference to one satisfactory only for a special kind of target practice.

While it is possible to fire a pistol with more or less accuracy from prone, kneeling or sitting positions, or with both hands, it will suffice here to discuss only the standing position as generally recognized and authorized in national and international competitions. Briefly stated this is with the body erect and free from support, the pistol being held in one hand with arm extended, so as to be free from the body. This position is the most practicable for all-around pistol shooting and is not limited to deliberate target practice. To avoid misunderstandings it is assumed throughout these instructions that pointing and firing are done with the right hand unless otherwise stated.

By studying the form used by our best pistol shots it will be found that they fall into two groups: namely, those who face the target while firing and those who face at right angles to it. Although a few very fine shots face directly toward the target or nearly so, the great majority of experts assume a position in which the body is faced between forty-five and ninety degrees to the left of the target. If the shooting is done with the left hand the position is reversed and the body then faces right or right oblique. Photographs of men in firing positions are often deceiving unless, while studying them, one keeps in mind the probable position of the target when the picture was taken. They are of value in studying details of form, rather than the position of the body in relation to the target. For this reason both diagrams and photographs showing positions and other details of correct form are herewith included in the hope that they will be of value to the beginner who may not have the advantage of instruction under the watchful eye of a good coach.

FEET:

The first question to consider is the position of the feet, for they are the main factors in determining the degree of body stability. Theoretically the farther you place them apart the better they will be able to resist any tendency toward top-heaviness resulting from holding a heavy weapon at arm's length. But when you go beyond the limit of comfort and separate your feet so far that you feel strained or uncomfortable, then the advantages of a good foundation are offset by the resulting discomfort and strain. The determining factor then, in deciding how far apart to place your feet, is your physique and especially the length of your legs. The position and distance apart of the feet and the equal distribution of the body weight are all important in maintaining equilibrium with a minimum expenditure of energy. For a man of average height the distance between the heels should be about sixteen inches and between the balls of the feet about twenty-two inches.

Consider next the position of the feet in relation to the direction the body faces while in shooting attitude. Take a shooting position facing directly toward a target, with body erect, heels on the same line and toes turned out equally. Now with your shooting arm extended and pistol or index finger pointing toward the target relax your muscles and observe the tendency of the body to sway toward and from the target. Now face ninety degrees to the left of this position with heels on a line parallel to your extended right arm, relax again and observe that you now sway at right angles to the direction in which you are pointing. A wind blowing from the direction in which you are facing in either case greatly increases the swaying movement.

Now maintaining this second position—facing to the left, feet separated a comfortable space and pistol pointing at the target—move your left foot from four to six inches to your front and turn your right toe slightly to the right. You will now find there is less tendency to sway. The new position reduces the tendency and renders it less disastrous to your score. Continuing the experiments a little further, now try turning the right toe farther to the right until you begin to feel a twisting strain in the muscles of the leg and thigh. Because of this strain it is better to have the toes turned out equally and at an angle of not over forty degrees. Do not attempt to make the right toe point directly toward the target as this may cause excessive muscle strain. The sketch below shows diagrammatically the location of the feet as the basis of a good shooting position.

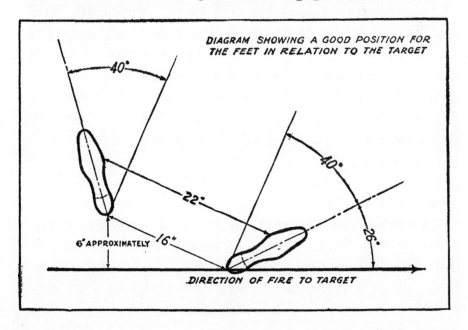

DIAGRAM SHOWING A GOOD POSITION FOR THE FEET IN RELATION TO THE TARGET

40°

40°

22°

26°

6" APPROXIMATELY

16"

DIRECTION OF FIRE TO TARGET

LEGS:

The legs should be straight without stiffness and ex-cept when firing in a wind or during strings of rapid fire with a large caliber pistol the muscles should be relaxed. Toward the end of a long match it is some-times advisable to tighten up the muscles in order to overcome the trembling that occasionally results from fatigue. The legs and knees are the barometers of a shooter's condition as regards nervousness and "buck fever." During competitions and if conditions of a match permit, they should be favored as much as possi-ble by sitting down between strings and even between shoots.

BODY:

To avoid unnecessary strain the body should be erect with the weight equally distributed on both legs. This of course requires that the feet be on practically level ground. Any tendency to lean forward or backward should be avoided. Holding a heavy pistol at arm's length has a tendency to cause one to lean back in order to counteract the weight. This should not be done, for the position soon becomes uncomfortable and strained, depending upon the strength and physical condition of the marksman.

ARMS:

The arms are the next members to consider in the problem of position. There again we find a considerable difference in practice. The left arm and hand are of little use to a right hand shot. Some shooters let this arm and hand hang loosely by the side, some prefer to place the hand on the left hip, others put it behind the back, while still others thrust it in the left hip or side trouser pocket. One prominent authority advocated letting the left hand hang by the side with the hand pressed firmly against the side. In recent years there has been a growing inclination among pistol shooters to put the left hand in the side trouser pocket and there is a good reason for the practice. The hand and arm should serve as a balance and should not be left to dangle by the side. It is certain to sway slightly and this affects the steadiness of the whole body. The hand should not be placed so high on the hip that it raises the left shoulder and brings into play muscles that should be at rest. But permitted to hang naturally, with the hand in the left side trouser pocket, a position is assumed that puts the smallest strain on the muscles. Placing the hand on the hip and bending the elbow does, however, assist in counterbalancing the shooting arm provided the body faces at right angles to the direction of fire.

The right or shooting arm should be fully and naturally extended, without rigidity and maintained in this position during the firing of each shot. The work of supporting the arm and pistol should be done chiefly by the heavy shoulder muscles rather than by those of the arm. This is accomplished by slightly raising the right shoulder. The great majority of our best pistol shots extend the arm fully but a few excellent ones use the arm partially bent. From actual count made at different times at our National Matches, during Olympic and International matches in Europe and at smaller competitions throughout the country the writer believes that

A comfortable, well balanced shooting position suitable for any style of target practice. The following details should be noted: Distribution of weight and position of the feet; right arm is fully extended without stiffness; right shoulder is raised slightly; grip is high on the revolver and the barrel is nearly in prolongation of the arm; left shoulder, arm and hand are at ease; head is erect and both eyes open.

over ninety per cent of good pistol shots extended the pistol arm fully. It is very likely, however, that for rapid fire with the revolver when the piece is cocked for each shot that an advantage may be derived in the use of a bent arm, in the increased ease and speed of cocking and aiming. If rapid firing is done with an automatic pistol or by using the double action of the revolver, there is not the same inducement to bend the arm. This will be discussed in the chapter on rapid fire.

HEAD:

The head should be erect and turned well to the right. Inclining the head forward to align the sights should be avoided; the gun arm should be raised high enough to enable the aim to be taken comfortably. Both eyes should be kept open.

GRIP:

The manner in which the pistol is held while firing, brings us to the point where muscular effort really begins and the muscles of the shoulder, arm, wrist and hand come into play. If up to this time you have accurately followed the instructions regarding the position to be taken, you will realize that you have done nothing to call for physical effort sufficient to cause fatigue or discomfort. If you are accustomed to ordinary work, and are normally developed in the arm and shoulder, you will feel that the effort to hold a pistol at arm's length makes no great demand on your strength. If your occupation or habits are such that you do not exercise these muscles much, you will find that the effort required to fire several five shot strings carefully is considerable, especially with a heavy pistol. When you make the attempt you soon find that the muscles tire and there is an

An excellent grip for this S. & W. target pistol fitted with a special stock.

A good method of holding the .38 Colt Officers' Model or any revolver of similar type. The index finger should be as low on the trigger as possible.

increasing shakiness and wobbling of the pistol. This depends largely on the manner in which you grip the

An excellent grip for medium and large caliber revolvers. The thumb is extended along the frame but is low enough to clear the cylinder when the recoil occurs.

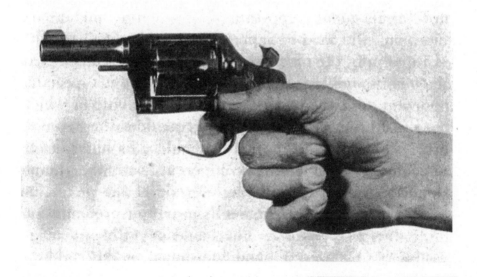

This grip is especially suited to revolvers of the type of the .38 Colt Police Positive Special which has a small grip and short space behind the guard. When used with the heavier factory loads, and a short barrel such as shown here, this revolver is unpleasant to shoot unless gripped as shown.

weapon and support it and the extended arm.   The
vibrations caused by the functioning of an automatic
pistol of. large caliber may further increase this shakiness.   By continual practice in aiming and squeezing the
trigger, combined perhaps with regular exercise of a
kind that will strengthen the muscles required in shooting, you will soon be able to get off more shots before
the effects of fatigue are apparent.

A fine exercise to strengthen and develop the muscles
of the forearm and hand and one that requires no special apparatus is as follows: Let the right arm with
muscles relaxed hang naturally by the side, palm to the
front.   With a slow rolling motion upward, beginning
with the tips of the fingers close the fist tightly as you
raise the forearm to the horizontal, meanwhile vigorously
tensing the muscles to your limit.   Continue the exercise
until tired and by repeating it frequently and at odd
times you will soon be surprised at the beneficial results.

In gripping the pistol care should be taken to see that
the stock is well seated in the hand.   This is especially
important with the service automatic, the butt of which
does not fit the hand as naturally as does the revolver
butt.   The grip on the pistol should be as high as the
particular weapon in use will permit, with the thumb
extended naturally along the left side of the piece, the
idea being to bring the barrel as nearly in prolongation
of the arm as possible.   The tendency with any large
weapon is to have the hand too much on the right of
the piece so that the barrel is not directly in line with
the forearm.   This is especially true when using a large
automatic.   The grip on the butt and its position in the
hand should always be the same.   Changing the grip

from shot to shot may result in changing the elevation of your hits on the target. The pressure on the grip should be only sufficient to hold it firmly, as firmly as one might hold an egg of questionable age; firm enough to be sure of not dropping it and yet not tight enough to crush it. The heavier the caliber and the greater the recoil the firmer must be the grip especially in rapid fire. It must, however, be constantly borne in mind that the tighter the grip on the weapon the greater the muscle strain and consequently the more nervous tremors in the hand.

HOLDING THE BREATH

As a part of the technique of firing with the pistol, the detail of holding the breath has, as a result of experience, become of great importance, especially in very deliberate shooting.

Tests made in psychological laboratories have proved that even in minor acts of precision a person involuntarily holds the breath for a very brief period. During delicate operations in surgery the operator will hold his breath in order to perform better a particular detail of his work. The same thing is true in various other acts of precision, at least until one becomes quite skillful in the art he practices.

Uninterrupted breathing causes a movement of the diaphragm and chest muscles as one inhales and exhales and this causes some unsteadiness of the body. For this reason marksmen in an effort to attain absolute steadiness, have learned to hold the breath while aiming and squeezing the trigger.

The breath can be held in two ways, one, by tensing the breathing muscles and the other, by their relaxation.

When muscles are tensed they are put under strain and if this is continued for any considerable length of time nervousness results. If muscles are relaxed they are at rest. Some effort is required to hold the breath, but it should be reduced to a minimum. We accomplish this by relaxing the muscles we ordinarily tense when we stop breathing, and hold the breath by merely closing the throat. This is not as simple as it sounds and it takes practice to do it easily and naturally because we are more accustomed to the other method. If we fill the lungs with air by taking a very deep breath we put certain muscles under strain. An attempt to hold the breath under this condition requires an appreciable effort. If, on the other hand we exhale until we have *nearly* emptied the lungs we find that we can close the throat, relax the abdominal muscles and hold the breath quite easily. A little careful practice will soon show the novice the advantages of this method.

The following procedure should be practiced until it becomes the natural way to hold the breath: Take an ordinary breath, exhale most of it, then with the lungs in a state of rest, close the throat, relax the abdominal muscles and hold the breath. Repeat this exercise during aiming, holding and trigger squeeze exercises. Holding the breath too long should be carefully avoided.

Chapter VI

HOLDING AND SQUEEZING

"HOLD 'em and Squeeze 'em," that ever popular slogan of the target range has much greater significance for the pistol shot than for any other marksman. To the beginner or those unacquainted with the language of the range this expression may have several meanings but, to the marksman who understands, it has only one interpretation. The experienced shot knows that his success in practice or competition depends largely on his ability to hold steadily and to squeeze his trigger when he fires. His shooting form may be excellent, he may be able to aim accurately, but if he is unable to hold closely and to squeeze properly while he is aiming, his shot will be a poor one. These two essentials of pistol shooting are so closely related that it seems wise to discuss them together rather than as independent actions.

Nerves and muscles untrained in the art of steady holding make this problem a difficult one for the novice. He soon finds that the muzzle of a pistol at the end of a fully extended arm does everything but remain stationary. To hold the sights properly aligned on the bottom of the bull's-eye seems more difficult for the beginner in the pistol shooting game than threading a fine needle is to the average man. If he does succeed in properly aligning the sights for an instant his difficulties are further increased by his attempts to squeeze the trigger and fire the piece. If not properly instructed at this point in his practice, he will by natural impulse do the wrong thing and that is pull or convulsively jerk the trigger when his aim appears to be correct for an instant. He should combat this tendency to the limit of his will power and by systematic drill in holding and trigger squeeze exercises, he will find that unsteady nerves and muscles are capable of a vast amount of training. He must not expect to train his muscles in a day or a week, but must approach his work of learning to hold with the idea of slowly improving, keeping in mind that he can make good scores with an unsteady pistol provided he gets his shots off with a proper trigger squeeze when his aim is correct. Close observation of some excellent shots will show that they have a very unsteady muzzle while aiming but that they have so mastered trigger squeeze that they make fine scores. The novice should realize that a movement of his shooting arm parallel to the line of aim can be considerable and if the trigger is squeezed properly the shots will still remain in an eight inch bull's-eye. If, however, there is the slightest angular movement of the pistol and arm from the line of aim, such as might be caused by a slight jerk of the trigger, the shot may be a very wild one.

For the purpose of improving his holding, and gaining confidence before attempting much trigger squeezing or firing, the beginner should practice holding exercises until he is satisfied by personal demonstration that he can hold his sights well enough aligned on the aiming point to insure a good score if the pistol was fired without deranging that aim. The following will gain the desired results if practiced sufficiently: Take the correct firing position 25 yards in front of a standard pistol target, or before one reduced to correspond to the distance at which it is most convenient to practice. After assuring yourself that your pistol is not loaded cock and extend it at the full length of the shooting arm. Aim carefully at six o'clock on the bull's-eye, hold the breath and without tensing the muscles of the arm, hand or shoulder try to maintain the sight alignment. Do not squeeze the trigger but let the index finger rest naturally on it. Hold the position for not to exceed 30 seconds and then return to the starting position. Repeat the exercise for the equivalent of twenty shots, resting between each five.

Holding is always affected by one's physical condition so it is well, even in practice, not to attempt to aim, hold or squeeze when one is nervous from mental agitation or from vigorous exercise. Slow deep breathing and a few minutes of relaxation before and between practice scores will have quite a steadying effect. After a reasonable amount of holding exercise when one is sure that he can hold his aim long enough to get off a shot, he can then take up a trigger squeeze exercise. Before attempting it however, he should be sure that he understands just what he should try to do and the proper method of doing it, for he is about to deal with the most important essential of the pistol game.

As control is to the pitcher, as putting is to the golfer, and as touch is to the blind so likewise is trigger squeeze to the pistol shot and no language however expressive, no oratory however eloquent can over-emphasize the importance of mastering by careful study, application and perseverance this essential of the art of pistol shooting.

A rifleman firing from the prone position with his rifle supported by both elbows and held immovable against his shoulder by the aid of a sling, may actually pull his trigger without deranging his aim, whereas the slightest movement of the finger on a pistol trigger has a tendency to cause an unsteadiness in the balance of the gun and a corresponding movement of the muzzle.

The trigger should be squeezed straight to the rear, with a pressure applied so gradually that the firer does not know when the pistol will fire and so carefully that the aim will not be disturbed by the movement of the trigger finger, and it should be squeezed, only when the aim is correct. It matters not whether the marksman is practicing deliberate slow fire or quick or rapid fire, the trigger should be squeezed steadily, straight back, when the sights are in alignment with the target. In rapid fire the pressure is applied in less time and more decisively than in slow fire. This statement does not mean that the trigger is ever pulled but that the good rapid fire shot has learned to contract his trigger finger smoothly and quickly when his aim is just right, and he does it so well that his sight alignment is not disturbed. The beginner will probably find when he takes up rapid firing for the first time that he will get some "fliers" or wild shots in each of his scores. These are due to the natural impulse to jerk rather than squeeze the trigger, especially when the aim can only be held on the target for an instant. This tendency will grow less as one's ability to hold closely increases.

When possible it is preferable to squeeze the trigger with the first joint of the index finger but if one must take an improper grip to do this, then he should squeeze with that part of the finger that rests on the trigger naturally and enables him to squeeze straight back. To determine this, cock the pistol, grip it properly, and with arm extended in firing position lay the index finger across the trigger as far as it will reach comfortably and squeeze lightly. You will find that you have a natural tendency to press against the right side of the trigger and the pistol frame. Now move your finger to the right until no part of it rests against the frame; then any squeeze or pressure you may exert will come on the face of the trigger, as it should. If your index finger is so short that the tip only rests on the trigger do not let this worry you for the only man who has ever won our National Individual Pistol Championship twice shot in this manner. I refer to the late Gunnery Sergeant J. M. Thomas, U.S.M.C.

As an aid to learning this important essential the beginner should practice a good trigger squeeze exercise carefully and frequently until squeezing becomes as second nature to him. The more he practices the greater will be his success, provided he does it correctly. The following is suggested: Take the correct firing position in front of your practice target, cock your pistol, extend your arm fully, hold your breath and try to align your sights on the bull's-eye. Whenever in the course of their movement across the target the sights are in alignment on the bottom of the bull's-eye squeeze slowly but steadily on the trigger. As the line of aim moves off the bull's-eye, from the unsteadiness of your holding, maintain the pressure you have on the trigger until the sights again come into alignment with the target and when this occurs squeeze a little more. At some one of these times, when your sights are in alignment, the hammer will fall and you can see that the shot would have been a good one, unless in applying the final pressure you disturbed the aim, or the fall of the hammer did so. Repeat as you did with the holding exercise, with frequent rests between shots. When you reach the point that you can call a reasonable number of your shots "Good" and the aim is not disturbed by the fall of the hammer, then it is soon enough to take up firing. Do not attempt to practice rapid squeezing until the muscles of your trigger finger become sufficiently trained to squeeze correctly in slow fire. When you begin firing you must concentrate more than ever on aiming, holding and squeezing the trigger, for the effects of the discharge and the resulting recoil will cause a mental and physical reaction which will have a tendency to cause you to flinch, and to flinch before the bullet has left the muzzle, courts disaster in the form of a wild shot. As correct trigger squeeze is the greatest asset to successful pistol shooting so is flinching the greatest obstacle to learning the game. If it was possible for a man to put out of his mind all thoughts of what was going to happen when the hammer fell or if he could fire mechanically he would then be able to eliminate flinching or at least to minimize the tendency so that he would have little to fear from that source. In this connection the reader is referred to the chapter on Shooting Psychology.

In all trigger squeeze or rapid fire exercises it is extremely desirable, in fact quite essential, to have a trigger adjusted so that it is free from "creep" and will release the hammer smoothly and cleanly.

Chapter VII

THE AIMING PROBLEM

To SOLVE the aiming problem in pistol shooting requires a knowledge of several factors all of which, though comparatively simple in principle, must be thoroughly understood by the novice if he desires to advance steadily and without unnecessary set-backs toward the goal of expert shooting. The correct method of aiming and of adjusting sights, the kind, size, shape and color of the latter, the matter of eyesight and shooting glasses, and the effects of different lights on aiming are some of the details that must be understood by a beginner in order to make rapid progress in the game.

PRINCIPLES AND METHODS

The principles of aiming are simple and easily learned. The purpose of this act is to point the pistol by means of the arm, the eyes and the sights so that the bullet will hit the target when the weapon is fired. This is accomplished by bringing the sights of the pistol into the line of sight from the master eye to the target. When the sights are brought into alignment correctly, they should present to the eye a certain picture or perspective view with the target in the background. This view of the sights and target should always be the same and any variation from it should be corrected before firing. The view of the sights properly aligned on

77

a bull's-eye target should show the front sight centered
in the notch of the rear sight with its top aligned with
the top edge of the rear sight and just tangent to the
bottom of the bull's-eye.   This is known as the normal
method of aiming.

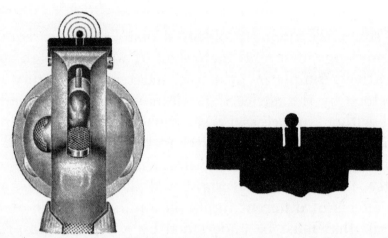

The appearance of bull's-eye and sights when correctly aligned by
the normal method of aiming. The top of both front sights should just
touch the bull's-eye.
(Left) A Colt's target revolver with Patridge sights.
(Right) A Tell free pistol.

With this method it must be remembered that, though
the point of aim is at the bottom edge of the bull's-eye,
the sights are constructed or adjusted to such a height
that the pistol when properly aimed and fired will place
its shots in the center of the bull's-eye. For game shooting or for target shooting at small objects, the pistol
should be sighted so that it will hit the spot at which
it is aimed.

Most good pistol shots keep both eyes open while
aiming and firing. The beginner should learn this
method of binocular aiming because of its natural advantages. The right-handed shooter, however, whose

left eye is his master eye, may find it difficult to aim easily with both eyes open and he then has the choice of closing the left eye while aiming or of learning to shoot with the left hand. Closing the left eye would be preferable.

To determine the master eye, extend the right arm and index finger. Keeping both eyes open, carefully align the top of the finger with a small object some distance away. Without moving the head, close the left eye and if the sight alignment between eye, finger and object appears the same as with both eyes open, the right eye is the master eye. If the finger appears to point to the left of the object, then the left eye is the master eye.

ADJUSTMENT OF SIGHTS

With target pistols and military weapons having adjustable sights, the normal method of aiming should always be used and errors in elevation corrected by raising or lowering the sights, without changing the aiming point. If the pistol has an adjustable rear sight, move it in the direction you wish to make the correction or the direction you wish your bullet to go. Remember always that your bullet will follow the direction of movement of the rear sight. If the sight adjustments are made on the front sight, the rule is reversed. Some target weapons have both sights adjustable, the front sight for elevation and the rear sight for direction. When using pistols thus sighted, care must be taken to follow the rules for making adjustments, or confusion and errors in sight setting will result. In using weapons of this kind make the correction for direction first by moving the rear sight and verify the adjustment with a few shots. Adjust for elevation by raising or lowering the front sight the proper amount, being careful to lower it if you wish to shoot higher, or to raise it if you wish to lower your shot group.

On military or pocket pistols having absolutely fixed sights, errors in elevation and direction due to the improper sighting of the weapon can be corrected only by changing the aiming point, or by altering the sights themselves. In the case of elevation trouble only, errors can be corrected by changing from the normal method of aiming to that of seeing more or less of the front sight in the rear sight notch.

At one time, in our military service, men were taught to take what was known as fine sight, half sight or full sight, if they wished to change the elevation of the shot on the target. Due to the uncertainty of taking the same amount of front sight when an attempt was made to take a fine or full sight, great inaccuracy sometimes occurred. With the half sight, the top of the front sight could be accurately aligned with the top of the rear sight and this method was retained as the correct one for aiming with open sights and was called the normal method of sighting or aiming.

It is well at this time to advise the novice to make no alterations in fixed sights until considerable experience and practice has convinced him that his pistol does not hit where it should when properly aimed and fired.

When he is certain that his pistol is not properly sighted for his manner of gripping, he should determine its errors by firing several five or ten shot groups at the range he expects to use the gun the most, and then calculate the distance of the center of impact of each group from the center of the bull's-eye. The mean error of these centers from the center of the bull's-eye should be the amount of correction to make on the sight. If the rear sight consists of a sight bar, and is not part of the frame or barrel of the weapon, elevation corrections can be made as follows: to increase elevation file off the

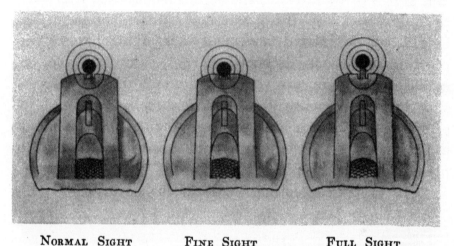

NORMAL SIGHT   FINE SIGHT   FULL SIGHT

This sketch shows three methods of aligning fixed revolver sights on a bull's-eye. Such a revolver should be sighted so that when a "normal sight" is taken at 6:00 o'clock on the bull's-eye the bullets will hit center. The same revolver will shoot low if a "fine sight" is taken and high if a "full sight" is used. Instead of changing the method of aligning the sights, it is better practice to change the aiming point to one above or below the bottom of the bull's-eye an amount equal to the correction necessary to center the shots in the black.

top of the front sight; to decrease elevation file off the top of the rear sight and deepen the notch; to correct for errors to the right or left or what are known as errors of direction, drive the sight bar with a small hammer in the direction you wish to make your correction.

If the rear sight is merely a notch cut in the frame or barrel of the pistol and the front sight is fixed, there is no way of decreasing the elevation. However, one can, by filing off the front sight, make the pistol shoot higher.

The best way to get such a pistol sighted to suit is to determine its errors in inches, both for elevation and direction, and then send the weapon back to the factory with instructions to have it resighted the way desired.

When making sight adjustments either with adjustable sights or by altering the sights themselves, it is well to understand and appreciate how a little change in the height, or the lateral movement of a sight changes the position of the bullets on the target. For example, let us assume that a revolver with sights 6 inches apart is shooting eight inches high and four inches to the right of the center of the bull's-eye at 50 yards. How much must we lower the rear sight and move it to the left to make it shoot center?

Let $x =$ the correction necessary for elevation,

then
$$\frac{x}{6} = \frac{8}{1800}$$

$$x = \frac{48}{1800} = .026 \text{ inches}$$

let $x =$ correction necessary for direction

$$\frac{x}{6} = \frac{4}{1800} = \frac{1}{75} = .013 \text{ inches}$$

From this it will be noted that the sight changes are small for a comparatively large change in the elevation and direction of the bullets.

SIGHTS

The question of the kind, shape, and size of sights for use in different conditions of light and background always has and probably always will provide a most interesting subject for experiment by the pistol enthusiast and one in which he can use his ingenuity to the limit of his interest.

Sights may be classified in a general way according to use and form, as military and non-military. The latter class may be again divided according to their use into target and sporting sights. Strictly speaking military sights should be open and fixed. They should be of a shape that permits a pistol to be readily drawn from a holster and they should be strongly and substantially made so as to stand the rough usage of general military service. Until the adoption of automatic pistols for military purposes, the rear sights on our military revolvers were cut in the frame of the weapon, but today many military automatic pistols have a rear sight that can be moved laterally and some even have sights adjustable for elevation.

Front sights may be grouped into two classes, as blade or bead, according to the cross-sectional view they present to the eye while aiming. Blade sights will usually be found on military and pocket pistols, while either blade or bead sights are in use on target or sporting pistols. The material generally used in the construction of the front sights is soft steel, or a combination of steel with German silver, bronze, ivory, or gold. These composite sights usually consist of a steel base with a bronze, silver, ivory or gold bead.

Rear sights vary from a notch cut in the pistol frame near the breech to accurately made sight bars, which are fitted to the barrel or frame in such a way as to permit their movement and adjustment for elevations and deflections. These adjustments are usually made by turning convenient set screws by means of a key or jeweler's screw-driver or by micrometer adjusting screws. The notches in the sight bars are usually bevelled toward the muzzle so they will always present a clean cut outline to the eye when aiming. Peep sights are seldom used in pistol shooting as they are impracticable except for experimental work or very deliberate slow fire shooting. They are not permitted in any of the pistol matches controlled by the National Rifle Association of America, the United States Revolver Association or the International Shooting Union.

While open sights have always been acknowledged as the most practicable for pistols, the shape, form, and size of these sights have been and will continue to be the subject of considerable study and controversy among pistol cranks.

As a general rule a sight should be large, and high enough to avoid being blurred by heat waves which rise from the heated barrel of a gun fired rapidly on a warm sunny day. This applies particularly to military pistols.

Large sights are advantageous because they are easy to see and align quickly. They are less affected by light changes, either natural or artificial, and they are not so easily bent, broken or displaced as fine sights. For these reasons probably, they have become very popular in late years, not only for military shooting but for very accurate target work, especially indoors under artificial light. Thirty years ago the bead front sight was the favorite for target work, but nowadays the pendulum has swung the other way and many more rectangular blade sights are in use for accurate target shooting, although the bead front sight still has its staunch advocates. Very fine pin head beads, while very accurate in favorable light, are most difficult to use in very bright light such as one encounters when shooting toward the west on a sunny afternoon.

Realizing that there is occasionally a necessity for changing one's aiming point when using fixed sights, it always seems easier to do this with a front sight whose top and sides are rectangular than with one whose outline is curved. Similarly it is easier to hold the top of such a sight centered under the bull's-eye at six o'clock than it is to do the same thing with a bead sight. Psychologically the latter procedure seems as difficult as balancing a large ball on top of a small one.

For target shooting at the customary bull's-eye target, a black sight is preferable, provided one aims at six o'clock on the bull's-eye, as his sights are then clearly outlined against the light colored background of the target. If, however, he is firing at a very large black bull's-eye or a black silhouette figure target and his aiming point is within the black, then a white, ivory, gold or silver front sight is highly desirable. If a rectangular front sight is used, it can be made more easily visible by coating or painting it with chalk or white paint. A small tube of Chinese White carried in one's shooting kit and carefully applied to the front sight will aid greatly when executing rapid or quick fire against a dark silhouette target. All members of the Winning American Olympic Pistol Team of 1924 used this method of illuminating their sights and it proved very successful. For shooting among the shades and shadows of the woods, the same scheme would be successful were it not for the fact that the color would be rubbed off while carrying the pistol in, or drawing it from a holster or pocket.

Though opinions differ as to the relative merits of ivory, german silver, bronze and gold beads for hunting or sporting purposes, the author firmly believes that a good gold alloy bead is superior to all others for general use. It is capable of being seen in most unfavorable lights and it can be blackened or smoked without harm, should its use be desired for shooting at the regular paper target. Though it is obviously undesirable to have the bead highly polished for use in bright sunlight, the contrary is true when it is used in the dark woods. Frequently when hunting in the thick fir forests of our Northwest or in the jungles of the tropics, I have been able, with the aid of the tiny point of gold gleaming from the center of my bead, to hit wonderfully concealed small game perched in the dark foliage. The chief disadvantage of gold beads is their softness, and they must therefore be handled carefully, or they get out of shape easily.

EYESIGHT AND SHOOTING GLASSES

Due to the short ranges at which pistol shooting is done and the large targets normally used, excellent eyesight is not so necessary to success as a novice might suppose. Normal vision without the aid of glasses is desirable though not absolutely necessary, for one may correct faulty vision by glasses so as to have it free from astigmatism and thus be able to pass the 20/20 optical test. Furthermore it has frequently been noted that eyes that are apparently normal and which can see

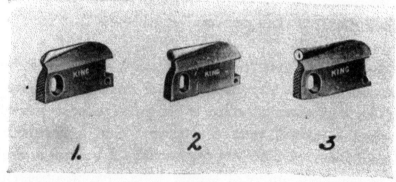

1 and 2 are King gold bead front sights for Colt's target pistols and revolvers. No. 1 is designed for use in a holster. 3 is an ivory head for the same weapons. 4, 5 and 6 are similar sights designed for S. & W. pistols and revolvers. 7 and 8 are Marble gold bead sights designed for S. & W. and Colt's pistols and revolvers.

well enough to aim easily and accurately in daylight have great difficulty in seeing the sights distinctly when shooting is done under artificial light. This results in errors of aiming that produce large shot groups regardless of how well the marksman may hold. To anyone who finds himself in this predicament and who desires to continue shooting under artificial light, as so many small bore pistol shots are now doing, the author offers

Standard sights issued on Colt's target pistols and revolvers.

an incident from his personal experience that may aid the discouraged.

When I first took up indoor pistol shooting, it was after considerable experience out of doors with military revolvers. My introduction to the game came as a result of being stationed near a city in which a flourishing rifle and revolver club was organized. I became a member of the club and was keenly interested in observing what to me was a new and interesting phase of pistol shooting, for the indoor season was then in full swing and the pistol shots of the club had discarded their heavy revolvers and were devoting their efforts to small bore matches.

On the advice of some of the older shots, I invested in a .22 caliber Smith and Wesson target pistol with 10 in. barrel and equipped with a thin blade front sight. The sights proved to be entirely unsuitable for indoor shooting as the front sight was but one thirty-second of an inch thick.

My eyesight at that time was normal except for a very slight astigmatism for which I used corrected glasses when reading or shooting.

My first attempts for a score at this new game, with my impracticable sights, resulted in a startling failure, for I found that my eyes could not accommodate themselves to the open sights and bull's-eye as seen in electric light and they soon began to water and feel strained. I then began to experiment with the lighting system and tried shooting from a dark firing point, but all to no avail. In talking over my troubles with brother shooters, I learned that all of them were using broad front sights; some used large beads but most of them the broad rectangular Patridge sight. Most of them aimed at six o'clock on the bull's-eye, but a few bisected it with the flat top of their rectangular front sights, which were just wide enough for the purpose. I changed my sights to a Patridge one-tenth inch rectangular front, and a square notched rear sight which helped somewhat, for I could then at least see my sights, though rather hazily and indistinctly. The bull's-eye, however, stood out clear and black.

After several evenings my scores showed little improvement and I became discouraged, especially when I found that my daily efforts developed eye strain and headaches. As a last resort I consulted an optician who had been recommended to me because of his interest in outdoor revolver shooting. He listened to my tale of woe, became quite interested in the problem and directed me to bring my pistol, shooting glasses and an indoor target to his office the next day. On keeping this appointment I found that he had arranged to simulate the condition of the indoor range. He placed me in a chair with a large mirror across the room in front of me and hung the paper target above and behind me with a light so arranged that I was somewhat in the dark and the target was brightly illuminated. After he had adjusted one of the ordinary optician's trial frames to my head, he directed me to aim at the target while he slipped various test lenses into the slots in front of my eyes. With lenses corresponding to those of my own glasses, I found the sights looked blurred and fuzzy as when shooting at the club. Other lenses were substituted until finally two were found that brought my sights into distinct focus but made the bull's-eye appear very slightly blurred, or out of focus. The prescription for these lenses was Right, Plus .50 sphere combined with plus .50 cylinder axis 90. Left, Plus .50 cylinder axis 90 and from this the optician had ground two lenses which he mounted in a pair of cheap nickel spectacles and gave me the next day with instructions to try them on the indoor range.

It was with feelings of mingled fear and doubt that I placed a target on the range that evening and from a darkened firing point aligned my sights on the bull's-eye. To my joy and relief the sights were clear and distinct and though the bull's-eye was slightly out of focus I found no difficulty in aiming accurately, and my scores thenceforth showed improvement in accordance with my ability to hold. The eye strain and head-aches I had been having after each evening's shooting, occurred no more. Those same nickel frames with the original lenses in them have now been in use for over sixteen years for indoor shooting under artificial light.

Frequently in the many pistol clubs with which my military service has brought me in contact, I have seen men experimenting with sights and lights in an attempt to get clearer definition of the former and to them I have told this story and provided a remedy, much to their relief and pleasure. Fortunately only a small proportion of men who follow this indoor pistol game have the same degree of eye trouble that I had, and it is to this small minority that I offer this incident.

LIGHT EFFECTS

Although some individuals have trouble with artificial light, others find that sunlight has a noticeable effect on their shooting at times. With open sights as used on pistols, there are frequently occasions when an unusual condition of light causes the shot group to be displaced materially from the center of a bull's-eye target. There is no absolute rule which governs and by which a marks-man can be certain of making proper corrections under all conditions of light.

It is generally believed that in using open sights in bright sunlight there is a tendency to shoot away from the sun. For example, when firing with the sun shining strongly from the right, the pistol will shoot to the left or with a bright sun overhead as at noon time the shot group will be low. This rule holds only for certain individuals, and the effects of bright sunlight on the sights vary with different kinds of sights. There is only one safe rule to follow and that is to "sight in your pistol" for different conditions of light, and to be absolutely certain that you know where it shoots under these conditions. As a safety precaution, be especially careful of your aim and hold for the first few shots of any competition you may enter. Then if you find that your shots are not centered properly when you call them "good," correct your direction or elevation accordingly. I once saw a man who had an excellent chance for the Pistol Championship of the World ruin that chance and his morale as well, by not raising his elevation when his sighters showed that his group was low. He continued to fire his first ten record shots with an elevation he had been accustomed to using and then, when it was too late, he raised his rear sight and centered his group. His low shots were not due to anything except a peculiar light condition which affected many competitors who fired at that time.

CALLING THE SHOT

Closely linked with aiming is an equally important essential of good marksmanship known as "Calling the Shot." It is the term used by shooters for indicating the location of a hit by the sight alignment at the instant the arm is fired, and before the actual bullet hole is seen by or indicated to the shooter. Its importance is not generally appreciated by beginners nor is the necessity for its proper performance fully understood by all experienced shots.

The reasons for calling the shot are:

1. To assure a marksman that he knows exactly where his pistol is aimed at the instant it is fired.
2. To determine whether or not the pistol is correctly sighted, that is whether it will hit the target when properly aimed.
3. To aid a novice in preventing and overcoming flinching.
4. To teach the necessity for close, steady holding until a shot is fired, for calling the shot is absolutely essential to the development of great accuracy in pistol marksmanship.

If a shooter cannot see where his pistol is aimed when it fires, the chances are that he shuts his eyes and flinches. The disposition to so do is the greatest obstacle to accurate marksmanship. If on the other hand, he can indicate the exact spot on the target on which his sights were aligned when the explosion occurred, he can then determine by the location of the bullet hole whether or not the gun shoots where it is aimed. If a novice will concentrate on aiming and calling his shot while he is holding and squeezing, it will aid him greatly in overcoming the tendency to flinch which is caused by letting the mind dwell on the explosion and its effects.

While firing a shot carefully, a marksman tries to hold his sights aligned on the target, and to squeeze his trigger when this alignment looks right. If he keeps his eyes open, he will, after a little practice, be able to see the exact spot on the target at which his weapon was aimed when it fired. Then without hesitation and without looking at the bullet hole, he should call his shot by saying to himself or to his coach, "It's high, It's low, It's right, It's left, It's good" as the case may be. As he becomes more experienced, he will be able to call his shots by saying; "It's an 8 at 3 o'clock" or "It's a close nine at 12 o'clock" or "It's a bull's-eye at 6 o'clock." When he can call his shots accurately by the clock system, that is by referring to the bull's-eye as though it were a clock and the points on its circumference in terms of the hours and fractions thereof, then, and only then will he get the full benefits from the practice. When a marksman realizes that to call a shot other than "Good" means a lower score than might have been, the psychological effect is to make him strive earnestly to aim, hold and squeeze so that he can call all of his shots "Good," and this in turn results in greater accuracy.

Chapter VIII

SHOOTING AGAINST TIME

ACCURATE rapid shooting is the true measure of one's skill and co-ordination in pistol shooting; skill in manipulating the pistol and co-ordination in aiming, holding, squeezing the trigger and calling the shot. It is not only the most practical kind of shooting to learn but is a highly advantageous adjunct to other kinds of firing and should be practiced to a certain extent at all times when one is training with the pistol. By rapid fire practice we develop co-ordination to a high degree and this aids greatly when we fire very deliberately as it keeps our mind and muscles from becoming sluggish and prevents the development of that fault or habit known as "freezing," that is, of being all set to fire and unable to squeeze the trigger.

During the tryouts to select pistol teams to represent the United States in the Olympic matches and the annual matches of the International Shooting Union in 1924 the practicability of rapid firing was clearly demonstrated. The Olympic matches consisted entirely of rapid firing, while those of the International Shooting Union of only deliberate firing with "free pistols" with practically an unlimited time allowance in which to fire sixty shots. The American tryout was participated in by pistol shots from many parts of the country as well as from Hawaii and the Panama Canal Zone and included National competition winners in both slow and rapid firing. The Olympic team tryout was held first, and the entire team selected, including substitutes, was composed of Army and Marine Corps men who were primarily military shots. Three of these men also won places on the International team. All pistol shots present tried out for both teams. It was quite evident that the old experienced deliberate fire shots were incapable of firing rapidly with accuracy, whereas the rapid fire specialists could do both kinds of shooting well. Incidentally those particular American teams shot the highest scores of any teams that had represented us in such matches up to that time.

Before the advent of the automatic or auto-loading pistol, accurate rapid firing against time consisted mainly of two problems. These were, aiming and squeezing the trigger, and cocking the revolver between shots. Success then depended largely on one's skill in solving the latter either by single or double action. The introduction of the automatic pistol simplified the problem of accurate rapid firing very much for with this weapon cocking by the shooter is eliminated and the entire time allowance can be devoted to aiming and squeezing the trigger.

Perhaps because of the popularity of the revolver and in order to encourage rapid fire practice by those who prefer this weapon the time allowance per shot in qualification and competition shooting has not been reduced, though this might well be done for automatic pistol shooting as the elimination of cocking allows a maximum of time for aiming and firing.

Depending upon his choice of weapons the novice may

learn rapid fire with either the revolver or the automatic pistol but if he chooses the former he will always be at some disadvantage when competing against men using automatics.

PRINCIPLES

There are three principles that must be understood and observed if one desires to secure the greatest results in rapid firing.

1. Every movement of pointing and aiming must be made in the quickest and most direct manner.
2. In rapid aiming the shooter should first establish his line of sight by fixing his master eye on the aiming point of the target and then bring the pistol sights into this line of sight. To attempt to align the sights first and then, by moving the pistol, to align the sights and the target is the wrong procedure.
3. In all rapid firing care should be taken to release the trigger fully after each shot.

Regardless of where the pistol is when we commence rapid firing it should be thrust into the firing position without unnecessary flourishes or other time wasting movements. In military and N.R.A. competitions in this country it is usual to start with the pistol in the position of "RAISE PISTOL" as prescribed in the U. S. Army Training Regulations for the pistol. This is, with the pistol held in the hand, six inches in front of the right shoulder, muzzle up, barrel to the rear and inclined to the front at an angle of 30 degrees.

In Europe, and the U.S.R.A., rapid fire competitions the rules require the marksman to hold the pistol with the arm extended toward the ground at an angle of 45 degrees with the body. Other rules sometime require the pistol to be in a holster until the signal to commence firing is given. In practice that simulates firing in self defense the pistol may be in a holster, in the pocket, or any other convenient place one may desire to carry it. In any case no time should be wasted in unnecessary movements of the gun into firing position. Even from "Raise Pistol" men frequently swing the pistol and forearm through the arc of a circle in taking the aiming position, instead of thrusting the hand straight toward the target and dropping the muzzle below the aiming point as they make the thrust. Quicker aim can be secured if the sights of a pistol can be brought into the line of sight from below rather than from above and through it. This can be done from "Raise Pistol" if the head is held erect and the muzzle kept below the line of sight. During the rapid firing of a string of shots on the same target the sights of the pistol should be held in alignment with the aiming point except when recoil or wind puffs derange the aim. Swinging the gun to a vertical position or similar flourishes between shots are always indicative of inexperienced shooters.

While it is always advisable to aim as accurately as time will permit obviously one cannot hope to align sights as carefully and exactly in rapid as in deliberate firing. As an aid to rapid aiming it is therefore desirable to have a front sight large enough to be quickly caught by the eye and a rear sight notch of sufficient width and depth to enable one to center the front sight within the notch easily. A combination of a broad blade front sight and a large U shaped rear sight with a horizontal upper edge is very satisfactory for quick and rapid firing.   Several of the newer military revolvers and pistols have sights of this form.

MANIPULATION

One of the first questions that arises when a novice begins firing with a revolver is that of using the double action.   While there are exceptions to the rule it is generally agreed that the most accurate rapid fire target shooting can be done with the revolver by cocking it for each shot as though it did not have the double action. The author however does not agree with many others who say that accurate rapid firing cannot be done using the double action.   The reason we do not become skillful in this method of firing is because we do not have to fire within a time limit that would make it difficult to get in all our shots if we used single action. A few years ago the Rapid Fire Championship at Camp Perry was won by a man using the double action and I have known two men who have developed uncanny skill in this method of firing simply because they specialized in it rather than in the popular method of firing.

If our purpose in learning to shoot a revolver is something more than mere target practice and we have the thought in mind that we may sometime have to use it in self-defense and at close quarters, then, we should by all means practice double action shooting, emphasizing quick drawing and pointing rather than aiming.   In emergencies like this it would be well for us to employ the tactics suggested by the words of a famous Confederate cavalry leader who said: "Always git thar fustest with the mostest."

To cock the revolver smoothly and with greatest speed

when using it as a single action weapon requires a little knowledge and a lot of practice. A person with a small hand may have considerable difficulty in manipulating a large caliber revolver, while one with an unusually large hand has diametrically opposite troubles in cocking small caliber weapons conveniently and speedily. With this in mind one of the three practical methods of cocking herein described and illustrated will be found

Cocking Method No. 1. Note that the grip is not changed while cocking in this manner.

suitable for almost any person except he be possessed of a very abnormal hand.

METHOD NO. 1: Hold the revolver in the proper normal grip with the hand high on the stock, three fingers around the butt and thumb along the left side of the frame in a position most convenient to the particular type of revolver used. With the thumb parallel to the barrel place the ball of the thumb on the cocking spur of the hammer, press downward and backward to cock the gun, at the same time turning the muzzle very slightly to the right without releasing the grip on the butt more than is absolutely necessary. The advantage of this method is that it assures one of retaining the same hold or position of the hand on the stock. It can be executed by an average sized hand and carries out the principle of keeping the sights aligned most of the time.

METHOD NO. 2: Hold the revolver as in Method No. 1. Flip the muzzle upward and to the right, at the same

Cocking Method No. 2. Showing the position of the thumb and the release of the grip between shots.

time placing the thumb across the hammer spur nearly at right angles to it and cocking the gun by pressing downward. The chief disadvantage of this method is that the grip must be entirely released and each succeeding shot may be fired with the hand in a different position unless time is taken to adjust it carefully. The advantages are that the work of cocking is made easy especially for small hands and that the recoil of the pistol helps the operation.

METHOD NO. 3: Grip the revolver with the little finger under the butt. Place the ball of the thumb firmly on the hammer spur, thumb parallel to the barrel, press down and cock the piece. If the thumb cannot reach the hammer it will be necessary to start the latter back by pressing firmly on the trigger until the hammer spur can be securely gripped by the thumb. The trigger is then released and the cocking completed by the thumb

Cocking Method No. 3. This shows the position of the thumb and little finger as the cocking begins. The grip is not changed at any time. Persons who cannot reach the spur with the thumb should start the hammer back by pressure on the trigger.

alone. The advantages are that the grip remains the same for each shot, the hammer can be easily cocked, the sights can be held more nearly in alignment and, when the thumb can reach the hammer and the double action be dispensed with, it is the fastest of all cocking methods. It has the disadvantages of requiring a lower grip on the pistol, a great deal of practice to execute smoothly when the double action is used and causes considerable strain on the wrist when firing is done with a heavy caliber revolver. To execute it most conveniently this method requires the arm to be slightly bent during the cocking and firing.

When he entered the military service the author was taught this method of holding and cocking the .38 caliber revolver then issued to the army. His instructor was an officer who had won the National Individual Pistol Match using this technique in both rapid and slow fire and as a result it was a favorite method for several years until the .45 caliber automatic pistol became the official side arm of the Service. This new pistol compelled the adoption of a higher grip because of the grip safety and the removal of the little finger from under the butt.

During a fairly wide experience in competition shooting the author has seen only two real rapid fire experts use Method No. 3 successfully, altho there have been several outstanding shots before his time who favored this practice. Of the two referred to, one of them probably has captured more rapid fire trophies than any other American on record. He uses the bent arm in all kinds of firing. As an aid to a more secure grip he has cut away the corners of the wooden stocks on some of his revolvers so that his little finger fits snugly and comfortably around the bottom of the butt.

RAPID FIRE EXERCISES

In practicing rapid fire exercises one should simulate as nearly as possible the conditions of actual firing, as regards size of target, starting position and time allowance for the string of shots to be fired. The purposes of the exercises are to develop quickness in manipulation, rapid co-ordination in aiming and squeezing, and regularity in firing. Quickness in manipulation is very essential when the single action of a revolver is used and its attainment depends entirely on practice. With automatic weapons this problem is greatly simplified. Co-ordination which will give uniform firing intervals and accurately placed shots, will be developed by practicing aiming and snapping systematically. The first shot of a string usually takes more time than the succeeding ones, and it is well therefore to devote considerable practice to snapping single shots from the position of "Raise Pistol." If one is slow in getting off the first shot it will cause hurry throughout the rest of the string with resulting inaccuracy and irregularity in the firing intervals. The novice should learn from snapping practice just how much time he requires to complete the string of shots and then by practice assure himself that he can get them all off well within the time limit. If he has learned by experience just how much time he has to spare, he has a comfortable feeling of confidence, when he is delayed in firing his first shot, because he knows he still has sufficient time to complete his string without sacrificing accuracy. The good rapid fire shot gets his first shot off in a minimum of time and the remaining ones with clock-like regularity, safely within the time allowed. The mediocre marksman fires his first shot either too fast or too slow and the others of the string at irregular intervals with absolute lack of smoothness; this results in very erratic shooting.

REVOLVER EXERCISES

Take the correct firing position in front of an appropriate sized sighting bull's-eye with the revolver at "Raise Pistol." The grip for rapid fire should be firmer than for slow fire and all slack taken up almost to the extent of partially squeezing the trigger when "Ready" is given.

At a signal or command for "Commence Firing" given by someone acting as a coach thrust the muzzle of the revolver directly toward the target and bring the sights into the line of sight, which should have been established by keeping the master eye fixed at six o'clock on the bull's-eye. Simulate firing by squeezing the trigger smoothly and decisively when the aim is correct. Cock the revolver quickly, maintaining the grip and the sight alignment as far as possible, and when the aim is again correct squeeze decisively as for the first shot. Repeat the procedure until five shots are fired. Rest a few minutes and repeat the exercise, being careful to execute it each time with care and attention. Start slowly at first and strive for smoothness in manipulation, that is, in cocking, squeezing, and especially in thrusting the revolver forward for the first shot. As smoothness is acquired speed will be developed and then the novice can concentrate on regularity and uniformity in snapping, which can best be acquired by snapping the piece at a regular interval of time regardless of accuracy of aim. This may be accomplished by having the coach call off the seconds to you or by counting to yourself—One and, Two and, Three and, up to Ten and, which should take ten seconds. Co-ordination will be developed by careful regular practice to the point where the squeeze will fire the piece at the instant the aim is correct and both will occur at regular intervals of time.

AUTOMATIC PISTOL EXERCISES

An automatic pistol that cannot be cocked conveniently while held in the firing position is impracticable for rapid fire exercises beyond the point of simulating the firing of the first shot of a string. Hammerless pistols and those without cocking spurs come in this category. With this fact in mind the novice who desires to train himself in the technique of rapid firing without expending ammunition will do well to select a pistol with a convenient hammer which can be readily cocked between shots either by the thumb method used on revolvers or by some other practical method. Actual practice in rapid firing may be held at small cost with the .22 caliber automatic pistols but to do this with large caliber weapons would be very expensive. The substitution of good rapid fire exercises in place of firing is highly desirable for several reasons.

Since its adoption in 1911 as the official side arm of our Army and Navy the .45 Caliber Automatic pistol, Model 1911 (Colt Government Model) is now more generally used throughout the country than all other automatics due to its wide distribution during and immediately following the World War and to the fact that government ammunition for it can be obtained readily at very reasonable prices. As a further incentive to practice with this pistol, all government qualification courses, the National Pistol Matches, and many other competitions, are limited to this pistol. In view of these facts the following exercise with this weapon is suggested:

Obtain a strong cord about four feet in length and of not to exceed one-eighth inch in diameter and tie one end securely to the cocking spur of the hammer with the knot on top. Hold the other end securely in the left hand near the left thigh and take the firing position opposite a sighting bull's-eye with gun cocked and at "Raise Pistol." At the signal for "Commence Firing" extend the right hand quickly and smoothly toward the target, align the sights, hold the breath, squeeze the trigger and call the shot. After the hammer has fallen recock it by a jerk on the cocking cord, so as to flip the muzzle upward, or by raising the pistol hand until the taut cord cocks the hammer, and immediately thereafter aim and squeeze the trigger for the second shot. Repeat until a string of five shots are snapped. Care should be taken to observe the principles of rapid aiming, squeezing straight to the rear and of releasing the trigger after each shot. This snapping practice should be done against time as described for the revolver.

The value of rapid fire snapping exercises cannot be overstressed for they are a most important factor in successfully shooting against time.

Chapter IX

FREE PISTOL SHOOTING

"FREE PISTOL" shooting originated in Europe and is the form of practice held under the rules of the International Shooting Union (Union Internationale de Tir). The name grew out of the custom of using pistols unrestricted as to caliber, length of barrel and weight of trigger pull in the competitions controlled by that organization. The name applied is not strictly accurate for there is one limitation placed on the arms used and that is that they must have open sights not containing glass. Regulations for this kind of shooting further provide that firing be done at fifty meters (about 55 yards) at the International target. The latter consists of ten rings, two and a half centimeters (.983 inches) apart, counting respectively one to ten points. It is shown in Chapter II. There is practically no time limit per shot as twenty-four hours is allowed in which to complete the course of fire for the International Free Pistol Match which consists of eighteen sighting and sixty record shots.

Twenty-eight nations are now represented in this international shooting organization, and pistol practice in accordance with its rules is increasing in popularity. This is due largely to the conditions under which firing is done. The use of a universal target, sheltered firing points, liberal time allowances, and free pistols makes it possible for marksmen of all nations to compare their skill under as near uniform and ideal conditions for accurate shooting as it is practical to devise. The use of free pistols stimulates initiative in the designing and perfecting of super-accurate target guns, and though they may be of little practical value for military purposes or for self-defense they do provide the pawns for a highly scientific game, which after all is a worthy

The shooting stand during the 1924 International Matches at Rheims, France. Note the comfort, convenience and completeness of the arrangements for the marksmen.

purpose in itself, and one which may eventually be the only legitimate reason for the possession and use of pistols by civilians.

Unquestionably this International style of shooting is the highest form of accurate pistol practice, and one which appeals particularly to the student of the game and to those who follow the sport as disciples of accuracy

and close holding. It is not spectacular nor does it carry
with it the thrills and excitement of other forms of practice, but bears much the same relation to them that bil-
liards does to pool, or that long range duck shooting does
to upland bird shooting. It demands a high degree of
skill, a carefully developed technique, the closest kind of
holding, and the finest and most accurate shooting equipment.

The target used is quite difficult, much more so than
the Standard American Target, and wild shots penalize
the marksman's score severely. The sighting bull's-eye
of slightly less than eight inches is not unreasonable and
the ten ring is about the minimum diameter within which
the best pistols and revolvers will group their shots.

Accuracy is the keynote of success in this game and
advantage is taken of every detail that will aid in securing it. Sheltered firing points are authorized as a means
to steady holding. Shooting must be done under natural
light, which, of course, is superior to artificial illumination. There is no time limit per shot to worry the firer
and cause him to hurry his work. Pistols especially
designed for fine shooting with long sighting radius,
long accurately bored barrels, set triggers adjustable
to the most delicate touch, very fast non-jarring actions,
and stocks and grips fitted to each individual's hand are
permitted and generally used for free pistol shooting for
it is decidedly disadvantageous to be otherwise equipped.

It is not the game for the novice in pistol firing, nor
the specialist in aerial snapshooting or quick and rapid
firing. It is, however, an advanced course for the deliberate fire shot and the military or police shot who has
had good training in slow firing. When one is able to

consistently average around ninety percent on the Standard American target it will be well worth while for him to try the International one at fifty meters and determine what average he can make on it with its closer spaced counting rings and smaller center.

The European type of free pistol is, to one accustomed to the familiar American models, a clumsy, cumbersome appearing arm, but a close inspection of a good model will quickly convince one of its efficiency for the work

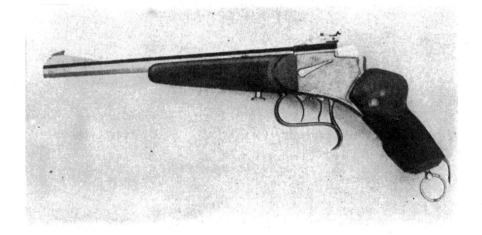

An older model "Tell" pistol.

to which it is adapted. This type of pistol generally weighs from two and a half to three pounds, and has octagonal barrels from twelve to fourteen and a half inches in length. The stocks appear quite unwieldy but this is due to their carefully shaped thumb, finger, and palm rests, which are made to fit and support all parts of the hand. As a further aid to holding, the trigger guard is provided with one or more spurs or finger holds, which when used as a part of the grip enables one to keep the arm nicely balanced with minimum muscular effort. Set triggers are the rule on these guns. Some have double triggers, the forward one being set by squeezing the rear one until it clicks. Other models have only one trigger which is set by means of a small lever on the side of the frame. The greatest asset of the European pistol is its action. The powerful leverage obtained by the cocking arm easily compresses a strong main spring and this, acting on a light hammer with a short

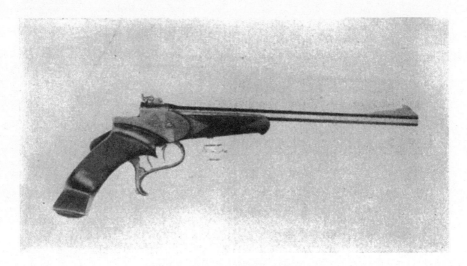

The Stotzer "Perfekt" pistol.

fall, gives a high speed action that is positive and yet so delicate that there is no jar given by the hammer striking the primer that can cause a disturbment of the sight alignment. The aiming equipment of these foreign pistols enables them to be shot with great accuracy as they have a long sighting radius which is sometimes increased by the addition of a rear sight bracket that extends well to the rear of the breach. The sights vary from delicate pin head beads, protected on both sides by metal wings, to the conventional broad rectangular blades. These are interchangeable and fit into a dovetail slot in the top of the barrel and are held there by a flat spring. The principle is good but the method of holding the front sight in place is not generally satisfactory. The rear sights have a broad horizontal upper edge of about an inch which is a great aid in the prevention of canting. They can be adjusted for elevation

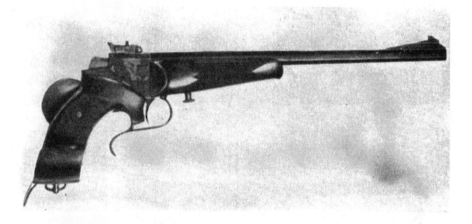

Here is shown a very late model of a System Büchel "Tell" Pistol. It has a 14¾" barrel and the grip is sloped at an angle to the barrel that is very similar to American pistols.

and deflection by means of substantial screws which are turned by small keys resembling those used to wind clocks. The latest means of sight adjustment is by a micrometer sight which gives a change in elevation of one-tenth of an inch, at fifty meters, for each click of the sight.

The technique of free pistol shooting is in general the same as slow fire practice with American pistols with the exception of a few distinctly different details, the most

important of these being the manner of holding or gripping the pistol and the method of using the set triggers.
Instead of gripping the butt of a free pistol with three

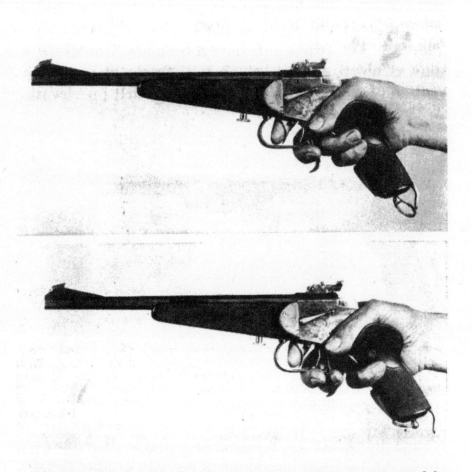

The two methods of holding the free pistol generally practiced by
European pistol men. The position of the thumb should be noted.
The shape of the thumb rest makes this position desirable if one
wishes to maintain the most comfortable and efficient grip on pistols
of this design.

fingers of the hand, as an American is accustomed to
doing, the foreigner hooks the second and sometimes the
third fingers also around the spur of the trigger guard,

leaving only one or two fingers, as the case may be, about the butt of the pistol. By doing this he is able to move the hand a little higher on the stock and to support the piece a little further forward so that it is perfectly balanced, in spite of the long barrel, and can be held with little effort while the trigger is touched or squeezed off.

A study of the illustrations will show that on the older model "Tell" and on the "Perfekt" pistol the shape of the grip and its slope or angle with the barrel is quite

The method used by some Americans for holding the free pistol. This is possible only with the later models which have the trigger guard shaped so as to permit a comfortable grip with three fingers around the butt. Even with these new pistols European shots prefer to hook one or two fingers over the trigger guard.

different from those found on most American pistols. It should also be noted that the rear support of the trigger guard of these models is so far back that it interferes with the second finger if one tries to hold the grip as he would an American pistol. The more modern guns have the rear support carefully shaped and further forward so that there is more space for the fingers that hold the stock, and the grip feels more natural to marksmen accustomed to our hand guns. It should also be noted that the stocks of the newer free pistols are better shaped and with an angle to the barrel more suited to us.

The most important detail for American shots to master in firing free pistols is the use of the set trigger. Our technique has been to squeeze the trigger rather than to touch it off and we have been accustomed to comparatively heavy pulls for so long that when we attempt to use a very light set trigger, which can barely be touched without firing the piece, there is at once presented a mental hazard which is very difficult to overcome. The pistol novice who takes up set trigger firing early in the game has one advantage over an old experienced shot because he can adapt himself to the peculiarities of this style of trigger without having to overcome a long developed habit of resting his finger on the trigger and applying a noticeable pressure before the gun will fire. Our European rivals have been brought up on set triggers and there is nothing about them they do not know and while they occasionally have accidental discharges they have learned to expect them and the results are not so startling or demoralizing.

There are two methods of releasing a set trigger. They are both used in free rifle shooting with very satisfactory results. The first is performed by a gentle tapping motion of the index finger pivoted from the second joint. When the aim is correct the shooter starts the movement of the finger and as long as the sights remain properly aligned he continues it until the trigger is touched and the rifle fired. One might think that this would develop flinching because the marksman knows that when he touches the trigger the explosion will occur. Perhaps it does, but apparently as a result of training, the set trigger expert develops a very delicate sense of touch and can with experience get his shots off as free from flinches as an American can who applies a steady pressure to the trigger.

The other method is to have a trigger set to such a weight that the index finger may be gently rested on it, until the aim is correct, when it can be released by a very light squeeze.

The latter method appears to be the more satisfactory for application to the pistol, but even then it is a more difficult problem than in free rifle firing and it is very necessary to have a support for the index finger such that very little pressure is put on the trigger until it is desired to release it. This is accomplished by extending the wooden stock as shown in the newer models of free pistols.

It is also quite practicable, with some models of European pistols to omit setting the trigger and to use it as one does an American trigger. The author found it very difficult to learn the use of set triggers after many years' experience with ordinary ones and finally by trigger adjustment experiments was able to secure a trigger pull of about a pound without using the set triggers as such. This weight is light enough for anyone and permits of squeezing the trigger in the normal American way and is offered as a suggestion to others who may find difficulty in using set triggers. While it is theoretically quite possible to adjust them to different weights, practically it is not so easy, for when one begins increasing the set trigger weight beyond a few ounces a decided creep or sponginess becomes evident in the trigger action.

Anyone who watches a free pistol match conducted by the International Shooting Union will be impressed with the leisurely manner in which the firing is done and will soon realize that the principle followed is to get every shot off with the greatest care and accuracy regardless of the time it takes. The participants take full advantage of favorable shooting conditions. If an incident occurs that upsets them they stop firing until their nerves are quite normal again. If they are not holding well they frequently take long rests between shots. If they think their pistols are not sighted properly they may fire a few sighters between their record strings, which is permissible under the rules. In simple language they take no chances.

The International game is not without its disadvantages, for to play it properly requires a range equipped with sheltered firing points. It might be argued that one could fire without this shelter, but a little experience with set triggers in a very moderate breeze will soon convince one to the contrary. The greater surface of free pistols causes them to be affected by wind to a greater degree than the more compact American hand guns. The best foreign pistols are quite expensive when one pays the high duty necessary to import them. The International target is quite satisfactory for fifty meter shooting but when reduced for twenty yard indoor practice the rings are so close together that the scores made thereon are not equivalent to those made on the full-size target at fifty meters but are generally several points higher.

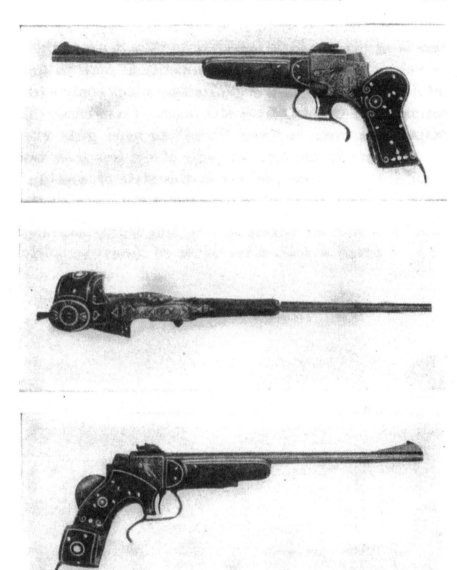

A beautiful "Tell" model Büchel pistol of most modern design. It is handsomely engraved and inlaid with gold and silver. The stock of Circassian walnut is carved with an oak leaf design inset with ivory acorns, and the forehand with a spread eagle. This masterpiece of the pistol markers' art is valued at $1000.00 and is owned by the B. H. Dyas Co., of Hollywood, California.

In America, free pistol shooting is in its infancy and there is at present little incentive to take it up as there are only a limited number of competitions open to free pistols, and the National organizations which control our National and State matches still insist on restricting the competitions open to "Any Pistol" to hand guns with ten inch barrels and trigger pulls of not less than two pounds. A few more defeats in this style of shooting, and a few more years of experience in the game on the part of our best deliberate fire shots will convince our pistol men that we should include this highly desirable form of practice with other kinds of American pistol shooting.

Chapter X

AERIAL PRACTICE

THERE is nothing magical or especially difficult about hitting objects in the air, providing one does not attempt the impossible by trying to perform feats that rightly belong in the field of shotgun shooting, or in the cleverly faked performances of the "movie" pistol shots. It is much easier to hit a moving target with a charge of shot, or with a rifle bullet than it is with one from a pistol. After the sights of a rifle have been aligned, this line of aim can be maintained by holding one's cheek firmly against the stock. The rifle barrel may then be swung until the line of aim becomes coincident with the aiming point of the moving target. This procedure is not as practicable with a pistol and consequently the same degree of accuracy cannot be expected as with a rifle. Nevertheless, one who has become moderately expert at rapid and quick firing using binocular aiming, and who has normal co-ordination should, with intelligent practice, soon develop skill in this fascinating and spectacular game. The habitual deliberate fire shot who lacks the faculty of rapid co-ordination in aiming and squeezing the trigger will probably have great difficulty in gaining even moderate skill at aerial shooting and had better stick to his specialty.

Discouragement followed by failure in this kind of shooting is usually due to three things, namely, lack of proper instruction, flinching, and practice at targets too difficult for the beginner. The novice at aerial practice should not expect to hit pennies tossed in the air or tin cans thrown rapidly across the field of fire. He should not attempt to fire more than a single shot during the flight of one target and it should be by single action, if a revolver is used. When he can hit easy targets with regularity and has acquired the knack of gun pointing with ease and smoothness, then he can take up the more difficult work with confidence.

There are three important factors that materially affect one's success in aerial practice. They are: (a) The fit and balance of the pistol. (b) The method of pointing and aiming employed. (c) The manner of throwing the targets.

A well fitted and nicely balanced pistol is more essential for aerial shooting than for any other kind of pistol practice with the possible exception of defensive firing in the dark.

The gun selected for the work may be either a revolver or an automatic, but like a shotgun used for shooting in thick cover, it must be capable of being pointed easily, accurately, and naturally. Such a pistol is one, which when held with a proper grip in a normal shooting position, will point naturally at the target with same degree of accuracy that one can point his index finger. Hand guns with a natural tendency to point high or low when properly held should be avoided for they are not well adapted to the gun pointing required in aerial work.

While it is possible to do good work with a gun that does not possess all the desirable attributes, the novice will make better progress if he selects a pistol that possesses as many of them as possible. He will find that a nicely balanced weapon of thirty-eight or smaller caliber, which fits his hand properly, weighs about two

Scoring on an ink bottle.

pounds, has a six inch barrel, and a clean, "sweet" trigger pull of not more than four pounds will probably give him the best results.

Aiming and Pointing are two different means for accomplishing the same purpose. They may be defined as the methods of giving direction to a gun with or without the use of sights, respectively,—that is we aim a weapon by aligning the master eye with the sights and the aiming point; we point a gun by natural instinct or habit without looking along the sights. If a pistol is aimed the line of sight is nearly parallel with the axis of the barrel whereas in pointing the angle between the line of sight and the axis of the barrel may be quite large, as for example when one shoots from the hip.

Among the first questions asked by a person beginning aerial practice is,—"Does one actually aim when shooting objects in the air?" The answer is "Yes," with certain exceptions to the rule. One celebrated exhibition shot says he aims every shot he fires at aerial targets. Inasmuch as he holds several records at this style of shooting a novice will not go wrong by following the example. It has been, however, the experience of the author that for relatively large targets a few feet from the muzzle, that a pistol may be pointed accurately enough without consciously aligning the sights with the eye. The natural instinct of a person to point accurately with the index finger combined with moderate practice in pistol pointing will enable one to do this quite satisfactorily if he has a well fitted and balanced pistol. Firing by pointing is the method used by some experienced shots when they wish to hit a large object in the air several times before it reaches a difficult range or falls to the ground.

The novice should try to align his sights for each shot and his success will be in accordance with his ability to catch his aim quickly and to fire the instant he does so. This requires training in pointing the pistol with fast, smooth movements and in squeezing the trigger rapidly without jerking it. Proper co-ordination can be developed by regular snapping practice at moving targets without using ammunition.

More uniformly accurate pointing will be done by fully extending the arm while aiming and firing than will be the case if the arm is bent. Experiments in shooting from the hip, that is, with the elbow at the hip, and then with the arm fully extended will quickly prove the truth of this statement. Smoothness in movements will be increased if the arm is first fully extended and then swung with the target until the aim is caught and the piece fired.

The value of binocular aiming is also evident in this practice for the target can be more quickly picked up, is more clearly seen, and appears closer and easier to hit than when one eye only is used in aiming. One should always aim at the bottom edge or slightly under an aerial target regardless of whether it is rising or falling. Aside from having the entire target visible above the sights, the reason for this may not be apparent but experience has taught that the best results will be obtained if this method is followed. In this practice sights should be adjusted so that the pistol will hit where it is aimed. Large sights are preferable.

There are two methods of executing the snapshooting that is necessary in aerial work. One is to thrust the pistol into position with the muzzle pointed at a spot ahead of the target and to press the trigger the instant the gun comes to a stop. To hit, demands an accurate estimate of the distance to aim ahead of the target. Shooting in this manner is advantageous only for large or slow moving targets, or after considerable experience

Throwing with the left hand and firing with the right.

and practice. The second and the best method, for beginners at least, is to let the master eye follow the bottom edge of the target, thrust the pistol upward until the sights come into alignment with the line of sight, press the trigger the instant the aim is correct and then continue to swing the arm with the target until the gun is fired. The latter method is snapshooting with a swing and is by far the best and most accurate way of hitting small objects. It takes a little more time but as one's skill in pointing develops and the sights are snapped into alignment more rapidly the swing becomes very short and actual snapshooting results.

Principles similar to those that govern the throwing of targets for trapshooting should apply in aerial pistol work. Clay birds are thrown within certain angles with a speed such that they will travel a certain distance and they have a rise not to exceed a certain height. The trap is sprung on command of the shooter who is in firing position a certain distance from it. By observing these rules trapshots are able to standardize their practice and compare their skill under fairly uniform conditions. If a pistol shot desires to make satisfactory progress at hitting objects in the air he must strive for uniformity in the throwing of his targets. In fact, targets for a beginner should not be thrown, they should be tossed. They should be tossed vertically to a height of not over fifteen feet and from a point a few feet in front of the shooter. The propelling of targets at once suggests the necessity of an assistant for the marksman. This is very desirable for the beginner but not an absolute necessity. A little practice with the left hand will soon enable one to toss suitable objects more satisfactorily than can be done by a person who is unaccustomed to the work. If one intends to specialize to any great extent and wants a mechanical means of projecting targets he can secure what is known as a rifle ball trap from manufacturers of shooting accessories. This device is built to throw balls or small objects vertically into the air and can be adjusted to vary the height of the targets. It is very convenient for exhibition shooting and more uniform in its action than a human trap.

A ball trap for aerial practice. This will toss a variety of targets.

The following points should be observed when using hand-propelled targets. For large objects no particular care is necessary except to see that they travel as nearly as possible in a vertical plane parallel to direction of fire. Targets should not be thrown across the front of a person firing until he has acquired skill in hitting those tossed overhead. Nor should they be tossed so that they will fall behind him. If clay birds, clam shells, coins or small disks are used they should be held between the thumb and first finger parallel to the ground and tossed upward with a slight spinning motion. If this is done properly they will always present their maximum diameter to the shooter. It sounds easy to do but requires some practice to perform correctly, especially if the marksman is doing the tossing with his left hand. There is always a tendency to spin the disks so that their edges are presented to the shooter. This is conducive to low scores and much annoyance and discouragement. Targets that do not tumble while travelling through the air are the easiest to hit and are less disconcerting to a novice. The action of gravity should never be lost sight of during aerial practice.

Very satisfactory results have been obtained by using the following procedure in teaching aerial shooting. Place the novice in his normal firing position with an empty, cocked pistol at "Raise Pistol" and caution him not to lower the muzzle below that position while snapping or firing at aerial targets. The coach places himself a few feet in front of and slightly to the right of the direction of fire. Start with a target about the size of a two quart tin can. Hold it in the right hand extended in front of the body and at the command "Ready" given by the pupil, toss it straight up to a height of not over fifteen feet, and so that in falling it can be caught by the coach without moving out of his position. As the target starts upward, the pupil should extend his arm with a smooth easy thrust and bring the sights into the line of sight from the eye to the bottom edge of the target. Care should be taken to keep the gun below this line of sight until the aim is caught. Try to catch the target as near the top of its rise as possible and before it starts to descend. As soon as the aim is caught the pupil should press the trigger decisively at the same time noting, as the hammer falls, whether or not he is on the target and then "call" his shot accordingly. When the pupil is able to call his shots "Good" the coach should permit him to load his pistol and fire a few shots. Unless flinching occurs, there should be no difficulty in the pupil hitting the can with reasonable regularity. Vary the work now by tossing a few clay pigeons overhead as previously explained. These will not go as high and will make good targets that will give the pupil a thrill when he breaks them. The first day's practice should be limited to twenty-five shots.

Either snapping or firing practice should be continued daily, starting each period with large targets and gradually changing to those of smaller dimensions. The first few lessons should be confined to such objects as large cans, clods of earth, and good sized bottles. Limit the disk shooting to clay birds. As skill develops change the targets to small cans, halves of bricks, blocks of wood, old tennis balls and objects of similar size. As a standard test of skill adopt a 2½ inch cube of wood as a target and keep a record of hits on these to check the progress in aerial work. Clam shells, iron washers with the holes covered with paper, lead disks, and large pennies make interesting targets until finally the pupil gets to the point where large marbles, small coins and even candy tablets can be hit frequently.

Some experts prefer to use large caliber revolvers and automatics for aerial work, claiming that they can obtain a better fit and balance in the larger weapons and because they are more effective in breaking targets. There is no doubt that more pleasure and satisfaction is obtained from seeing a target blown to pieces with a large bullet than there is in merely seeing it hit with a small bore pellet.

Position for Coach and Pupil.

An excellent cartridge for this work is the mid range, wad cutter or sharp shoulder bullet type. It is very pleasant to fire and when used against tin cans will sometimes lift them and enable the marksman to get in more shots than he otherwise could fire.

The novice will do well to use a small bore revolver or automatic until he has become skillful at the game for he will flinch less and can carry on much more practice for the equivalent cost of large caliber ammunition.

There is one very important point to be remembered in connection with aerial practice and that is the effect

A piece of coal hit by a .45 bullet.

that this or any other form of snapshooting may have on standardized target practice.

Snapshooting of any kind is not conducive to close holding and if practiced exclusively for long periods will spoil one's deliberate fire accuracy at paper targets.

A condition which frequently arises during aerial practice is the "flinching complex." This is more dangerous during firing at aerial targets because the habit is sometimes developed to a bad degree before it is realized. Every one has "off days" in shooting and when these occur in aerial work one is prone to believe he is not well co-ordinated in aiming, and squeezing. The chances are that he is flinching and does not know it because he cannot see how far he is missing his targets as he would if he were firing at a bull's-eye target. When one's average drops appreciably in aerial work he should investigate and remedy his trouble without delay or the consequences will be analogous to a baseball player "losing his batting eye." By using a gun loaded with both ball and dummy cartridges, or if dummies are not available, with empty shells, so that the shooter will not know when his piece will fire, one can soon discover if, and how badly he is flinching. If this fault has developed to any great extent practice should be limited to that with an empty gun and only an occasional ball cartridge. By firing a little slower and concentrating on calling the shot, and by a careful study of the chapter on shooting psychology this obstacle can be overcome readily.

Chapter XI

DEFENSIVE SHOOTING AND QUICK DRAWING

In this country, in this day and age one might logically think that the necessity for using a pistol for personal protection or for the protection of homes and property would be absolutely unnecessary. We might with similar reasoning believe that in our large cities there would be less necessity for other means of protection than the well organized police departments that are there maintained. To be perfectly honest, there is no necessity, or we might more accurately say there is little necessity, for citizens who live in well ordered communities to practice preparedness against crime to the extent of buying and learning to shoot a pistol, if there is adequate police protection provided by the municipality in which they reside. Unfortunately however, police protection does not keep pace with the demands upon it and a study of the records of police stations in any of our medium or larger sized cities will show that hold-ups, robberies, burglaries, thievery and malicious vandalism are as rampant today as they probably ever were, if not more so. My sympathy is all with the police, too, in this matter, for I know something of their problem and the efforts they make to solve it. It is a great deal like trying to maintain an adequate military establishment for national defense with inadequate funds and detrimental outside influences that prevent efficient, honest service. Let us grant for the sake of limiting discussion that there are many thousands of our civilian population who live where they have no need to fire a shot for personal protection any more than they have need for a practical knowledge of how to swim. Then stop and think of the thousands of communities where there is little or no active protection against the rougher elements of society. Think of the country stores and banks, of the isolated farmhouses and country homes, of the innumerable miles of automobile highways through forests, mountains and deserts where hold-ups are practical and help is absent. So vulnerable have small communities become to the depredations of organized bandits that "Vigilance Committees" have again been formed in certain sections of the country to combat banditry. Bankers' Associations of many states have offered large rewards for the capture or killing of these menaces to progress. Along the lanes of migration of that horde of undesirables who do not believe in working, the country is always subject to domestic unrest and depredations, as the changing seasons cause these vagrants to seek the more comfortable climates where they may exist as human parasites with greater ease and less exertion. The citizen who lives in the thickly populated sections of the country where, figuratively speaking, he is seldom out of hailing distance of a policeman, constable or sheriff, does not realize the conditions and situations that confront the hundreds of thousands who live in the vast, thinly settled areas of our land.

There are, in addition to this great class of our people who have occasional need for a pistol for protection, many others whose daily or nightly occupations require them to go armed and to be prepared to meet emergencies that threaten their lives and the treasure and property for which they may be responsible. I refer now to the guardians of the laws, though they be municipal ordinances, or state or federal statutes. County sheriffs and their deputies are responsible for the enforcement of laws in wide sections of our western states. These are quite different to the duties imposed on the city patrolman and there is a small army of men engaged in this work who have frequent need for skill in the handling of pistols. Even in our large cities where crime of the most flagrant type has flourished there are many who depend for protection on their skill in the use of weapons. If bank messengers, tellers, express and mail guards, special railway police, and night watchmen in general, were proficient in the use of pistols the effect on organized crime would be startling and quite adequate in stopping much of the robbery we read of daily.

The following paragraphs are intended for the two classes of our citizenry who may have need of instruction in the use of pistols for defensive purposes. For those good citizens who believe in preparedness for home and self defense and who are the possessors of that popular hand gun known as the "Bureau Drawer Model Assorted" which they may have occasion to use against the infrequent human night prowler, the second-story-worker, or the sneak thief, a brief course in the fundamentals of shooting is necessary. This should be followed by practice in quick and rapid firing against silhouette targets under conditions simulating those in which firing might be done. The scope of such a course could be covered in a few lessons and a very limited amount of practice, if the pupils would concentrate on the work for a short period and then occasionally practice position, aiming and trigger squeeze exercises to keep themselves acquainted with the technique of the game.

That group of men whose daily work assures the probable use of pistols frequently for the protection of their lives or of valuable property should learn the details of defensive shooting thoroughly and practice them regularly or they will be in the same predicament as deep-sea fishermen who cannot swim. The following instructions are intended primarily for them and for those pistol enthusiasts who wish to amuse themselves by learning methods of practical pistol practice. The essentials of quick drawing and shooting are:

(a) Suitable pistols.
(b) Accessible carrying positions.
(c) Properly made holsters.
(d) Skillful pistol manipulation.
(e) Natural accurate gunpointing.
(f) Coolness and self-control in action.

Defensive shooting presupposes the use of pistols at very close range and at comparatively large targets. Extreme accuracy of fire is not required but handiness in manipulating a gun, skill in gun-pointing, and rapid firing with weapons of good stopping power is most desirable. Weapons with long barrels, adjustable target sights and light trigger pulls are unnecessary and in fact disadvantageous for emergency shooting. Those with barrels of four inches or less, with circular blade front sights, rear sight notches cut in the frame and with trigger pulls of about four and one-half pounds are to be preferred because they aid in developing smoothness and rapidity in drawing, pointing and firing. Light triggers are treacherous when used for rapid work under excitement. Automatic pistols with awkwardly located safeties, revolvers with extremely heavy double actions, and either type of weapon if it be clumsy or poorly fitted and balanced is not well suited to the style of shooting under discussion here.

Large caliber belt guns with greater stopping power may be carried in belt holsters that are worn exposed, or under clothing that does not interfere with getting them into action quickly. If it is desired to conceal one's weapons this can be done best by carrying the pocket type of gun either in a pocket, shoulder or belt holster. Carrying a pistol in a pocket can be done successfully provided all projections on the gun are such that they will not catch on the clothing when the gun is withdrawn from the pocket. Hammerless pistols have advantages in this respect. It should be unnecessary to state that if a pocket is used as the resting place of a pistol it should be an outside one. If the coat is worn or an overcoat is the outside garment the pistol should be in the side pocket. If no coat is worn then the side trouser pockets are much preferable to the hip pockets. They should be made large. If firing through the pocket of a coat is contemplated a revolver will be more practical than an automatic as the latter may jam.

For many years a standard type of pocket revolver has been on the market along with a miscellaneous assortment of nondescript weapons. Today automatic weapons of small caliber are competing with the revolver for popularity. At one time the old style single or double barreled derringers were the most convenient weapons for personal protection but the unreliability of the rim fire ammunition used in them, and the later developments in pocket pistols has about caused the discontinuance of the use and manufacture of these short guns. Caliber for caliber, the automatic pistol is the more compact and as far as size alone is concerned better suited to pocket use than the revolver, but the factors of safety, reliability and stopping power favor the latter. Recently a "Detective Model" pocket gun has been put on the market by one of our reputable firms. This is a standard type of pocket revolver with a two inch barrel. It is convenient for pocket use but not pleasant to fire with full loads. For drawing from an outside belt holster, a pistol with a barrel of not more than six inches will give good results in speed and accurate pointing. For drawing from concealed positions a four inch or shorter barrel is best.

For several years the writer was privileged to observe and study the fine points of defensive shooting as practiced by Mr. J. H. FitzGerald, Colt's noted quick draw expert, who spent several days each summer with the service team of which the author was a member. At these times the latter did considerable experimenting with pocket guns and finally came to the conclusion that the Colt's Police Positive Special was the best gun for pocket use or for use with a small belt holster. It might be added in this connection that considerable firing was done with two, three, and four inch barrels, and the three inch size selected as the best all-around length, considering balance, accuracy, and facility in handling. This particular revolver is light, compact and adapted to the powerful .38 Special revolver cartridge. It can be used either single or double action and is accurate enough for all practical purposes. The grip is somewhat small for the average hand and the light weight of the gun when using full loads causes considerable unpleasant recoil. These disadvantages may be overcome, however, by gripping the gun with the little finger under the butt. The lighter caliber pocket guns lack stopping power while the heavier ones with better grips are slower in handling and not so convenient to carry and conceal. The S. & W. Safety Hammerless is a favorite pocket gun with many. It is made in two sizes, namely, for the .32 S. & W. Short or the .38 S. & W. and .38 Colt New Police cartridges.

The writer's favorite pocket gun is shown in the illustration. It is altered as shown to facilitate drawing and firing with either hand from a belt holster, and is a copy of the one owned and used by FitzGerald. The method of drawing this handy weapon is also shown in the illustration and I believe originated with him. The holster was designed by the writer and made by that expert leather worker and revolver shot, Captain A. H. Hardy of Beverly Hills, California. I have yet to see a faster combination.

To obtain speed in drawing, pistols must be carried where they are most readily accessible to the shooting hand and in a receptacle that retards the execution of drawing the least. A holster is the best method of "packing" a gun but its location on the body has long been a subject of controversy. Some experts, and most movie shots, prefer to carry their gun in a holster hung low on the thigh from a sagging cartridge belt and sometimes secured to the leg with a thong or strap. This equipment is suitable for fast work but is uncomfortable and cumbersome to wear, especially when dismounted. The Army tried this method of carrying pistols but

An excellent outfit for self-protection. The Author's altered .38 Police Positive Special revolver in specially designed quick draw holster made by Hardy. It is designed to be worn on the waist belt on the left side of the body. It is fast, compact and easily concealed.

scon went back to the more efficient one of swinging the holster from the belt in its normal position about the waist. The Army holsters are, however, still provided with thongs fastened to the lower end. Another popular place for the holster is on the right hip somewhat higher than the thigh position. With a holster properly designed and hung, this position permits a fairly rapid draw with the right hand. Another excellent manner of carrying a pistol is from a shoulder holster swung under the left arm pit. The gun can be well concealed under the coat in a comfortable carrying position. If

A Quick Draw holster for .38 caliber revolver with 6 inch barrel, in position for the draw-across-the-body. The holster may be worn further to the left if desired.

the holster is of the "Quick Draw" shoulder type, that is with a U-shaped retaining spring which permits the gun to be drawn from the side instead of the top, it can be drawn quite rapidly when one gets the knack. The height at which this holster is hung is also a factor in drawing. There is one type of shoulder holster that is equipped with a spring catch which locks the gun in

The thigh position. Good for quick drawing but inconvenient and cumbersome to wear.

place when it is seated in the holster and which must be pressed back by the index finger before the gun can be drawn. This type is not as suitable for fast work.

In weighing the matter of the best location for a quick draw holster we must consider several things. The inconvenience of the thigh or leg holster is one of them. Another is the question of where our shooting hand may be when we want to draw. It may be in our pocket, or perhaps holding the wheel of an automobile. It may be busy lighting a pipe or cigarette or even on a table in front of us as we read or write, and it is not unlikely that both our hands may be over our head. Another important factor we are likely to overlook, especially when we consider only the advantages of the leg holster, is the fact that no matter where we carry our gun this weapon must be raised to a good position for firing after it is drawn. If we wish to conceal our weapon we cannot do it as well when it is hanging low on the thigh.

Everything considered, the best location for a quick draw holster is on the waist belt to the left of the center of the body, with the butt of the pistol to the right. It is believed that a pistol in this position may be drawn and fired more rapidly with the right hand than from any other position, if the holster is properly hung. This method is known as the "draw-across-the-body" and can be done rapidly with the hand starting from almost any position and the pistol fired from the hip, the instant it leaves the holster. A pocket revolver or automatic may be carried as just described and concealed by the coat which is pulled aside by the left hand as the right reaches for the gun. The rule to keep in mind is, that any carrying position which requires the hand to function in a cramped, awkward manner is not the best

Illustrating the draw-across-the-body starting with the revolver in the quick draw holster and the coat buttoned. Note the short distance the gun travels from the holster to firing position. The revolver used is the Author's altered .38 Police Positive Special with 3 inch barrel.

(2)

(3)

suited to quick draw work. If this test is applied to questionable positions it will be convincing.

The subject of suitable holsters for defensive work will be discussed more in detail in a later chapter and it is sufficient to state here that holsters for this work must be properly designed, fitted and hung in order to give every advantage in their use. Flaps, straps, or thongs on a holster for keeping a gun seated therein are about as useful and unnecessary as a safety on a single barrel trap gun and might better be left off. These adjuncts may do on holsters for general service but those designed for quick draw purposes should be free from them. It should never be necessary to tie down a properly made and fitted holster for quick draw work if it is worn on a correctly made waist belt of proper weight.

Schemes for carrying concealed pistols are numerous and many amusing stories have been written about them. Criminals who are always expecting to be searched have been known to carry a pistol in the coat sleeve suspended by a cord passing across the shoulders and fastened to the opposite forearm. Carrying a gun in a newspaper, paper bag, or in an innocent appearing package in the hand has been known to give the possessor the drop on a surprised thug. Men who travel in places where human life is cheap, and there is always personal danger to prosperous appearing individuals, are not content with one gun but prefer to carry a battery composed of a convenient belt gun and a less accessible but carefully concealed pocket pistol.

Skillful manipulation of a pistol comes only with practice, a practice which requires training along the lines of juggling to attain real cleverness. The speed with which a gun can be drawn depends on: (a) the starting position of the hand, (b) the position and accessibility of the gun, (c) the skill and precision with which the operation is performed. While the right hand is drawing the gun the movement may be camouflaged by a feint with the other hand or by a twist of the body. The more complicated these movements are the more difficult it will be to attain smoothness and precision in their execution. It is as necessary in this form of practice to assume an efficient firing position as it is in standardized practice. Just what this position will be rests with the individual. He may draw and fire across the body with the left side toward the opponent, or he may step forward with his right foot as he draws, extend his arm and fire with either the right side or the front of the body exposed. Turning the body is a means of concealing the first movement of drawing. The beginner must be slow and precise in his movements. They must be carefully timed and exactly executed until they become smooth and natural. In drawing a single action revolver place the tip or fleshy part of the thumb firmly on the hammer cocking spur at the same time the hand grasps the butt. Cock the gun as the draw begins, letting the thumb drop to the left when the hammer is fully back. This also applies to a double action used as single action. Sufficient accuracy and greater speed will be obtained by using a double action as such. As a general rule automatics should be carried cocked, and with the safety on "Safe," although there is always some danger of it being shoved off. Certain automatics like the .45 Service gun may be carried with the hammer lowered and a cartridge in the chamber. If this is done

These pictures illustrate the reverse draw with the left hand. Note
trigger guard. This draw may be executed when the right hand

(2)

how the second finger falls across the trigger through the cut away is held or is otherwise out of action.

the gun may be cocked as it is drawn, in the manner just described. For automatics on "Safe," the thumb should be placed on the safety as the gun is gripped or drawn, and the safety shoved off as the muzzle clears the holster. The index finger should fall across the trigger as the gun starts out of the holster. It is not essential that the leather be cut entirely away from the trigger in order to place the finger on it before it moves or as the gun is gripped. Some shooters like to have holsters made so this can be done but it is not necessary for fast work.

The next step in defensive shooting is training in gun pointing. For those who are not reasonably proficient in aiming, holding and squeezing the trigger, sufficient of such preparatory work should be done to demonstrate the principles of shooting and to show the inaccuracy that will result if a pistol trigger is jerked or any form of flinching is done. Thereafter, practice should be done at silhouette targets at very close range, preferably under fifteen feet. Gun pointing without aligning the sights should be the practice now. If the target is placed in front of a hill or bank of dirt, one's errors will be quickly seen and the necessity for firing with a steady gun and trigger squeeze will be quickly shown and emphasized. Gun pointing practice should begin with single shots fired carefully after the gun has been drawn slowly and pointed without jerkiness. The trigger should be pressed decisively the instant the gun stops in the firing position. The pointing should be done with the arm fully extended at first and then with the elbow bent until finally one will be able to hit, without difficulty, a man sized silhouette, by firing from the hip. Experience and practice will teach, however, that better results will be obtained by firing with the arm extended. In extending the arm do not attempt to aim, but train yourself in gun pointing.

The last, and after all the most important essentials in defensive shooting, are coolness and self control. Without these attributes all the skill in the world will be of little value. Your draw may be phenomenally fast, your gun pointing extremely accurate and your rate of fire a maximum, but if you lose your head and become excited in an emergency you will bungle your efforts and your training and practice will all be wasted because of a lack of will power to concentrate on the problem before you.

Chapter XII

SUGGESTIONS FOR POLICE OFFICERS

THIS chapter is written for the purpose of emphasizing a few points that are of special interest to police officers or persons engaged in similar work requiring the use of pistols in emergencies such as those occasionally confronting members of police forces. Maintaining the fact that police practice is one of the three principal classes of pistol shooting and that its importance is second to none, the author has endeavored to make this entire book of value to the police. The practical pistol shot—and the police officer should certainly be one—can by a study of the principles and the technique herein discussed improve his skill for his personal benefit and also be of greater value to his unit.

Practical pistol practice does not consist of plugging holes in a stationary paper target at twenty or fifty yards at the rate of one shot a minute with a superaccurate single shot target pistol under ideal shooting conditions. Instead, it should be of a kind that may be turned to practical use in the performance of duty or the protection of lives and property. There is no question but that the basic principles of pistol shooting must be taught, and that sufficient slow fire practice be held to accomplish this mission. Once a person has reached the point however, where he understands and uses the approved methods of holding his pistol, squeezing the trigger and aiming, he should then be taken off slow fire or it should be combined with a course of practice that will simulate by the use of appropriate targets and rate of fire, the kind of shooting he may expect to do in professional practice. Very deliberate fire at a small bull's-eye target is of little value as training for quick shooting at moving targets, many of which may be in the dark.

The police officer has many other details in his training and daily work that require his attention besides pistol marksmanship. Like the army officer he is most likely to concentrate on those duties with which he is more intimately associated and let others go until such time as necessity requires him to pay more attention to those he has neglected. If his duties require him to use his pistol frequently he will be quite receptive to pistol instruction but if on the other hand, he feels that more reliance can be placed on his fists or his stick he may neglect marksmanship. The psychological time to arouse and create interest in pistol shooting in the mind of the recruit officer is when he is undergoing his training course and assembling his equipment. If he can at this time be given a course in pistol marksmanship he will be very likely to absorb the instruction in the proper spirit and to develop an interest in shooting that will be retained, if the means are provided for future participation in practice. It is quite evident from a study of the trend of police thought at this time that greater attention is being paid to the matter of pistol marksmanship for police officers. The appointment of instructors, the increase in the construction of ranges, the growing interest in the National Police Pistol Matches and the satisfactory results obtained by the well instructed departments, all indicate that the encouragement of pistol marksmanship is worth while. The well grounded officer cannot afford to neglect this part of his training regardless of the infrequent use he may have for actual demonstrations of his skill.

Instructors of police departments in pistol shooting should be men of recognized ability who can not only

The Running Man range. Police School, Camp Perry, Ohio, 1928.

shoot well but realize the necessity for work along practical lines. The courses of fire prescribed and the methods of teaching should be similar to those used for the military services, with greater attention paid to firing at disappearing silhouette targets under poor illumination. Silhouette practice should also include quick firing at very close range with the time limit per shot such that gun pointing and not aiming will be required to assure getting the shots off within the time allowed. For the purposes of training and to reduce expenses firing can be done with small bore pistols or revolvers provided sufficient firing is done with the gun the marksman expects to use eventually in his work, to assure his familiarity with its feel, balance and sighting. Quickness in drawing a pistol seldom enters into any row into which a police officer is involved, as the officer usually has his gun drawn when expecting trouble. It is well, however, not to neglect practice in this detail, for the unexpected does happen. The police officer should study the chapters on "Shooting Against Time" and "Defensive Shooting and Quick Drawing" in particular, and devote time to rapid firing and to rapid fire and gun pointing exercises.

Police officials will do well to encourage any form of pistol practice but should insist on a regular course for qualification which involves the kind of work described in the foregoing paragraphs. Several large cities have found it a good policy to encourage the development of police pistol teams for competition in sectional and National matches. The National Rifle Association and the U.S.R.A. conduct matches for the police that may be fired on home ranges and at Camp Perry, Ohio. Those cities that have done the most toward promoting pistol marksmanship make it a point to send a team to the National Matches frequently. The expenses of the trip are sometimes supported by popular subscriptions from members of the community represented. Certain municipalities award qualification badges and medals for successful participation in record practice and even in a few cases give additional pay for ratings as sharpshooter or pistol expert.

For the proper support of pistol work suitable ranges for practice are an absolute necessity. These may be installed indoors in conveniently located basements, or other available space or they may be constructed in city parks or any readily accessible public grounds where out-of-door practice may be held with safety. The ranges installed in National Guard Armories, at colleges and universities and at army posts are generally available for practice by police teams when not in use by military organizations assigned thereto, and every encouragement is usually given by military authorities to civilian organizations who desire to use these facilities. Plans for the construction of indoor ranges can be obtained from the N.R.A. and from certain of the large arms and ammunition manufacturers.

In addition to skill in marksmanship the police officer should know and practice certain tactics that go hand in hand with shooting and he may find that the use of a little knowledge and headwork in occasional emergencies are worth more than his ability to hit his man. If his skill in shooting is not what it should be he may find that a knowledge of how to fire from the kneeling, sitting, or prone position may be useful not only in increasing his hits but in giving him protection against the fire of gunmen and rioters. Ability to shoot with either hand may at times be necessary as in firing around corners or when one hand is disabled. When engaged in a shooting fray involving several opponents timely advantage should be taken of the best available cover and protection afforded by position or surroundings. The military principle of guarding one's rear or flanks holds good in police tactics. The smaller a target one presents to an enemy and the better protection one has the better will be his chances of gaining fire superiority and eventual victory.

While covering a crook with your gun do not permit your attention to be diverted from the task at hand until you have either disarmed or secured your man. Keep just far enough away from him to be sure of hitting, if necessity requires you to shoot, and not close enough for him to kick, knock or otherwise displace the gun from your hand or put you out before you can deliver your fire. If it becomes necessary to fire at a running man do not attempt this while moving yourself. Take a good position and fire carefully.

If at any time you are covered by the gun of a criminal and are considering a disarming attack, the first principle to be observed is that of diverting the muzzle from your direction and then disarming your opponent. The closer you are to the gun the better are the chances of success. Quick thinking and acting officers have frequently disarmed less alert opponents by reason of a knowledge and practice in these tactics. A loaded but uncocked revolver may be prevented from firing by grasping it firmly about the cylinder so as to prevent the latter from revolving and the hammer from rising. A very slight parrying movement will turn the muzzle sufficiently to cause a shot to miss and this should be done before one attempts to take a weapon away from an opponent. Then a firm grasp of the weapon with the hand and a quick twist to the left, (if the gun was held in the right hand) will probably bend or break the opponent's index finger by the pressure of the trigger guard so that the gun will be released.

Firing with both hands holding the pistol has been done very successfully and is a means of improving the hitting of persons who are not skillful with one hand. This method is not approved by pistol experts for it is believed that all police officers should be well enough trained to use the pistol efficiently with one hand. Using the two hands is a makeshift method. It is slow, clumsy, and impracticable except where time is not a factor, and that is seldom the case where police firing is done. For those who are not expert, and this applies to a large majority of the police of the country, firing with a rest or support will improve poor shooting and for this reason methods of using the pistol in this manner are included here.

Keeping in mind that the purpose of two-handed shooting is to improve the holding and to prevent flinching and the attendant bad effects of pulling or jerking the trigger, the holds used should be those that will insure the greatest steadiness and the best support for the gun. This will not be obtained by grasping the shooting wrist with the other hand as the gun is still allowed to wobble with the wrist joint as a pivot. It is much better to support the firing hand with the other one by grasping it in such a manner as to support it underneath and at the same time steady both the hand and the wrist. There are several methods advocated by men who profess to have done considerable of this kind of work. The best method to use is that most suitably adapted to the gun in use. These are illustrated and explained. The one the author is inclined to favor for general use with any arm is merely to grasp the

A good two-handed grip that is very satisfactory to use with or without a rest.

A good grip for the .45 Service Automatic.

shooting hand with the other one after the regular normal grip is taken of the gun by the firing hand. If firing with the right hand the left should be placed under the right with the thumb nearly vertical and hooked across the top of the second finger of the right hand. The butt of the left hand supports the firing wrist. This method can also be used when a rest is available as the left hand forms a cushion for the gun to recoil against

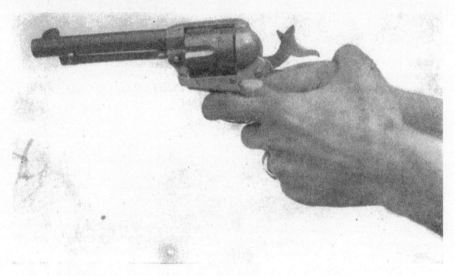

A satisfactory grip for the .45 Single Action Army Revolver.

instead of permitting it to rest on a hard surface which will change the impact of the bullets.

Another method of supporting the gun is to grasp it normally and then hook the left index finger, if it is long enough, in front of the trigger guard and the left thumb either over or under the right thumb, as shown in the illustrations. This method can be, and has been used extensively with the old favorite "Peacemaker" single action revolver. It was first demonstrated to me by a brother officer whose father had used it frequently as a sheriff in Frontier Days.

A study of the illustrations will also show the manner of taking advantage of the arms, elbows and knees in

An excellent prone position.

supporting the gun in the sitting, kneeling and prone positions.

For officers armed with automatic or double action revolvers there is always a great natural inclination to fire with maximum rapidity as soon as an emergency

This position is steady and comfortable. Both elbows are supported
by the knees.

arises and if a revolver is used to fire it double action. Even experts, who have never been under fire, have a

A good two-handed standing position.

desire to empty their guns as fast as possible when someone is firing at them and even though they have had

The proper way to kneel and fire.

little or no training in double action work they will, under the strain of excitement, use that method of firing with results corresponding to their lack of training in this kind of fire. For this reason officers must school themselves in double action so that they can hit with certainty when it becomes necessary to fire with great speed.

The revolver range of the Los Angeles Police Department.

The Author has made it a habit to ask police officers where he has been how they carry their guns and the different methods used have been astonishing. Many older officers still carry their pistols in pocket holsters in the hip pocket but this method seems less popular than formerly. Many officers who carry pocket revolvers do so in small belt holsters. Men who use guns with five to six inch barrels, and it is surprising how many officers are carrying such guns, do so in belt holsters on their right or left hip and let the end of the scabbard rest in the hip pocket. As a result of interviewing makers of holsters it is quite evident that the shoulder holster is rapidly becoming the favorite for both uniformed and plain clothes' officers. There are several types of these now available and they can be worn with comfort and convenience. The Hardy Shoulder is of excellent design and can be worn either high under the arm pit with plain clothes or lower down for convenient

The Sheriffs' pistol range, Los Angeles County, California.

use under a uniform. The secret of its success is in the materials of which it is made and particularly the spring that holds the pistol securely in place and yet permits its rapid drawing. The main defect of many of the spring type of shoulder holster is that the springs are too stiff and the method of fastening them in the holster so unsatisfactory that it soon gives way. The pouch type of shoulder holster is not nearly as suitable for police use as the spring type just described. The police of one West Coast city I visited were using a holster made of pliable four ounce leather worn on the inside of the waist band of the trousers, between the left suspender buttons. The holster was held down by passing the waist belt thru a loop made of the upper part of the front leather and bent forward over the top of the trousers. The inside leather of the holster was extended upward in the shape of a triangle and at the apex there was a ring to which the suspender was fastened instead of the usual button straps. This holster seemed to be very satisfactory for pocket guns with not to exceed four inch barrels.

Chapter XIII

EXHIBITION SHOOTING

WHEN one has become an all-around pistol shot of more than average skill and has played the game from slow fire to aerial practice, it is but natural that he should feel the desire to demonstrate to others the talent he has developed and to exhibit in an interesting manner the variations in a versatile sport. As a most enthusiastic follower of the game he may merely wish to show others the possibilities in the sport, with the purpose of encouraging them to take it up, or to make greater efforts to excell in it, if they are already participants. But not infrequently, in every line of sport we find individuals who, after they have mastered a game, wish to see if it has more material rewards to offer than the satisfaction and pleasure that comes from success. They have made, in the form of years of study and practice, certain investments in a game and they would like to know if there are any monetary dividends coming to them, even though they may never have considered this point when they took up the sport. There are no ethics that should prevent a marksman from entering the field of exhibition shooting, either as an amateur or a professional, if he desires to do so, as long as he plays the game in such a way as to encourage and create interest in it and at the same time provide healthful amusement and entertainment to satisfied audiences.

Many times we find amateurs putting on a few stunts at the close of a day's practice at the range or the gun club and these add to the interest in the sport. A marksman is always interested in the work of other shots and particularly enjoys witnessing any specialties a brother shooter may have perfected in the pistol game. This holds true of all sportsmen but more particularly of those who shoot and can appreciate skill with arms. It matters little whether they be disciples of Samuel Colt, artists with the scatter gun, or mere riflemen, they all enjoy a good shooting exhibition. The ardent fight, football, or baseball fan is not even mildly interested in watching a rifle or pistol competition where firing is done against the usual paper target. He wants something more exciting, something that will bring him to his feet yelling and cheering. The only kind of shooting that will cause him to cross the street is something that partakes of the spectacular, or appeals to his sporting instinct, as for example, a live turkey shoot where skill and chance play strong parts and the rewards are of a material nature that he can fully appreciate. By far the largest class of spectators to whom one may expect to exhibit his skill is that variable multitude of pleasure seekers who attend anything that offers the probability of varied amusement. The revolver and pistol always have had, and probably always will have a romantic appeal to Americans because of the part they have played in our national life and history. It is therefore not difficult to arouse interest in an exhibition of skill in the use of these weapons, but to maintain this interest the exhibitor must furnish a much different program than that seen at competitions with hand guns. From those who attend charity affairs, civic carnivals, bazaars and similar entertainments the demands for high class exhibitions are not as exacting as those made by a theater-going crowd who expect to see not only first grade skill but also spectacular and thrilling performances. This kind of an audience does not care whether or not the stunts are all legitimate, nor do they appreciate, with a few exceptions, real shooting skill of the target variety, but they do enjoy the spectacular and if some of the feats are of a mystifying nature so much the better, for many people like to be fooled, so that they may try to determine just how this was done.

If one watches and analyzes the occasional shooting number that appears on our vaudeville stage, or is shown in connection with some circus side-show or wild west performance he will soon realize that either the performer is a marvelous shot or that there is something wrong with the way he accomplishes the feats he passes off on the crowd.   A genuine marksman goes away from such an exhibition with nothing but disgust and ridicule for the performer who is getting credit for fine shooting.   He loses sight of the fact however, that though the show may be a farce from a target shooting standpoint, it is, from a showman's way of looking, quite satisfactory, for it has given the audience an exhibition that is spectacular, amusing, and perhaps surprising and mysterious.   The expert in shooting may also think that the few stunts or shots that he witnessed which were not faked were very easy and that a good shot would be ashamed to pan off on an unsuspecting assembly such mediocre work under the guise of expertness.   He is wrong again, for the average citizen has no conception of what good shooting consists. Distances on a stage always appear greater than elsewhere and a good stage set-up for shooting is very deceiving. And regardless of the distance at which the firing is done the audience will applaud the marksman if he handles his pistols with dexterity and breaks objects rapidly, cleanly, and with mechanical regularity, for this demonstrates skill of a kind. As for the ease of doing these stunts I suggest that the critic try some of them himself before a crowd, even though it be composed only of his shooting friends, and see how well he gets away with them. He has something in the nature of a surprise coming to him and his respect for the stage shot will be greatly increased after he has tried to put on a show of his own, however brief it may be. It is one thing to be a good target shot when practicing alone or even in the presence of other shooters, and a horse of quite a different color, to do the same things when you know that the eyes of a large crowd are on you, and on you alone, and that they are ready to laugh at your failures or applaud your good work. Then the element of time again enters the problem. No crowd will be at all interested in watching you plug holes in a bull's-eye at the rate of a shot a minute, at least no crowd that is out to be amused. They want action and skillful action at that.

A musical artist rendering a concert, may have a fair percentage of his audience who appreciate his fine technique and a much larger part that is not educated up to his art. If he wishes to have his concert enjoyed in such a way as to react fully to his benefit he must include enough popular or familiar numbers to please the less musically inclined. And so it is with the exhibition shot. He may include in his program a few stunts that show the experts that he can do fine shooting and then he must make up the rest to amuse the majority of his audience. If he is clever and gives sufficient thought to his work he can, with apologies to Barnum, please all of the people some of the time. If, on the other hand one intends to give an exhibition before a group of shooters he should cut out the easy stunts and try only shots that show real skill. To make a real impression, it is well to try feats that individuals in the crowd are not in the habit of practicing. It does not usually pay to play a man at his own game.

The stage shot should keep in mind the fact that he is entering the realm of the entertainer and must make a study of means of showing his skill to the best advantage with the primary mission of pleasing his patrons always before him. A cardinal principle to observe is to carefully prepare the program and rehearse it frequently so that there will be no question about the time it takes and the smoothness with which it is conducted. This is one place where alibis are not permitted and failures are costly to one's prestige. We find in this specialty as in others, there is no place for the slow deliberate shot and only the versatile marksman will be successful. A friend, whom I knew as a fine military shot at Camp Perry, has recently taken up exhibition shooting as a means of supplementing his income so that he may be enabled to meet the increasing expense of his hobby without drawing too deeply on the family budget. He has worked out a series of stunts that combine expert skill with amusing and interesting entertainment, and is making a success because there are so few in the field

who can give a good exhibition with the pistol and revolver. His stage setting consists of a room containing

Shooting with the revolver reversed. The arm must be held so that
the wrist does not interfere with the line of aim and the trigger should
be squeezed with the little finger.

an old fashioned fire place, which forms his backstop, and
about which are grouped various fixtures cleverly ar-

ranged to make good targets. Imitation light bulbs, ornaments made of toy balloons, and the usual light colored composition balls furnish targets that are unique in appearance and that go to pieces in a blaze of glory when hit. Among other things he shoots out candles, and lights from different positions, and with either hand. He works a few tricks that keep the marksman guessing and which look quite marvellous to the layman. The point to be made is that he plays the game from the showman's viewpoint and yet gives enough of a demonstration of real skill to make his work appreciated by all who witness it.

The novice at this game should go slowly and try out a few stunts at a time with his regular practice so as to keep his hand in at all-around work. The feats that amuse and entertain are those that involve breaking objects, for an audience likes to see the result of the shot immediately. Shooting done on a stage must, of necessity, be limited to that performed against a backstop but for an out-of-door exhibition a greater variety can be given to the show. Indoor work introduces the problem of securing satisfactory lighting which must be perfected or the difficulty of the work will be greatly increased. Fifteen feet is about the usual distance for indoor shooting and when done on a stage appears much farther.

There are certain stunts that may be well called standard because they are practiced by many exhibitors and these are what are usually seen at a show put on by a real shot. They consist of hitting the old favorite glass or asphalt balls in rapid succession with the pistol held in different positions. To shoot with the gun turned sideways and upside down is not difficult if one remembers where to aim as the aiming point varies with the different positions of the gun. Firing with the pistol inverted is done by squeezing the trigger with the little finger. Hitting two objects simultaneously calls for more skill and also care in placing the targets so that the hands are not too far apart. This shot requires steady holding and good co-ordination in aiming and squeezing. A more difficult stunt is to hit simultaneously one object that is stationary and another swinging. These should be arranged so that the guns are close together and stationary when fired and the swinging target is at one end of its swing. The farther apart the targets are the more difficult the shots become. Shooting corks out of bottles without breaking the latter is a good stunt. Splitting cards held with the edge exposed like a vertical line is not difficult, but to do it when the card is horizontal is not as easy. This stunt is made easier by using large caliber revolvers and square shoulder bullets, as the latter will cut the card almost as though a knife had been drawn through it. Mid-range cartridges are the best to use in this case as the noise and recoil is less than with full loads. Breaking objects with a piece of cardboard placed over the muzzle so that the sights cannot be aligned with the target is a mysterious stunt to those who do not understand it. This is accomplished by shooting with both eyes open and cannot be done by the one-eyed shot. The binocular shot finds that when he attempts to aim, his right eye will align the sights and his left eye will make it possible for this alignment to coincide with the target. If the card on the muzzle is so wide that in aiming the left eye cannot see

(1)

Two simple methods of making mirror shots.   More difficult positions

(2)

can be assumed with practice.

the target then the stunt cannot be done with certainty. This shot demonstrates an advantage in using both eyes in shooting. Another favorite is the mirror shot. It consists in aligning the sights by using a mirror and firing without looking directly at the target. The easiest way to do this is to hold the revolver across the body and rest the shooting hand on the left arm at the elbow, then with a small mirror held in the left hand in rear of the hammer the sights can be aligned. This takes a little practice to master and can be done best by first getting the sights aligned in the mirror and then bringing the alignment on the target by a movement of the body instead of the gun only. To split a card while shooting in this manner is not an easy shot.

Fancy shooting of the William Tell variety is generally condemned by writers on this subject and yet I venture to say that all good exhibition shots attempt it at some time or other until they lose their nerve by reason of a loss of skill or because of an accident. Ira Paine, who perhaps distinguished himself as one of the greatest pistol shots of all time by his international exhibitions, did shooting of this nature. He would shoot objects off the head of an assistant or held in their fingers. A protest against this form of exhibition work was made against his work in England and not without reason, for it was there that legal action to recover damages was taken against him by an assistant who lost part of a finger while holding an object for Paine to fire at. This is only one of many accidents on record in this kind of shooting and while it is spectacular and always brings a "hand" when done successfully it is not to be recommended. Aside from the question of skill there is always a chance that a cartridge may be defective and the accident be entirely due to it. If you must practice stunts of this kind do it by placing the target on your watch or some other valuable object so that human injuries will not result should you have an accident.

If shooting out of doors aerial stunts will always please and can be practiced with small bore ammunition with little danger of the falling bullets injuring anyone. Do not be too ambitious in this work for the audience expects you to hit, and failures will always bring forth derisive comments from certain types of individuals. It is better to try only shots that are easy for you and there are enough stunts of this kind that can be done to make your exhibition worth while. Breaking clay pigeons tossed in the air in rapid succession will bring applause. To pick up a bottle from the ground, toss it in the air and then draw a concealed pistol and break the glass with a bullet is real shooting and will demonstrate quick drawing as well. To do this requires considerable practice but for a good aerial shot is not difficult. Breaking inch marbles or hitting golf balls in the air with a bullet are other aerial stunts of high class. A golf ball hit squarely from below with a .38 bullet will astonish the crowd by the height to which it will fly.

A favorite stunt of some expert fancy rifle shots is to outline profiles of well known characters with .22 rifle bullets fired rapidly from an automatic rifle. An Indian head is one of the usual models cut out. This not only requires good shooting but artistic ability as well. While it is not recommended that this kind of work be done with a pistol the same idea can be carried out and simple designs made using a pair of automatic pistols. This is a neat and effective stunt.

Place a bottle on top of a tumbler or glass jar. Hit the jar and then the bottle before it reaches the ground and see how easy it is. Don't try this before a crowd until you have mastered it.

As a climax to an aerial exhibition release several toy balloons and burst them by shots fired with guns held in both hands. If they get too far away have a revolver loaded with shot cartridges to finish them off.

If, as you run through your program before an audience that has been educated in fancy shooting by the cleverly faked performances of movie stars, you hear disparaging remarks when you miss an occasional difficult shot do not let it upset you, for the ignorant critic is always present.

Chapter XIV

SHOOTING PSYCHOLOGY

ON THE subject of shooting psychology, much has been said and little written, so that the novice as he advances in his study and practice of shooting soon comes in contact with problems which at first appear to be entirely of a physical nature but soon develop into mental obstacles of no small proportions.

While it is true that the physical and mental conditions affecting one's shooting are very closely related, nevertheless there comes a time in the progress of learning this game when the physical problems such as aiming and holding are fairly well mastered in practice, and if it were not for the mental hazards that crop out and obstruct one's advance, the attainment of success would be made much easier.

Not infrequently the degree of one's success is measured by one's ability to solve the mental problems of shooting rather than those of a purely physical nature. As one advances to the stage of competition shooting, the mental problems presented become increasingly difficult. Often the difference between the good competitive shot and the poor one is determined by his ability to solve these mental problems and to overcome the difficulties they present. The novice will probably find that as he begins his practice, the fundamental principles which he must learn are few but it is in the application of these principles that he finds difficulty. Most of his efforts will be required in training his muscles and nerves to hold his pistol steadily aligned on the target while he squeezes the trigger. At this time the physical effort required will be so great that all his energy, physical and mental, will be devoted to the work. As his nerves and muscles become trained and the problem of holding becomes easier and simpler, his mind then finds time to dwell on other details of his shooting not directly connected with the operation of firing, and perhaps he finds himself thinking of such things as the score he is going to make, or of the poor one he has just made or possibly of the actions of someone else on the firing line or in rear of it. With the beginning of qualification or competition shooting, it becomes more difficult to concentrate on the problem of aiming, holding, squeezing the trigger, and calling the shot, for the greater responsibility of making a good score is apt to be felt with its accompanied tendency to unnerve. A football player waiting for the whistle before an important game experiences a certain amount of nervousness which in practice causes him to fumble the ball, to forget his signals or which otherwise demonstrates itself by his nervous actions. After the whistle has blown however, and the first bodily contact is made in the scrimmage line, this nervousness disappears and probably is experienced no more during the game. The player was not required to exercise much will power or self control to overcome this nervousness nor did the nervousness materially affect his game. The pistol shot has the same cause for nervousness before an important match, and however slight this may be, it is greatly magnified at the muzzle of an extended pistol.

Should firing be commenced while this condition exists, the effects of such nervousness will be quickly and conclusively demonstrated in the score. Unless the shooter through the exercise of self-control can soon overcome his nervousness, his score will quickly be ruined beyond hope of redemption. If his nervousness increases, the shooter may "blow up" with the subsequent lowering of his score, and his morale, as well as that of his team, if a team match is being shot.

The causes and remedies of this condition which affects perfectly normal, healthy men at most inopportune times and frequently for slightly apparent reasons, and which in shooting parlance has come to be known as the "buck" short for "buck ague," are well worth study and consideration rather than the popular attitude which ignores them and treats the subject as of small consequence.

Recently, while sitting about a campfire during a deer hunting trip in the Cascade Mountains of Washington, the author listened to the experience of a member of the party which illustrates a case of typical "buck fever" the like of which probably gave the name to the disease. The story teller was a man of over sixty-four years of age, a rifleman of national reputation, who a few years previously had established a world's record at the Camp Perry National Matches. A big game hunter all his life, he had shot many trophies so that the sight of game was a mere incident of little importance to him. The previous year while climbing the steep side of a Chelan mountain on the track of an immense mule-tail deer which he had been tracking in the snow for several hours, he suddenly saw above him through the thin foliage of

a group of small fir trees, the antlers and partial outline of the largest buck he had ever come upon in his
long hunting career. The left shoulder and part of the
neck of the animal were exposed to view and the range
was only two score yards. In his own words he described his actions: "I realized that there stood the
finest buck I had ever seen, and that due to the thick
cover, steep slope of the mountain, and the direction of
the wind, the animal had not yet discovered my presence. The shot was easy enough for a child to make
and yet as I raised my Springfield and tried to align the
sights on the massive neck, my knees suddenly grew
weak, my heart pounded like an air compressor and my
rifle muzzle described circles and rectangles about the
entire frame of the buck. Probably a realization that
to fire under these conditions was fatal to my success was
the only thing that saved me. I lowered the piece,
breathed deeply and concentrated on controlling my
palsy-like movements, and in what seemed minutes and
probably were only seconds, I regained control sufficiently to aim and press the trigger while the sights settled with reasonable steadiness on the vital spot on the
buck's neck. The roar of the rifle as it echoed and re-
echoed among the mountains and the crash of the falling deer put an end to the 'buck fever' but the memory
of those few seconds will remain with me as long as I
live."

To the target shot, the symptoms of the "buck" are
unmistakable and usually manifest themselves by causing
at first a feeling of unsteadiness and uneasiness which
increases to the extent of causing one to desire to move
about rather than sit still. In exaggerated cases when

the shooter takes his position on the firing line, he experiences a sinking sensation in the pit of the stomach and a weakness in the knees which tremble and shake noticeably. A feeling of irritation and a tendency to lose control of one's temper are also present at times.

The causes of this condition which closely resembles the stage fright experienced by public speakers when first appearing on a platform, may be traced to many sources, some of them apparently trivial while others are more reasonable. Certain marksmen when given team responsibility on a team that has a good chance to win an important match become extremely nervous as that event approaches, and fail to shoot well as a result. They will shoot well in individual matches occasionally, until they reach the point in their career when they are especially anxious to win a coveted cup or medal. Then their anxiety to win unnerves them and they go to pieces in the critical stages of the match.

There is a certain temperament which causes the possessor to be irritated to the point of losing his self-control so that his temper finally flares up at some trivial incident occurring on the firing line, and his score goes down correspondingly. I have in mind a rifleman who while preparing to shoot or during his match becomes decidedly agitated at most unexpected times and incidents. His mind is such, that in addition to watching the details of his shooting technique, he seems able to take in many, if not all, the minor events occurring in his vicinity, such as the remarks of spectators, the actions and exclamations of adjacent shooters, the instructions of nearby coaches to other contestants and verbal controversies between shooters and range officers. He is always too ready to snap up any remark, action, or suggestion within hearing that he conceives as being in the least annoying to himself or team. Such a temperament is a person's worst competitor and until he can learn to control and subdue it, he will never become a really successful shot, especially with the pistol. This, in addition to the natural nervousness resulting from normal causes preceding and arising during a competition keeps him always on the ragged edge of an eruption. The mere thought of going on a competitive firing line upsets some marksmen, while others grow more and more nervous as they continue in a competition. In cases like the latter, this increased nervousness is frequently due to a poor start or to a very brilliant one. Either condition may upset certain temperaments and contrarily a poor start occasionally spurs on some men to greater efforts and better shooting as they approach the end of a match. Irritating, provocative, or annoying noises or comments overheard from the side lines, or the attitude and decisions of an over-zealous range official all have a tendency to keep one on edge and are the immediate causes of extreme nervousness at times, unless carefully guarded against. It might be well at this time to call attention to the fact that this form of nervousness is different from that experienced as one's muscles become tired toward the end of a long match. Tired muscles and nerves cause unsteadiness in holding but this is due entirely to the strain of shooting and not to the causes which produce "buck fever." Short periods of rest and relaxation, if time is available, may remedy this unsteadiness, but only the exercise of mental effort or will power will stop the effects of the "buck."

While there is no panacea for this disorder, and what may be a remedy for one may prove ineffective for another, it is well to study the causes of the ailment so as to avoid them. In addition to this it is well to have in mind certain expedients which can be resorted to in an emergency when a touch of the trouble is present. It never pays to lose one's temper over the fact that one is suffering from an attack of this kind, for this will probably only exaggerate the nervousness. Rather one should exercise all his self-control toward overcoming it. Being caused entirely by the agitation of the mind due to some exterior incident, the effect will be stopped only when the mind is again at ease. Therefore, the cause of the excitement must be expelled from the mind, and every mental effort made to concentrate on the immediate task at hand, usually that of aiming, holding, squeezing, and calling the shot. A coach may frequently assist by calling the attention of the shooter to something that will take his mind from his condition. A joke, a humorous reference to anything about the range or even a mild ridiculing of the shooter's condition will sometimes relieve the strain by causing the one disturbed to laugh and relax. Sitting down, resting, and slow deep breathing for a minute or two sometimes have a wonderfully quieting effect on the nerves and heart action. But most important of all, if one could put out of his mind everything except the immediate operation of firing, he would find that the "buck" would at once disappear.

To accomplish this, one must first of all decide that he is not going to let anything disturb him mentally. It is a fundamental principle of psychology that interference with any behavior arouses emotion. He is not going to let his imagination run riot and cause him to ponder over the results of his shooting; he is not going to think of the effect on his team of his individual score, no matter whether it be good or poor; he is not going to anticipate the trophy he hopes to win; he is not going to think about the comments of his friends or rivals should he win or lose. He should avoid all controversies with range officials, scorers or competitors. If necessary to make a protest, he should do it in a quiet, self-possessed manner and accept the decision in the same way. He may assume that certain individuals, friendly or otherwise, will attempt by the power of suggestion and comments to "get his goat" and should therefore ignore their remarks or laugh at their strategy as being very crude. If you start poorly don't worry about it but shoot each shot thereafter as though it alone counted. Nearly everyone has a bad string somewhere in his match and your competitor is having his troubles while you are having yours. Above all things do not take the matter too seriously as it is not a matter of life or death. Shoot carefully, work hard, but not too hard. Determine to make each shot good, and the closer you get to the end of your match the greater will be the necessity for the exercise of your determination and will power to prevent a relaxation of effort and subsequent wild shots. Your last shot may win for you so make it good. Realize that there is such a thing as the "buck" but also rest assured that it can be readily controlled if understood thoroughly. Side step as far as possible the numerous causes that bring it on and if still subject to it under certain conditions such as in competition shooting, put yourself under these conditions as frequently as possible until competition has no terrors for you. Seek every opportunity for keen competition until you reach the point where you prefer such work to mere practice and then your worth as a shooter will be recognized and your system nearly immune to the "buck."

"FREEZING"

Sooner or later the novice will reach a time in his practice at slow fire when he finds that he is frequently able to hold his sights aligned on his target for a perceptible time but that he is unable to squeeze the trigger and fire the piece at this time. This condition is known among shooters as being "frozen" and is encountered most frequently by men who follow chiefly the slow or deliberate fire game. It is not due to the weight of trigger pull for its effects are felt when using either a heavy, slow trigger, or a very light set trigger. A number of years ago the author was a member of a pistol team which that year won second place in the National Indoor League matches conducted by the United States Revolver Association. The team was composed of a number of very excellent deliberate fire shots whose shooting was done with the .22 caliber long barreled target pistol with a minimum trigger pull of two pounds. About the middle of the season when everyone was shooting at his best, this condition of being unable to squeeze off a shot when the hold was perfect became very noticeable to nearly all the team and frequently members had to make several attempts before each shot was fired. This resulted in a loss of valuable time and frequently made it necessary for certain members to fire their last shots hurriedly in order to complete a match within the time limit, which was a minute a shot. This particular group affected were old experienced shots, most of them having devoted their attention largely to the deliberate form of pistol shooting rather than to timed or rapid firing. The development of the condition was brought about by a slowly acquired habit of shooting very carefully, deliberately, and with the emphasis placed on making a shot good regardless of the time required. The immediate psychological cause was mutual inhibition, or the partial checking or complete blocking of one nervous impulse by another nearly simultaneous impulse. This phenomenon is brought about when an individual lacks the decision or will power necessary to complete the operation of firing through a fear that his aim or hold is not perfect. During the firing of a shot, the marksman aligns his sights on the bull's-eye, holds his pistol as nearly immovable as possible and then squeezes his trigger when the sights appear perfectly aligned. If at this instant he has perfect co-ordination of nerves and muscles his pistol will be fired and his shot will be a good one. To explain it according to psychology, at the instant the eye registers his perfect aim the proper external stimulus is given, his brain gives an impulse to certain nerves and the muscles with which they are connected; this impulse causes the trigger to be squeezed and the shot is fired. If a shooter can develop this habit of always squeezing without hesitation or fear when his aim is good he will eventually establish a strong path of nervous impulse which will develop co-ordination and assure him of excellent results in his shooting. Now, consider the opposite case. If at the instant the sights appear aligned correctly and the brain gives the nervous impulse to the proper muscles to squeeze the trigger, there is a doubt in the mind of the shooter, or a fear that perhaps the aim or hold might be better, there will then be a partial checking or a complete blocking of the first impulse by a nearly simultaneous impulse which acts along a different path or set of muscles and these prevent the squeezing muscles from firing the pistol. Thus exists a condition in which one set of nerves and muscles is attempting to squeeze and another checking the operation. If, through habit the inhibitory or checking nerves and muscles are developed, it will be very difficult for a shooter to get his shot off and he will have to extend and lower his arm many times before the shot is finally fired satisfactorily. Shooting under this condition requires a great deal more energy than when the shots can be fired on first attempt, and may cause a shooter to weaken materially toward the end of a fifty or sixty shot match.

To avoid the dangers of this habit, the best advice to the novice is to remind him that "an ounce of prevention is worth a pound of cure." The development of the habit can be largely prevented if understood and if at times it does cause trouble in spite of all efforts to the contrary then there are certain practical schemes that help to overcome it.

For one desiring to make a success of rapid firing after he has become reasonably advanced in slow firing, it is highly desirable to develop decisiveness in squeezing while practicing slow fire. No person can ever hope to shoot accurately in rapid fire who lacks the power to squeeze decisively when his sights appear to be aligned satisfactorily on his target. Realizing therefore the importance of this fact, everyone who hopes to reach a high plane in all-around pistol shooting should determine, when they begin practice, to get off their shots on first attempt without lowering the arm. Faithful practice and adherence to this principle will do more to prevent the development of pottering in shooting and the resultant condition of "freezing" than any other thing. On the other hand, toward the end of a long series of shots when tired nerves and muscles have about reached their limits of endurance and the arm has become shaky, it may be occasionally necessary to lower it rather than "pull" or "flinch" the shot. For more experienced shots who are afflicted by this "frozen" condition, the following remedies are suggested: During practice determine to follow the plan outlined above of getting your shot off on first attempt and note whether your scores suffer, also note how much less energy is required to fire a string of shots. To assist the squeezing impulse it will help some to hold in the left hand a small object such as a pocket knife, and when the sights are properly aligned to emphasize the act of squeezing by saying to oneself "now" and at the same time squeezing both the trigger and the pocket knife. If you become "frozen" in an important competition, as the author once did in an international match, it will help to overcome the trouble temporarily if you can lay aside your pistol for a few minutes and snap a few times at the target with a gun having a heavier trigger pull. Also exercise the muscles of the shooting hand by slowly closing and opening it a few times between shots.

At the pistol matches conducted by the International

Shooting Union at Rheims, France, in 1924, the author sat behind M. Paul Van Asbroeck of Belgium while the latter fired his 60 shots in the International match of that year, and noted among other things that this celebrated deliberate fire shot who had several times previously won the World's Free Pistol Championship, invariably got his shots off on the first attempt until toward the end of his shooting when, his arm becoming tired, he found it necessary to lower it occasionally without firing and make a second attempt after a short rest.

Plenty of snapping practice and a fair amount of rapid fire are also invaluable to a young shooter as a preventative to the development of pottering and the habit of "freezing" during slow fire.

FLINCHING

The greatest obstacle the novice has to overcome when he begins firing is that of flinching. He will soon learn to aim, hold and squeeze well enough to make respectable scores but will find that he frequently gets erratic shots because he flinches. More annoyance, discouragement and failures in pistol shooting are blamable to flinching than to any other problems of the game. This phenomenon may be defined as the sudden, involuntary nervous reaction experienced while firing, which causes spasmodic movements of certain muscles which derange the aim and produce wild shots.

The normal reaction of one's nervous system to a startling noise or blow is to cause the body to suddenly shrink from or attempt to avoid the disturbing action. The violence and rapidity of this reaction depends largely on one's temperament,—the more nervous it is the greater the reaction. The nervous system not only reacts after a disturbance, but frequently does it in anticipation of expected injury. The sensation of heat as one's hand unexpectedly nears a hot stove causes it to be involuntarily withdrawn before any harm is done. The tendency to shrink from the explosion of a large firecracker after the fuse has been lighted is involuntary. These are examples of the nervous system's reaction to anticipated danger. Accordingly, when a novice begins firing, his system reacts to the noise of the discharge in his ears and the jar of the recoil on the muscles of his hand. The greater the noise of the discharge and the heavier the recoil the greater will be the effect of the reaction. At first the reaction occurs immediately after the explosion and recoil of the gun and in such a case the flinching does not cause an erratic shot as the bullet has left the gun before the flinch begins. After a few shots however, the nervous system may anticipate the effect and react just about the time the trigger is squeezed, causing the muscles of the shooting arm to spasmodically jerk the trigger or thrust the hand forward to meet the expected shock of recoil. In this case the reaction occurs before the bullet leaves the muzzle, deranges the aim and causes a wild shot. It is this form of flinching that is detrimental to the progress of the beginner and unless he knows how to prevent and overcome it he will continue indefinitely to flinch and his shooting remain mediocre, except that increased shooting experience and the gradual accustoming of the nervous system to the noise and the recoil of discharge will decrease the tendency. It is well to understand that flinching is not confined to the beginner but is quite prevalent among old and experienced shots, to a much lesser degree however. It cannot be blamed entirely to fear of noise or recoil but sometimes occurs to a pistol shot when through over-anxiety he attempts to hurry a shot. It occurs more frequently as a result of a disordered digestive system, due to indiscretions of eating and drinking or when mental worries combined with stomach disorders give one a case of "jumpy" nerves. At such times when the nervous system is "keyed up to a high pitch" very small incidents cause one to flinch badly. The proximity on the firing line of a careless shooter, who while loading points his weapon in your direction or who frequently makes startling exclamations or otherwise conducts himself as a nuisance, is likely to make one nervous and cause flinching. Hair triggers or very heavy, creepy triggers, because they are treacherous and uncertain, are very conducive to flinching and are a constant worry to anyone who is not thoroughly accustomed to them. They are especially bad for rapid fire, for it is very difficult to squeeze uniformly and get good co-ordination with them when firing rapidly.

If we consider flinching from a psychological standpoint and realize that it is more of a mental than physical problem, we will readily appreciate the advisability of preventing it by giving the mind so much to do during the operation of firing that it will not be able to think of or anticipate the effects of the explosion or recoil. This can be accomplished by training the mind to absolutely concentrate on aiming, holding, squeezing and most important of all in preventing flinching at least, on calling the shot. If a novice will bring himself to think only of these four essentials his mind will be so occupied that he will see only the alignment of the sights at the instant the explosion occurs and if he flinches at all it will be after the bullet has left the barrel. After the marksman has taken his firing position, aligned his sights, held his breath and begun squeezing he should put out of his mind everything except calling the shot until the explosion occurs and if he does this he will soon find that his flinches become fewer and his scores greatly improved.

To sum up, flinching will be prevented or reduced to a minimum by a careful observance of the following:

1. Keep the nervous system in a normal healthy condition by sensible exercise and diet.
2. While firing concentrate on aiming, holding, squeezing and *calling the shots* until the habits become mechanical.
3. Do not fire many shots at each practice period while learning the game or until the muscles and nerves become thoroughly accustomed to the noise and recoil. Too much shooting is conducive to carelessness and flinching.
4. Know your pistol, especially its cocking action and trigger pull and avoid treacherous and uncertain triggers and actions.

THE RELATIONSHIP OF MAN TO GUN

There is another psychological side to pistol shooting on which I wish to touch and that is the relationship between the weapon and the person using it. The technique of shooting—the proper stance, the correct manner of aiming, holding and firing the pistol—has been emphasized over and over and may be defined as the outward or visible technique of shooting. There is, however, another form of technique which could well be termed the inward or invisible technique and, as has been shown already, it bears an important relationship to one's success in the sport. The point to be made is that we must not only have complete mastery over the pistol to obtain the greatest success in marksmanship but we must also have absolute control of it at all times to insure complete personal safety.

The pistol, either as an instrument for the development of skill or as a weapon for defensive purposes, is a splendid servant in the hands of him who masters it, but it is a dangerous enemy in the hands of anybody who is mastered by it. It might be compared to a spirited horse in the hands of its master: under control he performs and behaves beautifully; out of control he throws his rider. No doubt Lindbergh's "Spirit of St. Louis" became a very human personality to him long before he reached Europe, but the plane out of control would have meant his death. So it is with a pistol, for if one practices intelligently and faithfully until he masters the art of shooting it, there will come times—though they may be rare—when it seems almost human in the way it responds to impulse of mind and nerves. When these occasions occur it seems as though the perfect coordination that exists between man and gun causes the latter to function as though it were part of the body and mind and not as a separate external mechanism. There are however, occasions when an entirely different relationship may occur and then the gun becomes the master of the man. I will illustrate by two incidents recently told me by a friend.

"During the War my brother trained with a machine gun battalion and told me afterwards that he had become so familiar with his machine gun and his automatic pistol that he could almost take them apart and reassemble them in the dark. For some years after his return from France he kept his pistol at our Mother's home and during one Thanksgiving vacation, while visiting there from the University of Wisconsin, where he was an instructor in history, he decided that he would get out his automatic and do some target shooting in a quarry nearby. Five minutes after he had secured an oil can, a rag and a hairpin from our Mother the pistol went off and he was instantly killed,—shot through the head. Of course we do not know what happened. There was, however, every evidence that it was an accident, and I do know that my brother was tired through overstudy.

"Another incident was that of a young man in the literary department of a large publishing firm some years ago. He had come to the firm at a very high salary and with the understanding that he was to achieve certain results. He was there about a year or more when it became apparent both to the firm and to himself that he was not likely to succeed in what he had undertaken to do. There was no question that he worried very much and that at times his frail health was the result of that worry. One Saturday, while leaving early to go to his country home, he remarked to one of his associates that he was discouraged and that he felt that the best thing he could do was to resign. That afternoon, while out hunting in the company of two or three friends, he stepped over a low stone wall and carelessly dragged his gun after him. The gun went off and he was killed instantly."

These two incidents are, to my mind, significant of something similar to what is called, in the game of chess, a blind spot in the brain. It is well established that even the great artists of chess have been known to leave a piece exposed or to overlook an open threat which would be obvious to the most amateurish player, simply, because in that fraction of a second, there is a blind spot which prevents the player from seeing anything. I wonder whether many of the accidents resulting from the careless handling of firearms are not the result of something similar.

The point to be made is that firearms are always dangerous to any person handling them who is below his normal powers. It is highly necessary that anyone using a pistol—or any other fire-arm for that matter—be at the peak of his efficiency in all departments of his being, so that he shall be master of the weapon and insure the most efficient results from the use of it. Conversely, it is apparent that when a person is below his normal powers, he is inferior to the weapon which becomes increasingly dangerous in his hands. He must, therefore, be master of it or he will be well advised to leave it alone, especially should he be worried or despondent. A lover of firearms may, in periods of stress and worry, be inclined to turn for comfort to those companions of many happy hours, his pistols, with the idea of attempting to get his mind off his worries and, not being as alert and careful with them as usual, accidents may result.

Chapter XV

COMPETITION SHOOTING

COMPETITIONS in pistol shooting as in other sports, are the great incentives to continued efforts after one has learned the rudiments and developed a certain skill in the game. When the novelty and primary interest in a new sport wears off Americans lose their inclination to "carry on" unless they have an objective or ambition which spurs their will to greater efforts. Competitions have always furnished this incentive and we have now reached the point where we seldom engage in any sport for the pure love of the game, but instead we play it only to win. This is a national characteristic and the pistol shooting fraternity is not excepted.

The novice who can be convinced that his greatest pleasure will come from competition shooting and that the thrills and satisfaction he gets from good shooting in practice are not to be compared with those which come as the result of a keenly contested match, will be a much better competition shot or team man than the person who practices all the time and then enters a competition much as he would a mental examination. To develop a match shot the novice should be given a thorough course in pistol shooting with the policy continually stressed and followed of ignoring the scores made until fairly good groups can be shot. The scores will take care of themselves after one has learned, by thorough preliminary training, the technique of aiming, holding, squeezing and calling. When reasonably good groups can be made, it then becomes desirable and necessary, in order to record and stimulate progress, to keep tabs on all the firing done. This is best accomplished by keeping a score book in which all firing is recorded. By keeping an accurate record of all scores made the novice can note his progress or set backs. Recording only the good scores is of little value. From his score book he can, by analyzing his work, determine when he does his best shooting. This may occur after he has fired ten shots or it may take several scores to steady him down to good holding. He can also compare his practice and match scores.

Many times we hear marksmen say they can do better work in matches than in practice but this is usually "bunk." Where one man is found who can do this there are ninety-nine who will not do nearly as well when they have something worth while at stake. Aside from the exceptional score occasionally made in a match, a pistol shot's average will be lower in competition than in practice. He should however, strive to maintain his average at all times both in practice and competition. The novice should believe that there is more satisfaction and better practice in match shooting, even though the effort he makes, the strain he undergoes, and the disappointments he experiences may have a tendency to discourage him. He should realize that practice scores are merely for "sighting in" pistols and for checking their sight setting and that the only worth-while shooting is that done against a real opponent with a prize for which to shoot. He should endeavor to shoot a match with someone every time he fires and better progress will be made if this shooting is done against someone who is slightly better than himself. Shooting for qualification badges and medals, for merchandise prizes in club matches, in local turkey and chicken shoots, and in sectional contests is excellent competition training. Re-entry matches in which unlimited entries are permitted are not as desirable as single entry ones, for they encourage marksmen to keep only their good scores and to cease firing on a target when they make a poor shot.

About the time a novice gets interested in comparing his skill with others he naturally studies the question of what constitutes good shooting. He wants to know what scores he must make in the various kinds of fire in order to have a chance in competitions against pistol men with ambitions similar to his own. Specifically he would like to know what percentage he should strive for in deliberate fire or in rapid and timed fire at the standard bull's-eye or silhouette targets. The young man who lives on a farm, ranch, or in a small community where there is little opportunity for competing in local matches because of the scarcity of persons interested in his favorite sport, needs especially some means of testing his skill under match conditions. The United States Revolver Association and the National Rifle Association, realizing the need, have provided for it in the most practical manner. They conduct competitions by mail in which contestants can fire on their home ranges at their own time and pleasure. Such competitions are held twice a year and consist of outdoor and indoor matches during the appropriate season. Qualification matches are also conducted and a shooter may, by making certain scores, determine whether he should be rated as a "Marksman," "Sharpshooter" or "Expert." The match conditions and ratings are not the same in both organizations, however. By participating in the competitions of either or both of the associations the novice will soon learn what constitutes good target shooting. Memberships in these national shooting organizations are open to any one interested in shooting and the dues are very nominal.

To enable those who may not be able to benefit from matches of the shooting societies just mentioned, the author offers the following as a reasonable basis for grading pistol practice.

In deliberate shooting, or slow fire as it is generally called, any person who can average 90% on the Standard American target at fifty yards out of doors, with good average shooting conditions or on the reduced target at 20 yards indoors under artificial light is an excellent shot regardless of the kind of pistol he uses. Such a shot can compete favorably in any competitions conducted in this class of fire. This is a broad statement, but it must be remembered that pistol shooting is a game of opportunity to the extent that all pistol shots have their good and bad days and a score that would place several points below the winner today might win in a similar contest tomorrow. To average between 80 and 85% would constitute good shooting and between 85 and 90% very good work under the same conditions given above.

Shooting against time can be rated in a similar manner. If the 50 yard Standard American Target is used at 25 yards, as is the normal procedure for rapid or timed fire, the difficulties incident to shooting against time will be compensated for by the shorter range. For rapid fire, in which 5 shots are. fired in ten seconds, "good," "very good," and "excellent" ratings are justifiable for percentage scores of 80, 85 and 90 respectively. For timed fire at a rate of 5 shots in 15 or 20 seconds one should be able to increase his scores by about 5% in order to be entitled to the same ratings. For military work using the prescribed service targets

The firing line at Camp Perry, Ohio, during the pistol matches of the National Rifle Association.

and heavy caliber military pistols the same percentage would still stand, by way of comparison, even though the ranges are shorter and the targets easier, especially the silhouettes.

In general it is more difficult to shoot well with the larger caliber revolvers than it is with small bore target pistols, so that a marksman using the former weapons should be entitled to the ratings given above even though his scores average several points lower than the standards here established. By using the percentages indicated for each kind of fire one should be able to estimate what should constitute an excellent total score for any match composed of slow, timed and rapid fire.

There is one feature about pistol matches that is unsatisfactory. If a shooter may fire wherever and whenever he chooses there is bound to be a lack of uniformity in the shooting conditions of all competitors which may materially affect their scores so that the best shot does not always win. We have all seen the type of marksman who does excellent shooting locked up by himself or with a lone friend to witness his scores, but who makes a miserable showing in shoulder to shoulder competitions in the open with strange faces and stranger conditions about him. A man training for competitions should do so in company with as many marksmen as possible, for in important matches he will ultimately be required to shoot on a firing line with many other contestants, if he goes very far in the sport.

When one begins intensive preparations for an important competition or series of matches he naturally asks himself the question, "What kind and amount of exercise, if any, shall I take to fit myself properly for the work ahead?" Pistol shooting does not require a highly developed muscular system. It does not require great physical endurance. It does not want nerves keyed to the highest pitch, but, to assure the greatest success for the participant it does demand general good health and enough exercise to maintain the nervous system in a good normal condition. For the person who lives an active outdoor life, is temperate in his habits, and whose physical condition is good, no special training is necessary except that incidental to the firing done in preparation for the matches. For persons of sedentary occupations who expect to attend an out-of-door competition for any length of time, such as the National Matches, it would be wise for them to accustom themselves to plenty of fresh air and more exercise than they normally take or they may find that the sudden change from an indoor existence to an active one in the open air will upset them temporarily and their shooting will suffer accordingly.

There has always been considerable discussion on the question of the effect on a marksman's shooting, of his use of tobacco, alcoholic liquors or other stimulants, during a training or competition period. After studying the different opinions and methods of team captains and coaches of several successful National and International rifle and pistol teams and as the result of his personal experience, the author has come to the following conclusions on this subject, in so far as pistol shots are concerned and affected.

Smoking in moderation—with emphasis on moderation—is not harmful. To suddenly require a man accustomed to the use of tobacco to give it up entirely will do more harm than to allow him to continue the habit, for he may become discontented, irritable or otherwise nervously upset. The coffee drinking habit is much worse than smoking, especially for persons of nervous temperaments, as the caffein is very stimulating to some nervous systems.

The use of alcoholic stimulants should be absolutely avoided to get the best results in pistol shooting. Other dissipations which adversely affect the nerves should be eliminated.

The most important factor in the conditioning of a pistol shot is the diet. There are two parts of his system that must be right. They are his digestion and elimination. Indulgence in anything that upsets the digestion is bad and the failure of the bowels to function properly with good daily movements is even worse and may unnerve a good pistol shot so thoroughly and quickly that his scores will look like those of a novice.

A well balanced diet with plenty of fruit, vegetables and other roughage which will stimulate the intestines to movement is what is needed to maintain the nervous system in a normal healthy condition. During the National Matches at Camp Perry, Ohio, in 1921 the entire camp was affected by an epidemic popularly known as "Water Sickness" which caused the latrines to be about as well occupied as the firing line. The effect of this diarrhoea was certainly not adverse to the shooting, for more records were made that year than have ever been made there before or since that time. This incident should be taken for what it is worth.

It must be remembered that pistol shooting is a great strain on, and demands more of, the nerves and will power than any other form of shooting and anything that causes mental or physical irritation will be quickly indicated through the nerves to the muzzle of the pistol. The effect of too much sleep is quite noticeable at times. As a result, one's nerves become so keen and keyed up that occasionally a marksman finds himself too much on edge in the morning to do his best shooting then, and that his scores are better when fired later in the day after his system has settled down.

Particular care should be taken of the eyes, especially if one is doing much indoor shooting under artificial light. Shooting in poor light or in brilliant sunshine may cause eyestrain and for this reason the eyes should not be required to do more close work than is absolutely necessary during competitions. Shooting glasses with amber colored lenses will be found beneficial in bright light, if they are ground to fit the eyes. It should be unnecessary to say that the shooting hand and arm should be protected against injury at all times. Scuffling, wrestling and similar pastimes should be avoided at these times.

TRAINING PERIOD

The time to be devoted to training for a particular competition will depend on whether the participant is entirely out of practice when he begins preparation, the nature and extent of the match he expects to enter, and his personal equation. For one who does a little shooting throughout the year at frequent intervals, and keeps in practice reasonably well the intensive training period need not be long. For older men and those who drop pistol work during half of the year to indulge in other seasonable sports, a greater time is required to get into shape. Young men, because of greater versatility, flexibility, and quicker co-ordination can round into form in less time than older men, although the latter, due to greater experience, may have certain other advantages in match shooting.

If one anticipates attending the National Matches,

and every enthusiastic pistol shot should make this his Mecca at least once after he has qualified as an expert shot, he should study the match program, decide on what contests he prefers and then practice for them under conditions as laid down by the rules. The Camp Perry matches cover contests in every style of pistol shooting with more attention paid to contests open to the service pistol. Trophies in the form of cups, medals and cash are offered as prizes, but the opportunities to exchange opinions with pistol experts from all parts of the country and elsewhere, the chance to observe the work of celebrated shots, to inspect the latest developments in hand guns and accessories, and to experience the ups and downs of a large competition will be of inestimable benefit to the young shot in future years.

The nature of the competition should govern the amount of time spent at each practice period. If one expects to fire a fifty shot match he should frequently fire that number of shots under match conditions as nearly as he can arrange them. If rapid as well as slow firing is expected then both kinds should be practiced with special attention to the former. Daily practice in firing a few scores is better than longer periods of practice fired at irregular intervals. If opportunities are limited for range practice the marksman should not fail to hold daily trigger squeeze and rapid fire exercises, to supplement his firing. If a marksman can devote all of his time to training for a short period before the matches it would be an excellent thing to do. Then he can plan a daily schedule with sufficient rest periods to enable him to do all the practicing he requires without overshooting. This assumes that one is preparing for a series of competitions such as the National or International matches.

Teams representing the different branches of the regular military and naval services usually train for about two months before assembling at Camp Perry. Their daily practice varies. Some teams fire only in the afternoons, others both mornings and afternoons. Practice consists of firing through the National Pistol Match course at least once, and more often twice, then working on the class of fire in which individual members are weakest or at slow fire work with small bore pistols.

As a man reaches his peak he should be careful not to shoot too much or he will become stale and perhaps have a slump, to recover from which, it takes time, a rest and change of routine. Assuming that a marksman is enthusiastic and conscientious in preparing for a competition and willing to work hard, he should be careful to note the time when his interest wanes, his practice becomes much like work, he feels irritable and fed up on the game, and his scores fall off or get erratic. Then is the time to take a rest and change, if only for a couple of days, rather than to grit one's teeth and keep plugging along, and incidently, worrying about one's progress. Fighting for a place on a national team, for a state or national championship or for any important trophy is nerve-trying business and worry is a big obstacle to success. Our nervous system which is the controlling factor in our success must be favored continually and not overstrained. By starting his practice with a few scores and gradually increasing it until he can fire through the equivalent of his hardest match without fatigue will get better results for a marksman than burning up much ammunition with the idea of hardening himself quickly.

Firing in a moderate breeze should be practiced, for one may have to fire his match under similar conditions, but practicing on very windy days is of no value. Instead it is a waste of time, energy and ammunition.

When using large caliber pistols less firing should be done at a practice period than if small bore guns are used. Do not practice with an old favorite pistol and then change to a new one just before a match. It will not feel or function the same. It is also well to use a heavier trigger pull than that required by the rules as triggers do wear, some quite rapidly, and it is better to play safe than to be disqualified.

Before entering a match one should be sure he has all his equipment ready so as to avoid haste and confusion on the firing line and the bad effects this may have on one's shooting. If for some unavoidable reason a competitor is late in arriving on the line he should not permit himself to become excited and hurry his final preparations even though others may attempt to rush him on the line or into a relay that is about to fire.

Sights should be checked carefully to see that they are not bent, broken or loose. In the case of adjustable sights see that the setting is correct and watch it like a hawk throughout the match. One of the greatest weaknesses of certain American pistols is the sight adjusting screws which work loose repeatedly during firing. If there is a graduated scale on the sights, the setting should be recorded in a score book for fear a doubt may arise in the mind concerning the proper elevation or deflection for a particular range, light or ammunition load. Smoke or paint the sights and be careful not to rub them off.

Inspect the ammunition to be used to see that there is powder in the cartridges and that they are not deformed in any way or the shells split. The most reputable firms occasionally turn out a lot of ammunition that is not up to standard, or one may get hold of some old stuff that has deteriorated. In case one gets hang fires, keyholes, fliers, frequent misfires, or unusually low groups, the ammunition causing them should be discarded and another kind used.

Tighten all loose screws and have a screwdriver handy to keep them tight. If one cannot afford to have an extra pistol available in case the one in use fails during a match program, he should provide himself with spare parts, properly adjusted beforehand, for those which have a tendency to fail. Firing pins crystallize, springs weaken or break, extractors and ejectors wear badly, triggers go bad suddenly, and unfortunately these malfunctions occur at most inopportune times, much to the annoyance of the marksman.

The matter of blackening sights is important and a marksman is foolish to fire in any match with shiny sights. They may be effectively blackened in two ways, —by smoking them, or by painting them with a dead-black quick-drying paint. The paint if applied with a brush, is convenient to use and is fairly lasting but it may become lumpy and thick and present ragged and blurry appearing sights for aiming. Smoke can be applied more evenly and leaves the sights sharp and clean cut. Anything that gives a black smoke can be used, from a match or candle to a kerosene or pitch pine

torch.   Camphor gum gives a heavy smoke but leaves
the sights grayish black.   Splinters of good pitch pine
or fir give off excellent smoke.   Kerosene smoke is good.
In recent years rifle and pistol men of the Services have
been carrying a small carbide lamp in their kits.   These
lights give the finest kind of black smoke, can be used
in breezy weather with ease, and permit the application of the smoke uniformly and quickly.   If the smoke
is applied too long the black gets too thick and falls off in
tiny flakes.   The lamps and necessary carbide for re-
charging them are a little bulky and inconvenient to
carry about.

In smoking sights it is well to blacken any part of
the gun which may reflect bright light into the eyes
while aiming.   Sights should be free from grease when
the smoke is applied or the results will not be satisfactory.

To avoid needless arguments and delays one should
know the order of numbering the targets and firing
points, the manner in which competitors are squadded
or assigned to firing relays, range officers in charge, the
methods of marking and scoring targets, the commands
or signals for "Commence Firing" or "Cease Firing"
and in fact everything covered by the rules governing
the competition.   Individuals who are continually ask-
ing questions or making groundless protests on points
with which they should be familiar are a source of annoyance to others on the firing line.

When marking is done in the pits and scoring at the
firing line, one must never fail to check the scorer by
seeing that he calls out and records the score indicated
by the marker and in case of a re-mark, that the proper

score is entered on the score card. One should check his scorebook against the scorer's record before leaving the firing line. The marking of shots should be verified either by an inspection of the target or by spotting the bullet holes with a telescope or good pair of binoculars as the marker indicates their location. If convinced that you are not getting the score to which you are entitled, that score should be challenged. In case of close, questionable shots remember that the marker in the pits is in a better position than the marksman to determine whether or not a bullet cuts the ring or the edge of the bull's-eye. If in rapid fire one is so unfortunate as to put a bullet cleanly through another bullet hole without any indication of this fact do not rave and tear your hair when you get a zero for that shot. It sometimes happens and the range officer can only approve scores for the number of bullet holes found in the target. The method of scoring that is the most satisfactory for all concerned, is to issue separate match targets to each contestant and as they are completed have them scored and recorded and filed by an official scorer, at the same time permitting the shooter to inspect his target and check the score.

When actually on the firing line contestants should be very careful to observe all instructions given by range officers especially those regarding safety regulations. If officials act "hard boiled" and critical it is usually the result of misconduct and carelessness on the part of cantankerous marksmen who annoy and endanger the lives of others by their actions.

When rapid or timed fire is the order, listen carefully for the commands of the range officer or you may discover that the targets, in the case of disappearing ones, have appeared and that you are not ready to fire. This occurred to a contestant in the last Olympic Matches and he got one miss as a result.

As a final word of advice in match shooting, do not take the matter too seriously. If you have had previous experience in competition work there is no occasion for worry or nervousness. If you are a novice at the game put your mind on the work at hand and forget your surroundings. No one is watching you in particular. Others marksmen are busy with their own firing. Concentrate on the details of aiming, holding, squeezing, calling your shot and keeping your scorebook. You have no time to be thinking about other matters or to let your imagination work and your mind wander.

The following is a check list of equipment necessary or advisable to have on the firing line:

Pistols
Ammunition
Screwdriver with interchangeable bits.
Sight blackening materials.
Telescope with mount, or binoculars.
Scorebook and pencil.
Cartridge block for .22 ammunition.
Cleaning materials.
Camp stool.
Shooting glasses, amber.
Small pad of powdered resin.
Copy of match rules.
Targets, if not furnished.
Ear protectors or absorbent cotton.

Chapter XVI

COACHING AND TEAMWORK

As ONE's interest in pistol shooting grows and his knowledge and skill increases there comes a time when all students of the game feel a natural desire to impart knowledge of their hobby to others. They do this not because of an egotistical tendency to show their knowledge but because they want others to enjoy with them the advantages and pleasures of the sport that has been profitable to themselves. It is this desire to instruct others that keeps the game alive, for the success of any sport depends to a large degree upon the men who do the coaching of the novices when they first feel its appeal. The inherent desire to teach also adds to one's pleasure in a sport by giving the instructor an opportunity to watch the development of a pupil of promise. Athletic coaching is the life work of many men and women and they do it primarily because of their interest and love for the work. It is probable that the pleasure and satisfaction they get out of developing worthy representatives in a sport is greater than any other rewards they may receive. Teaching a beginner the elements of pistol shooting and then carrying him through the more difficult problems is an excellent test of one's ability and knowledge. In the process one may find that there are many details to which he has given little thought. A study of these will be of value to the teacher.

218

Successful team coaching for pistol competitions is largely a matter of good individual coaching and not of intensive training in teamwork. The spirit of team-work must prevail in any successful pistol team, but, like trackwork, the winning points will depend largely on the individual and his instruction, coaching and training. The good coach must possess knowledge of the finer points of the game and be either a good shot or have been one in the not too distant past. Shooters are all too prone to ignore the advice of men who cannot demon-strate, or at least who have not been able to demonstrate what they preach. Even though one may have an en-viable record, we frequently find in coaching young men that there are some of the latter who, because they are able to shoot better than their coach at that particular time, indicate by their actions and attitude that they feel they know more about the game than men long in experi-ence in competition work. Self-control, patience and tact, the primary requisites of a good coach, are needed in dealing with such men.

In the coaching of individuals better results will be ob-tained if the coach makes a careful study of the charac-teristic traits of each person he is instructing. Shooters are like musicians. They are all too frequently tempera-mental and have to be handled tactfully to secure their enthusiastic support and retain their best efforts. As regards disposition and temperament marksmen may be divided into two groups. Perhaps the majority of shooters may be said to have nervous temperaments, while those really phlegmatic are in the minority. There is not a distinct dividing line between the two groups and we cannot always place an individual by appearances or first performances. Basically, persons with nervous temperaments are apt to be high strung, physically and mentally energetic, quick tempered, easily excited and irritated. They are inclined to be talkative when things are going well and moody when blue or displeased. With these inherent characteristics it would seem that persons of this class would make poor pistol shots, but this is not the case for there are many examples of distinguished marksmen who by perseverance in training themselves in self-control and the psychology of shooting have mastered the art, and through the force of their will power travelled farther along the road to success than many of their less energetic, phlegmatic brothers. In handling men of this type care should be taken to see that they do not over shoot, that they are paired off with congenial shooting partners and that they fire their matches at such times of day as a study of their work shows they do their best shooting. Firing under conditions that will assist in training them to overcome the tendency toward irritation at trivial things should be prescribed without the purpose being known to the marksman. The training routine should include plenty of competitions. In coaching this type of shooter praise will accomplish much more than criticism and censure.

As a rule a man with a phlegmatic temperament is excellent material for a pistol shot and should make a good team man. His calm, imperturbable disposition, which makes him slow to anger or irritate, his well controlled nerves that accomplish marvels in steady holding, his reliability and confidence in his ability to produce a good score at any time, are all assets to be desired. Usually he lacks imagination and consequently is not easily upset or worried over the results of a poor start in a match or of the possible glory that will be his should he win. He makes a splendid anchor for a team. There are of course extremes among this group that are not desirable for marksmen. They are too easy going. Some are so lazy that they lack sufficient energy to make them ambitious enough to do really good work and they may be so dull witted as to be unable to absorb, understand and apply the principles taught.

Between the distinctly nervous and phlegmatic types there is a large field of material that possesses many of the good points of both groups. They are energetic without being highstrung, they have reasonable self control and are not easily upset. They may not become as good deliberate fire shots as their more phlegmatic brothers, but they learn more readily and are more versatile in manipulating revolvers in all-around practice. I have in mind a shot of international fame who is phlegmatic to a high degree and who has tried repeatedly to learn aerial shooting without success.

There are three distinct dispositions that are worthy of mention here. The first is the pessimist who is always "on the rocks," who has little or no confidence in his ability to improve and who is constantly worrying about future matches. There is always danger in giving such a man a place on a team until he has proved that he can stand the gaff of competition and not "blow up" when he gets in a pinch.

The optimist is always going to do better, at any rate he thinks he is. If he does improve, the chances are he will become over-confident and he then presents a big problem. It is difficult to teach him anything and he spends so much time explaining away his poor shooting and offering tiresome alibis that he has no time for studying his weaknesses and improving his work. A few good drubbings at the hands of some of his straighter shooting teammates may take the conceit out of him and show him the error of his ways so that he will settle down and shoot instead of talk.

Another extreme type of personality is the ornery individual, if I may be permitted to use this term. He is extremely temperamental, which accurately defined might be called meanness. He is always carrying a chip on his shoulder, is never quite satisfied with anything about him and his noisy tongue and disagreeable presence make him a decided bore and a source of constant irritation to his teammates. He may be a very good shot but if his manners and conduct bring discord and discontent among the team his ability to shoot well will not be as valuable as his absence.

The chances are that a coach will find among his team material men of each type who may cause him worry because of the different problems they present. The majority however will give little trouble and no especial attention need be paid to their dispositions. In his first conference with the squad it is well for a coach to announce, among other items of policy, that temperament will not be tolerated on the team, in order to forestall any attempts on the part of the individuals to use temperament as an alibi for favoritism or for poor work they may do.

The first important thing in the preparation and training of a team for competitions is the selection and appointment of officials and the organization of the squad. The plan followed by teams attending the National Matches at Camp Perry has proven to be very efficient without being cumbersome. It provides for a team captain, team coach, a supply officer, and the shooting members. For minor local competitions this scheme may be unnecessary and can be modified accordingly. For competitions such as sectional, national and international contests involving travel, messing and supply problems, organized training periods, and other extensive preparations, it is well, in fact essential, that a good organization be provided to carry on the work. The team captain should be in command as the administrative head and the go-between for conducting all business between the team and the officials of the matches. He should be well qualified to coach, and should have tact and diplomacy for acting as an arbitrator when difficulties arise. He should make himself responsible for everything pertaining to the welfare of the team except the coaching, and in this he should not interfere save in exceptional situations. Any differences of opinion regarding coaching methods and training can always be amicably settled by a quiet conference between the team captain and coach provided they are the right kind of men for the jobs. If they are not they should not be selected as team officials. To have a team captain and a coach with decidedly different ideas regarding the training of a team cannot help but be disastrous. Of equal harm is the policy of carrying joy-riding dead wood and figure heads among the team officials. This usually results in the shirking of responsibility by some and the carrying of the entire burden of team administration and coaching by one man.

The team supply officer under the supervision of the team captain should provide those things necessary for the team as a whole. Cleaning materials, stationery, scorebooks, ear protectors or absorbent cotton, trigger testing weights, sight blackening materials, target supplies, spotting telescopes and ammunition are among the things he should be responsible for.

An important item in regard to military, police and semi-military teams is that the team captain should be the senior officer present. I have in mind a fine police team that was in charge of a patrolman of long experience in the shooting game. Among the shooting members was a police captain who was perhaps the best shot and who thought he knew more about the game than any one else. He did not loyally support the patrolman in charge and there was dissension in the team, for the patrolman, thinking perhaps of the future, did not like to oppose his superior in rank although he had the better ideas and methods. Situations of this kind should be avoided.

The team coach is responsible for the coaching and training of the team. He should be relieved from other work and devote all his energies to his specific duties. He should by reason of his knowledge of the individual characteristics of team members be better able to make the final selection of the team or recommend it to a team captain. An official scorebook should be kept which shows the work of the team in detail. Failure to keep an accurate record of all scores made during the try-out period will result in an inaccurate record of the relative standing of the team members. Shooters are inclined to remember the good scores they make and forget the poor ones so that their average seems better to them than it actually is. Each man should also keep his own record as a check and for his convenience in determining his progress or setbacks. In order to carry out this plan of showing a relative standing of team members, all should fire the same record courses each day. Daily standings should be posted on a bulletin board after each day's practice. Weekly standings should also be compiled and be posted so that men may see their relative progress with that of other members. The plotting of curves for each man, showing his progress in each kind of fire, is an excellent way to indicate a man's ups and downs. This should be done by making a graphic chart on cross section paper with the scores as ordinates and the dates as abscissas. I have seen the members of a team watch their charts with keen interest and fight their hardest to keep their curves pointing upward. Records of all inter-team or other matches should be kept separately and special study made of work done in these competitions for it is the ability to shoot well in matches that counts the most in the final analysis and selection of the team.

The final selection of a team may be difficult if the race for places is a close one. There are other things to be considered besides scores, but the safest plan to use, if the questions of favoritism are to be avoided, is the record made in competition and secondarily in practice. If it is impracticable to conduct matches with keen competition it may be desirable to have several try-outs among the members to select the team. These will be of such importance to the shooters as to provide a good test of their ability under strain. They should be completed several days before the matches for which the team is selected. The greatest error I ever saw a team captain make was to hold a final try-out for the selection of a very important team the day before the big match. The candidates put every effort into the try-outs and worked so hard for their place on the team that the reaction of mind and muscles the next day lowered the scores in the match materially below what they should have been, and the men actually shot poorer than they did in the try-out or had done for some time previously. It is well to remember that some men simply cannot shoot well in team competitions and they should never be selected to fire in an important team match unless there is no one else available, this regardless of how well they show up in practice.

In the matter of prescribing a schedule for practice, exercise, meals, sleep and similar details the reader is referred to the chapter on competition shooting. Good judgment should be exercised in these details.

Among the first things to be done by a coach when a team assembles for training is to inspect each member's shooting equipment to see that it complies with competition rules and if not that it be altered or replaced at once to avoid lost motion. Practicing with unauthorized sights, with trigger pulls below weight and similar evasions should not be tolerated. The coach should also assure himself that all guns are properly sighted.

COACHING ON THE LINE

Much depends on the attitude the coach takes on the firing line and the critiques he may hold after practice. He should school himself to be always patient, to be ready to assist no matter how tired he may feel, to be encouraging at all times, to be cheerful though he may not feel that way, and when it is necessary to criticize, to temper that criticism with some praise for the shooter's efforts. In running a firing line the less loud talk, hurry and bustle there is the better it will be for all present. Many annoying delays occur that test one's patience when getting relays on the line and the loss of temper by a coach may cause some shooter to be so upset as to ruin his work for the day and lower his morale accordingly. Men should be cautioned that good discipline on the line is necessary in order to make the work run smoothly and that if they wish to avoid later unpleasantness with over zealous or "hard boiled" range officers at competitions they should practice promptness in getting on the line and preparing to fire. In observing and coaching a shooter, instructions should be given in a low tone and an unhurried manner. The coach's self control will have a good effect on the shooter whereas any excitement on his part will only increase the nervousness of the pupil. Do not divert a man's attention from his work while he is actually firing. That is no time for giving instructions other than an occasional word of caution. When new men are inclined to be flinching and their minds leave the problem of squeezing and aiming to think about the noise or recoil of the gun they can be helped by repeating quietly "Squeeze"—"Call your shot." This will aid in bringing their mind back to the work at hand and they forget to anticipate the explosion. It is poor psychology to say "Don't flinch" at such times, as the power of suggestion may cause them to do the thing you mention.

A study of each man's shooting technique should be made before prescribing rules for his observance. If he is not using good form and his scores correspond then it is well to make some changes. If he is shooting well be careful about suggesting changes in his form. With new men it is a different matter entirely and is the duty of the coach to see that they get started correctly. He should insist on proper methods being followed. Frequent inspections of guns for creepy triggers, loose or bent sights and similar defects should be made by the coach. This should be done far enough ahead of a match date to insure equipment being in first class shape. A good motto for a coach is "Patience, more patience and still more patience."

Chapter XVII

ON INSTRUCTING LADIES

TEACHING a woman to shoot a pistol is a great deal like teaching a child to swim. Before either can make progress she must have confidence. The child must be assured that there is nothing dangerous about the water by permitting her to play around in it until she feels at home there. Most women have an inherent dread of firearms and the sight of them will at once arouse nervousness and sometimes bring on hysterics. If pistols are flourished about, pointed promiscuously or otherwise mishandled, it will invariably have the effect of discouraging a woman from having anything to do with them. The obstacle, therefore, that must be overcome by ladies who desire to learn to shoot is the fear of firearms.

The author has taught over three hundred women to shoot, most of them university students, and during the time so engaged learned some things of value to an instructor in this work. During the time these girls' classes were being conducted, he was also instructing college boys in rifle and pistol marksmanship and discovered that the girls learned more quickly than the boys and up to a certain point in their progress, with the rifle at least, the young women did better work than the young men. The reason for this was that the girls were openminded and intensely interested in learning to shoot. They admitted that they knew nothing about the game when they began and were willing to do, without question, exactly what the instructor told them to do. Most of the boys on the other hand were taking the instruction as part of the required military training of their institution. The big majority of them had done some shooting at an earlier date and felt that they knew how to do it. They invariably showed the lack or absence of proper instruction and had acquired enough bad habits to require a lot of correcting which was difficult with the average college sophomore.

After a few trying experiences with the first classes of young women, in which one had hysterics, another fainted, and a third almost shot an instructor, the necessity for very close supervision, individual coaching, and a carefully thought out plan of instruction, was an absolute necessity if accidents were to be avoided and confidence and enthusiasm developed in the pupils.

The following plan proved to be very successful and no further trouble was experienced after it was put into effect. Each class was assembled in a lecture room and seated about a large table on which an assortment of pistols was placed. After assuring the group that all the weapons were empty and that there were no loaded cartridges in the room, the instructor spoke briefly on the subject of hand guns and the safety precautions necessary to their proper use. The main characteristics of pistols, revolvers and auto-loading pistols or automatics, as they are commonly called, were explained and the operation of each type demonstrated by simulating the loading, unloading, cocking and firing of each. Every pupil was then required to perform the same operations and where no harm was done to the guns by snapping them, this also was permitted and encouraged. The instruction at this point was quite informal and the girls were allowed to move about the table, examine and operate each gun and required to observe the primary precaution of not pointing the pistols at anyone while they were snapping them or simulating loading them. It was not long before every girl knew how to handle the guns in a business-like manner and they took great delight in doing it. When they saw how simple the mechanisms appeared and found out that there was really nothing mysterious or dangerous about their functioning, their fear of them vanished. Nothing further was attempted in the first day's instruction.

Having overcome their fear of the guns themselves, the next steps were to teach the principles of aiming, holding, squeezing, and calling the shot. This was done in the order given, but each day the pupils were allowed to play with the guns until the time came for them to fire them.

The first shooting was a critical point in the game and great care was taken to prevent dangerous reactions due to high strung nerves. The loading and firing was first demonstrated and then each pupil was coached as she attempted to hit the target. Single shot target pistols were used, supplemented by revolvers in which only one cartridge was placed at a time. All were of small caliber, and were fired against targets with comparatively large bull's-eyes. The thrills a girl got from seeing her shot in the bull's-eye were often enough to cause her to turn quickly about with the gun in her hand and acclaim her success to her neighbors on the firing line or in rear of it. This could not be tolerated and it did not take long to show the necessity of keeping the guns always pointed toward the targets and never brought back through the shooting windows of the indoor range.

Toward the end of the course all pupils were required to fire larger caliber pistols and revolvers with the object in mind of training them to fire weapons such as they might use in self-defense. The principles were taught and all target firing was done with small bore target pistols and revolvers. Shooting against time was of course done with multi-loading weapons.

There are many reasons why a woman should know how to shoot and if she is given a good opportunity to learn, she will become an interested pupil provided the instruction is properly conducted. Aside from the prospect of possibly having to use a gun in self-defense or in the protection of her home or children, there are benefits to be derived from the game as a sport or pastime and there is no reason why a lady should not enjoy them. There is also little reason for her not becoming a good shot. She has a more delicate nervous system and will have to develop self control to a higher degree than most women succeed in doing in normal life, but this in itself is of value to her and not hard to do. If the principles and methods as outlined in the preceding chapters are followed and only small bore guns are used for practice until reasonable skill is developed, then there is no reason why she cannot go as far as she likes in the game. There have been some very fine pistol shots among women and if they were given greater encouragement there would be many more. I have seen one lady, the wife of a Chief of Police, stand up with a police team and shoot through the National Match course with a .38 caliber military revolver and make a score that would make many men envious. The pistol and revolver championship of Texas was won by a woman using the .45 Colt automatic pistol a few years ago. The great growth of rifle shooting among high school and college girls since the war, indicates the interest they take in that game and it is only the lack of instructors and facilities for pistol shooting that keep them from taking an equal interest in pistol work. Though it is much more convenient to practice than rifle shooting, the latter game frequently draws young women away from the pistol because it is easier to learn than the hand gun game.

Because they do have, as a general rule, a nervous temperament and less strength than the average man, ladies should use light pistols both in weight and caliber. The easier it is to hold and fire a gun and the lighter the noise and recoil, the better will it be suited to a lady's use, provided of course it has the necessary qualifications of efficiency, safety and accuracy. This applies particularly to target work and not so much to firing for defensive purposes. For personal protection the twenty-two caliber guns are of much less value than the larger calibers. It is not, however, advisable for a woman to go beyond the .32 caliber weapons if it is necessary for her to carry one for this purpose. Guns larger than this caliber are not nearly as convenient to carry and their increased effectiveness in stopping power is not worth the trouble the larger weapon will give her. After all is said, the fact that she is armed and can demonstrate by her actions that she knows how to handle and fire a pistol efficiently, will be all that is needed in any emergency in which she would ordinarily be involved.

The improved Colt .25 Automatic, Pocket Model Hammerless, with the magazine safety, is the most convenient of any of the pocket guns for a lady to carry. It weighs only thirteen ounces and its small size and compactness is such that it can be easily concealed in a hand bag or purse. Its great disadvantage is its lack of stopping power. Next in point of convenience are the .32 caliber revolvers and automatics and of these the following can be recommended: Colt's Pocket Model Hammerless automatic in .32 caliber; Smith and Wesson's Pocket automatic, caliber .32; Colt's Pocket Positive revolver, caliber .32 with a 2 inch barrel; Smith and Wesson's .32 caliber "Hand Ejector" revolver and the Smith and Wesson Safety Hammerless revolver in .32 caliber. In choosing between revolvers and automatics the latter will be found to be more compact in size and shape and therefore more convenient to carry but against these advantages the revolver's strong points of safety and reliability must be considered. When it comes to carrying and using pocket guns, the author always favors the revolvers even though they are not quite so convenient to carry. The S. & W. Safety Hammerless revolver has advantages in shape, contour and safety that the other revolvers do not possess, but the trigger pull is so long and heavy that it takes more strength to fire it than many women can produce, especially should they be weakened by fear or sudden fright. Before deciding on a weapon for personal protection, a lady should have assembled, in a reliable gun shop, all the guns above recommended and then compare them for size, weight, safety devices and facility of loading and firing. By doing this she will be better able to come to a logical decision.

In the search for target guns the field is more limited. If a single shot pistol is desired the Smith and Wesson perfected model with its 10 inch barrel is the best suited for a lady's use. The manufacture of this gun has been discontinued at present, but if one can be purchased from the stocks on hand in some of the larger sporting goods houses, the money will be well spent. This pistol, while it has always been used as the best target pistol of American manufacture until recently, has had the disadvantage of having a small grip which is too small for the average man's hand. It is, however, an excellent size and shape for a lady. It is very accurate and its light weight of twenty-four ounces make it easy for a lady to hold and fire. In the target revolvers the S. & W. .22-.32 Heavy Frame with a grip similar to that on the S. & W. pistol is the best .22 target revolver made for a lady's use. The Colt .22 Police Positive target revolver and the Colt "Woodsman" target automatic guns are also suitable for women. All of these are excellent target guns for general practice.

Pistol shooting is a sport well suited to a lady in many ways. It does not require great muscular development or special physical endurance as do some of the more strenuous sports. It does not demand that one dress especially for it, or bathe and dress after practice to remove the effects of the exercise it gives, as one has to do after tennis or golf. Hundreds of acres of park or country-side are not needed to furnish facilities for practice. The shooting equipment required for practice or competition can be carried very conveniently in a small leather case without exciting comment or attracting attention to the shooter.

Accessible places to shoot a pistol can usually be found without difficulty, unless one lives in the larger cities and then it takes more time to reach them unless there are ranges within the city itself. Persons living in the country, at the sea-shore, in the mountains, and in that part of our country known as the "land of magnificent distances" will find no difficulty in establishing a fifty yard range that is perfectly safe to use and convenient to reach. With interest in police practice increasing, there are many attractive ranges being installed in city parks or other public municipal grounds for the use of police officers, and there is little doubt that these will be opened to local clubs if the demand for their use is great enough. Many pistol enthusiasts have in recent years included indoor ranges in the plans of their new homes in order that their families may all enjoy the game.

To many young ladies there is a feeling of satisfaction in being able to excell in a sport that is out of the ordinary pursuits of women and especially is this true if it is one in which her brothers or father participate. Pistol shooting does carry with it a certain distinction, for among many its proper performance is considered extremely difficult. Let a lady establish a reputation as an enthusiastic pistol shot and the chances are it will cling to her wherever she goes. Her person, property and home will thereby receive valuable insurance against molestation that it would otherwise be without.

Chapter XVIII

GAME SHOOTING

THERE have been many occasions when big game hunters, trappers, cowboys, miners and even fishermen have had opportunities to shoot game with a pistol, and because of their lack of skill with the hand gun have passed up chances to secure trophies, or to provide a much needed change in the camp menu by the addition of a toothsome grouse or rabbit. There have been other critical times, fewer in number but more impressive in memory, when men have had to depend on their skill with the pistol to save themselves from the sudden attacks of big game that has been wounded or suddenly brought to bay by surprise or fright. A State hunter of one of our western states, whose main occupation is the hunting and killing of cougars and wildcats as one of the means of conserving the deer of that section, has claimed that he has killed many of these mountain lions with the old .45 Single Action Colt after they had been treed by his dogs. His use of the revolver was no doubt mainly due to the fact that it was much easier to "pack" during the long strenuous climb on the mountainous trails than a rifle would have been.

In some sections of the country where big game can still be hunted each fall, it is quite customary for the hunter to carry a small bore revolver or pistol to shoot grouse or rabbits for the pot during the course of his day's hunt after deer or moose. He may do this because he does not wish to use his heavy rifle for fear of alarming the game he is hunting, or because he knows that to hit a partridge with a high powered soft nose rifle bullet in any place but the head or neck will result disastrously and be a waste of good food and ammunition.

Trappers running their trap lines have found it much easier to carry a pistol than a rifle with which to despatch wounded fur bearers and they, too, take advantage of the hand gun to secure an occasional meal which offers itself in the form of small game, in the course of the day's work. Many a coyote has been brought to earth with a pistol bullet fired by a cowboy in his rambles about the range and even the husky timber wolf has been put out of business by the same men, while their cattle have been pastured in the mountains in the summer. At one time in the open country of Montana, it was a favorite Sunday sport to get together a crowd of cow punchers and run down coyotes. When the prairie wolf was overtaken, the last act of the play was to see which rider could kill him with his six shooter, as he scurried about or doubled back through the sage brush. It was no easy matter to hit this dodging streak of fur when shooting from the back of a horse running at break-neck speed over rough uneven ground. A trout fisherman I once knew in Washington always carried a target revolver with him when whipping his favorite mountain streams in the early fall, when the blue grouse season was open, and he seldom failed to bring in a mixed bag of cut throats and birds to show for his day's excursion. Not infrequently we read inquiries in the sporting magazines from men who expect to do hunting in

Alaska, the Canadian Rockies or the few places in our
western country where big game can still be found, ask-
ing which kind of side arm is the best to carry for emergency use on such expeditions. These queries may be
encouraged by the advertising matter circulated by some
of our large pistol manufacturers in the form of vividly
painted scenes in which a hunter or fisherman is being
charged by a grizzly bear or by a springing lion or some
other member of the cat family. Incidents of this kind
have occurred and there are a few places in the world
today where they might happen again, but carrying
heavy revolvers or automatic pistols, primarily for one's
protection against wild animals, is not nearly as essential
as it is to carry them for protection against human animals, in certain sections of the world.

There are various reasons for supporting game shooting with pistols and for touching on the points in the
game that the paper target shot seldom thinks of when
popping away at a clearly defined bull's-eye under favorable natural or artificial light. The first consideration
has already been touched on and that is game shooting
with a hand gun to supplement the larder while one is
engaged on a big game hunting trip or a fishing or
camping trip during the open seasons for small game.
Even fifteen years ago, while deer and moose hunting
in Maine, I recall quite clearly the efforts of the guides
to prevent any promiscuous target practice with large
caliber rifles, because of its effect on the game we were
hunting. They believed that rifles should be "sighted
in" before entering the game country and that if small
game was to be killed it should be done with small bore
weapons that could not be heard for any distance. And

they were quite right, too. At that time the bag limit on ruffed grouse was five birds a day or ten birds in one's possession at a time. The birds were reasonably plentiful and they certainly did improve the camp meals during the time we were in the woods and they made a nice bag to take home, especially if one was not successful in getting his deer or moose. While hunting there I carried a small bore single shot target pistol in a shoulder holster, rather than resort to using my rifle on the birds. A companion who accompanied me one day pointed out a grouse in the underbrush as we were returning to camp, and suggested we try for it. It was off about fifteen yards, standing alert but immovable and watching us as we passed, as the partridge will often do. My friend thought he was enough of a marksman to hit the bird's head and wanted to shoot it with his big rifle while I was anxious to try for it with the pistol. He took the chance and when he fired the grouse simply exploded and all we could find were its extremities, for the 220 grain soft nose bullet he was using had hit it in the body and simply blew it to pieces. After that experience we depended on the pistol for birds.

Considering game shooting with the hand gun as a sporting proposition there is much to be said in its favor provided proper guns are used for the purpose. An enthusiastic pistol shot may hunt game in much the same spirit that an archer does. He is not intent on merely killing his quarry or he would pursue it with rifle or shotgun, either of which will accomplish the results much easier. He believes, with the archer, that there is much more satisfaction to be experienced in bagging a game bird or animal as the result of careful stalking and accurate shooting than there is in killing it at easy ranges with weapons that give the hunted little chance for its life. There is no doubt that if game shooting is done with the pistol the game will be conserved, for there are few more difficult things to do in the shooting line than to hit a carefully concealed and camouflaged bird or animal in his native environment. Because it is difficult to do, it is conducive to the development of greater skill and this makes better pistol marksmen.

Success in hunting with the pistol also requires a study of the habits of the game hunted, in order that it may be found and approached in a manner that will afford a reasonable shot for the weapon in hand. This acquirement of skill in stalking introduces a factor in the sport that is not always present when one uses other weapons in the field. As an example, take squirrel shooting with its problems and fascinations. One may take a shotgun and walk along the small creeks and bottomlands of Eastern Kansas where walnut trees abound, and stumble on many chances at the scampering fox and gray squirrels as they rush for cover when surprised. To bag them with a charge of shot is not difficult, but if one hopes to get them with a pistol he must station himself under the trees, possess his soul with patience, and await quietly until the watchful little rascals come out of their nests and resume their interrupted operations. In time the hunter may be able to discern a small head beset with two shining eyes alertly watching from over a high limb apparently believing itself unobserved. If the shooter's movements are very deliberate, his pistol accurately sighted and his skill of a high order, he may be able to aim carefully, squeeze slowly and at the crack of his gun have the satisfaction of seeing a limp ball of fur tumble to the ground. If he is only an average shot and unaccustomed to the squirrel shooting game, he will probably see the head disappear as the little watchful-waiter flattens himself out on the safe side of the tree, or scampers away to his nest. Ofttimes better shots will be afforded and no one should complain of a target such as a full grown gray or fox squirrel offers as he perches on a branch and busily gnaws away at a choice nut.

Game shooting also introduces a psychological factor that does not enter into target work. A person may blaze away all day at a paper target and do very fine shooting without once becoming mildly excited over the prospect of making clean bull's-eyes. Let him prepare to fire at an animate object, especially if it be small game that he is anxious to bag and that he knows may move any instant and his system experiences a different sensation than that felt when firing at a bull's-eye. There is always a thrill of anticipation in game shooting, no matter how small the game, that will usually cause a noticeable decrease in a marksman's skill. The element of time has something to do with this for the inexperienced hunter may hurry his shots with the usual results.

Small and difficult targets like these present another phase of the aiming problem that is not always thought about when paper targets are used and that is the matter of getting clear definition of the target and of sighting a pistol properly for this work. To do accurate work it is of course necessary that the sights be seen and in order to do this in the shades and shadows of the woods it is obvious that they must be of a color different from the background of the target or its surroundings. Pistols must also be sighted so that the bullet will hit the aiming point and not a few inches above it, as is usually the case when one practices against the standard paper targets. It will not take a novice in game shooting long to learn that black sights are generally the least desirable for the purpose and that instead, a gold or ivory faced front sight is much to be preferred for the average background. The relative merits of these two kinds of beads has long been discussed and both have their adherents. The beginner can only determine which is the best for his use by trying out both kinds in the particular environment in which he expects to do his hunting.

One accustomed to normal practice at paper targets will often be surprised at the ease with which he misses small game perched directly overhead in a high tree or on the face of a cliff. There is always a tendency to overshoot when firing at such targets but the effect is not so great as with a rifle, because of the comparatively shorter ranges at which the firing is done. It is an acknowledged principle of gunnery that a rifle or pistol, sighted to hit a target in the same horizontal plane, will overshoot the same target if it is placed directly above or below the gun. If a shot is fired from a pistol or rifle with the barrel horizontal the bullet will begin to drop the instant it leaves the muzzle due to the action of gravity on it. To overcome the effect of gravity we must therefore incline the barrel upward an amount sufficient to equal the drop of the bullet. This is done by raising the rear sight or lowering the front sight which makes an angle between the line of aim and the axis of the bore. Then when we aim at an object in a horizontal plane the barrel is actually pointing above it. If we were to shoot straight up the action of gravity would be directly down and if we had our sights set with an angle between the line of aim and the axis of the barrel we would be aiming at a point vertically overhead while our barrel would be pointed behind the aiming point and we would hit there. If we fire at any object not directly overhead we will shoot above it and the more nearly it is to the horizontal the closer we will come to it. The same rule applies to shooting at targets below the pistol. At the ranges at which one would be likely to fire at game with a pistol there would not be much tendency for a pistol to overshoot, if it was first sighted in a horizontal plane to hit the point at which it was aimed. There is however a tendency for a shooter to aim higher when firing at objects above or below him and this combined with the effect of the gun overshooting may make a considerable error in the impact of the bullet. The reason for this may be largely psychological but it exists nevertheless and many a bird, squirrel and rabbit has been lost by overshooting, whereas if a little more care had been taken in aiming, the results would have been more satisfactory.

Of equal importance with the aiming problems is that of using the right gun and ammunition for this class of shooting. I now have little patience when I see writers advocate shooting small game with any old kind of small bore guns and cartridges. Two incidents are indelibly stamped on my memory in this connection. On one of those hunts in Maine previously mentioned I was again armed for small game with the .22 single shot pistol carried in a soft leather shoulder holster, when I saw a grouse about fifteen yards away clearly outlined against the ground and rigid as a statue. There was no under-brush and the rains had soaked the leaves underfoot. I drew the pistol, sighted deliberately and fired carefully. The bird crumpled up on the ground apparently stone dead. I stood my rifle against a tree and replaced the pistol in the holster having some difficulty in doing this because of its position and the lack of stiffness in the soft leather. Turning to pick up the bird I discovered he was not in sight and a hasty search availed nothing. To make a short story of it, I spent about twenty min-utes carefully combing the open ground where he had fallen and finally found him in the hollow stump of a tree nearby where he had crawled, though he had been shot squarely through the body. While packing into a deer camp on the Elwah River in the Olympics one fall, I carried a .22 target revolver for small game and used the long rifle cartridge. During the day I had many chances at the large blue grouse of that locality and after shooting five of the big birds out of tall fir trees so that they hit the ground with a solid thumb and only securing three I stopped trying for them. Then as never before I realized that the little 40 grain bullet was not large enough to immediately kill such large birds and when only wounded they get away easily in the dense underbrush. Since that time I have never used small bore pistols for the blue or ruffed grouse or for sage chicken and rabbits and I have killed many of these with the pistol. I will grant that the hollow point bullet will do better execution than the solid nose .22 but still I prefer something heavier. There is one class of small game that it is permissible to use small bore cartridges on and that is the lowly but delectable bull-frog and incidentally he furnishes great sport in localities where he abounds.

In selecting a suitable pistol for small game shooting, one must consider whether he wants it as an adjunct to his big game rifle or as his only hunting weapon. He must consider weight, convenience of wearing, ease of cleaning, weight of ammunition, accuracy, killing power, and the number of shots available. At one time I thought the single shot pistol with its long barrel and sighting radius was the best side arm to take on a big game hunt and as a consequence used one for three years in Maine. After several annoying experiences with it and in the light of greater knowledge I now state that I think it is the poorest arm for the purpose that one can pack around. It has the one advantage already mentioned but to offset this it is inconvenient to carry either on a belt or in a shoulder holster because of its length. It is slow to manipulate and has only one shot without reloading. Ever so often one runs into a covey of partridges and frequently several shots will be afforded if too much time is not taken between shots. The single shot pistol is certainly not the most desirable arm to have at times like this. With only one hand free to draw and fire a pistol, assuming that the other one holds a rifle or some other equipment it is an advantage to have a gun that can be manipulated without the use of two hands. A good target revolver or automatic pistol is much better for the purpose. If one believes in the .22 hand gun for small game then he cannot do better than to secure either the S. & W. .22–.32 Heavy Frame target revolver, the Colt .22 Woodsman Automatic or the Colt Police Positive Target revolver. The automatic has the advantage of more shots without reloading and of only the barrel to clean at the end of the day, which incidentally is worth something when one is tired. Any of these guns is light, convenient and very accurate and can be easily fitted with gold or ivory front sights if desired. There are other small bore pistols that can be used, but I consider these three the best in their class. For those who do not believe in small bore guns for game shooting, and there are many who think as I do in this regard, there are several suitable large calibers, or perhaps we had better say medium calibers, that are qualified as game getters. One summer in Wyoming I used a .32–.20 S. & W. revolver for sage chicken shooting from the saddle and found it quite satisfactory. In hunting from horseback I was able to approach closer to the birds than when I was afoot. In several cases however, when using this gun I have shot a bird through the body and have had it travel some distance before collapsing. Some one whom I do not recall, has recommended the .32–.20 for game shooting but using in it the .32 S. & W. short and long cartridges, claiming that while the cylinder was not chambered for these cartridges they give very good accuracy at small game ranges.

Personally I have but one choice as the result of much small game shooting and that is a good .38 caliber target revolver using the .38 Special cartridge and the mid range loads of the same caliber. This gun is not too heavy to pack around, it has splendid accuracy, good stopping power when used with the full factory loaded cartridge with square shoulder bullet against game up to the size of deer, and for small game the mid range wad cutter ammunition is ideal. This last cartridge

will drop the big blue grouse "deader than a door nail."
As to particular revolvers there is little choice between
the Colt and S. & W. target models and either are excellent weapons. One fits my hand better than the other so
I use it, although I have owned and used both makes.
Like good automobiles they both have their strong points
and a few weaknesses. I would not be covering the game
fully if I didn't mention that at times there have been
advocates of game shooting with hand guns who have
had made smooth bore single shot pistols and revolvers
in which they use shot cartridges. The late Walter
Winans, a noted international pistol shot used a specially
made duelling pistol with a .32 bore ten inch barrel, in
which he fired a charge of $\frac{3}{8}$ ounce of shot and $1\frac{1}{4}$
drams of black powder. He claims this was quite successful for live pigeon shooting up to 12 yards rise. I
venture to say that many large caliber revolvers have
been altered to shoot shot cartridges both for game
shooting and for exhibition work. This can be done successfully and is a means of using an old gun and barrel
when it has passed the stage of usefulness for which it
was intended. The large calibers such as the .45 Colt
and the .44–.40 (.44 Winchester) with a $7\frac{1}{2}$ inch barrel
are the best to convert into shot revolvers. These weapons must be rebored into choked smooth bores and the
ammunition specially loaded to get the best patterns.

In anticipation of small game hunting it is well for the
marksman to give himself training in this kind of shooting by practice at targets made to resemble the game
he expects to shoot. Silhouettes of birds and animals
colored to look like the real thing and then placed in the
trees or underbrush where they will be concealed in a

manner that will make them as difficult to see and hit as the game in its native environment will afford splen-

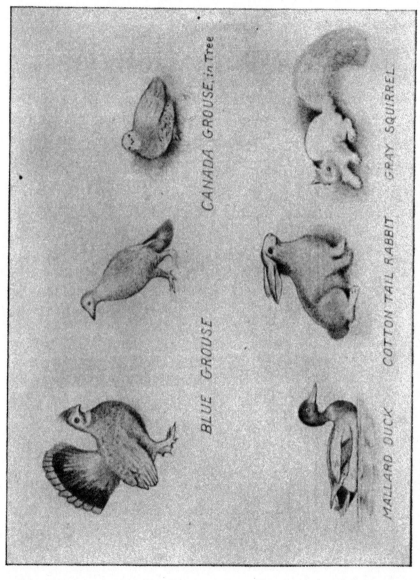

CANADA GROUSE, in Tree

GRAY SQUIRREL

BLUE GROUSE

COTTON TAIL RABBIT

MALLARD DUCK

Suitable silhouettes for practice in small game shooting.

did practice and be something out of the ordinary run of target work.

Chapter XIX

LONG RANGE POSSIBILITIES

EVER so often the subject of long range work with pistols crops up in the columns of the sporting magazines, usually in the form of a story on some remarkable shooting that has been done by an individual or club. The story is very likely to start a controversy, for every "doubting Thomas" in the pistol game—and there are many who know very little about the possibilities in this line of shooting—at once gets up and howls that it can't be done. He then rushes madly into print to prove his contention which is based entirely on the fact that he has never been able to make even a fair showing at this special game.

The author holds no brief for those enthusiastic revolver shots who would like to convince others that the pistol is an effective long range weapon but he does feel that there are possibilities in the game that are extremely fascinating and worthy of study and practice by those who really wish to enjoy pistol work to the fullest. If one approaches the subject with an open mind and is willing to spend time and money in experimental work he will find that the results are worth the efforts he puts into the tests. Anyone who has gone through the discouraging stages of thousand yard rifle shooting on a windy, tricky range will get an idea of what to expect in long range pistol practice. The difficulties of the problem make it interesting and when good scores are finally made the satisfaction obtained thereby is quite gratifying. A rifleman when he first tries to hit the 36 inch bull's-eye at a thousand yards on a range that is noted for its changing conditions of wind and light, runs into snags he never anticipated. He finds that there is much more to rifle work than he realized and that hitting the bull's-eye is now a matter of not only holding well but one to make his sight corrections accordingly. He soon learns of being able to read the conditions before each shot and that failure to observe the changes from bright sunlight to cloudiness will cause him to hit the target one minute and to go over or under the next. He finds that if he cannot judge the wind by reading the mirage and catch the changes from one direction to the other he may go from one side of the ten foot target to the other on alternate shots. He will also find that to do the very best work at long ranges requires the greatest care in sight adjusting and in the selection of ammunition, as well as in holding and squeezing. And so it is with long range pistol work but to a less degree. Special care must be taken in the matter of sights and their adjustment. The weapons used must be of the best and preferably target revolvers or single shot pistols adapted to the most accurate pistol ammunition. The targets used should be proportionate to the range or the impossible will be attempted. Wind and light must be studied and care taken not to fire in unfavorable conditions. Even then, in spite of all his efforts, the marksman may find the work discouraging until experience has taught him the finer points of the game.

Quite a number of years ago a most interesting booklet was written by Mr. W. B. Altsheler entitled "The Long Shooters." It was a narrative describing the experiences of certain members of the Louisville, Kentucky Revolver Club in old fashioned turkey shoots with revolvers. The original story, "The Turkey Shoot," I understand created somewhat of a sensation among pistol men and resulted in much talk and much more shooting to verify the results obtained by the Louisville experts. Since that time several pistol shots of national reputation have gone on record as having accomplished equally remarkable results and yet whenever the subject is mentioned there are many who believe it is next to impossible. Capt. A. H. Hardy of Denver, Colorado, to prove it could be done, hit the silhouette of a turkey against a white background three times in fifteen shots at 300 yards using an S. & W. Target revolver with 6 inch barrel, chambered for the .38 Special cartridge. The shooting done by the Louisville experts was at ranges up to 300 yards and their favorite weapon seemed to be the revolver using the .38 and .44 Special cartridges.

A well known exhibition shot of one of our ammunition companies always includes some long range pistol stunts in his work if facilities permit it. He rather astonishes the spectators by hitting small barrels, "man targets" and similar objects with revolver bullets at ranges at which they have trouble hitting with a rifle. An army officer of my acquaintance gets great fun out of competing with the riflemen of his organization when they fire their qualification course offhand at 200 yards. Soldiers as a rule are poor offhand shots and this officer using a .38 Colt revolver and .38 S. & W. Special cartridges has no trouble holding his own and frequently beating his men in firing on the "A" target with its 10-inch bull's-eye and 26-inch four ring.

Shortly after the National Matches of 1925 the author secured a case of new .38 Special ammunition of excellent reputation with the idea of specializing in long shooting. He was in good trim as a result of the matches and was holding well, and had had made a special high rear sight for his Colt Officer's Model revolver. The rifle range used was well protected from wind and free from tricky air currents. Firing was done at one and two hundred yards against ten- and twenty-inch bull's-eyes and prone and kneeling silhouettes. Several hundred rounds were fired but the results were so discouraging that the tests were discontinued. Every few shots there would be an unaccountable one that would strike low in the butts at 200 yards and ruin an otherwise good score. At first these shots were believed to be due to flinching and poor holding as it takes very little movement of the muzzle to miss the target entirely at that range. As these bad shots invariably went low, and many of them were called "Good" the ammunition was suspected and it proved to be the correct alibi as firing from a six point rest soon demonstrated. Discussing the matter with an authority on small arms ballistics who usually represents one of the large ammunition firms in the tests held for the selection of ammunition for the National Matches, he was informed that revolver ammunition never had been designed for long range work and that it was foolish to attempt or hope for satisfactory results beyond 75 yards. In view of this advice and his experience the author did as many others have done, let the tests drop with the mental reservation that it would be taken up again when a suitable opportunity presented itself and different ammunition could be secured.

In the Spring of 1928 while on leave of absence in California the author had the chance to discuss long range revolver shooting with the Capt. Hardy mentioned in the foregoing paragraphs and this resulted in our conducting tests covering three days' firing. The work was done on the rifle and revolver range used by the Sheriffs of Los Angeles County and the Alhambra Rifle and Revolver Club, and was witnessed at times by various interested revolver shots. This range is laid out among the brown California hills but mostly in a ravine through which bothersome puffy breezes prevail in the afternoons and to a less extent in the mornings. The range runs about East and West. The Colt Police Silhouette Target was used by cutting out the silhouette and pasting it to a brown paper background four feet high and six feet wide. This paper was then mounted on a rifle target frame. Firing was done at 300 yards with an Officer's Model Colt with 7½–inch barrel and special high rear sight. Peters .38 S. & W. Special cartridges were used.

Each shot that hit the paper target was marked with a three-inch spotter which was left in the bullet hole until the next shot was fired. A spotting telescope was used to read mirage and dope the wind and great care was taken to get the shots off under the most favorable conditions, that is, when there was a lull in the wind at the firing point and when the mirage at the target seemed to be running steadily and in the same direction for each shot. The "sighting in" was necessarily slow and was

done from a substantial rest using the left hand as a support and cushion for the shooting hand. After the
sights had been adjusted approximately, the final setting was determined by offhand firing. Due to a difference in eyesight or holding, it was found necessary to
use a higher sight setting for Captain Hardy than for
myself with the result that each time we alternated in
firing we had to reset and check our sights.

The results of the first day's firing were very encouraging, not from the standpoint of scores made, but because of the performance of the ammunition, which
seemed remarkable after my previous experiences. Not
a shot fell short and in fact not one hit in front of the
target all day. Several hit the wooden target frame and
tore through two inches of wood as though it were a
shingle. Lack of practice in real close holding combined
with the effects of a puffy breeze showed that we were
not doing as good shooting as we knew we could do, and
at the end of the day we found that we had averaged
slightly better than one hit on the silhouette out of every
five shots.

The second day's experiments under very similar conditions raised the score to an average of two hits out of
every five shots. On the third day all the firing was done
in the morning with a little less breeze but a bad light
as the sun came over the back of the target shading it
badly. On this day each of us averaged three hits out of
five shots and we felt that these results were quite satisfactory. The shooting did not seem difficult, in fact not
nearly as hard as trying to hit the two inch center of the
International bull's-eye at fifty meters, although the
black silhouette as an aiming point was relatively smaller

than the eight-inch bull's-eye and was on a darker background.

There is no doubt that under the best conditions an excellent revolver shot in good practice will make better scores than we did, but at that, three hits out of five shots at 300 yards on the half silhouette of an average sized man is not such bad work for revolvers and revolver ammunition.

One very noticeable detail about the grouping of the shots was that the vertical dispersion was much less than the horizontal errors. This may have been due to wind or to the natural tendency to have greater deflection errors in pistol shooting than errors in elevation. This point supported our contention that it was a big advantage to have a good coach when the wind and light conditions are variable and that perhaps the most important detail to master in this game is to know when not to shoot.

Prior to the firing just described we had determined the approximate height it was necessary to aim in order to hit at 300 yards with a revolver sighted for fifty yards. Using the silhouette target mounted as explained in the foregoing paragraphs we erected an aiming point on a pole above the target and when we had raised it to twenty feet we could get hits on the silhouette. The revolver used was a Colt's Army Special .38 Cal. with 6-inch barrel. This test showed that the bullet fell approximately twenty feet below the line of aim at 300 yards.

Some firing was also done with a .22 Single Shot S. & W. Target pistol with an adjustable rear sight and the best score made was three hits out of five shots. This test was so limited on account of time that I am not prepared to say what can be done with this cartridge at 300 yards.

I have used it very successfully at 200 yards with both pistol and rifle and have every reason to think that it will hold up, but undoubtedly the little 40-grain bullet is affected much more by wind currents than the heavier calibers, and more care must be taken in getting off the shots under uniform conditions. As in using the .38 Special ammunition, a good coach qualified to dope the wind and light conditions will be a great help in making good scores with the .22 Long Rifle ammunition.

If one contemplates long range firing and wishes to get the maximum satisfaction with a minimum of discouragement he will do well to consider carefully the equipment and ammunition he uses. There are a few revolver cartridges that will produce satisfactory results at long ranges and there is little to be gained by trying others. The same rule can be applied to pistols and revolvers. Problems of aiming are more difficult at long ranges because of the inherent defects of eyesight which make it impossible to avoid errors in aiming with open sights at long distances. The greater the range the greater the error. Obviously the longer sight radius we use the greater the accuracy and ease of aiming. The sight radius must necessarily be limited by the length of barrel that can be used, so we must consider not only this factor but the weight and balance of the pistol and the effect of wind on long barreled guns. The free pistols of Europe give every advantage in aiming, for with their long barrels and rear sight extension arm they have a sighting radius as long as some rifles. They also have excellent adjustable rear sights which simplify the problem of getting correct elevation. However, if used with set triggers, they are difficult to hold in a breeze and touch off at the instant the aim is correct. On still days or when firing from sheltered firing points they make good long range pistols, if chambered and rifled to use American long range .22 Long Rifle cartridges.

When it comes to the selection of revolvers for this class of work we should again resort to target guns with adjustable sights and even then it may be necessary to use higher rear sights than are issued by the factory. It is so much a matter of personal taste and the better revolvers are so nearly equal in accuracy that to say that one is the best for long range shooting is like making a decision on the best automobile. However, the accuracy of revolvers, other things being equal, depends on the ammunition for which they are designed and this limits the selection of guns to those using a few particular cartridges. There is no question about the superior ballistics of the .38 and .44 S. & W. Special cartridges when properly loaded. Any manufacturer may turn out an occasional bad lot of cartridges, as I have already indicated.

These two cartridges have frequently proven what can be done with them in long shooting and no doubt exists as to their accuracy for this work. The marksman should assure himself that whatever ammunition he uses is new and not some that has been in storage a long time under varying and extreme changes of temperature.

Going back to the question of revolvers, there are several that can be recommended. The .38 Officer's Model Colt with 7½ inch barrel, the .38 S. & W. Military and Police Target with 6 inch barrel, the S. & W. .44 Target with 6½ inch barrel and the Colt New Service Target with 7½ inch barrel chambered for the .44 S. & W.

Special cartridge are all suitable revolvers for long range work. The "Super .38 Colt Automatic Pistol," using the latest high velocity .38 A.C.P. cartridges is also quite satisfactory for long range pistol work. This cartridge is being improved and may soon equal the .38 and .44 Special cartridges in accuracy. Smith & Wesson contend that no better shooting is possible with a 7½ inch barrel than with one of 6 inches in length and that the longer length makes holding more difficult and tends to make the arm muzzle heavy. In general the writer concurs in this statement and for ordinary target practice up to 50 yards, including slow, rapid, and timed fire, the six inch barrel is the best all-around length. For deliberate fire at 50 yards and for special practice at long ranges it is believed that the 7½ inch barrel aids materially in aiming and consequently in scoring, to say nothing of giving a slight increase in muzzle velocity with the .38 and .44 Special cartridges. Experience is the best teacher in this matter and as I have always been able to do better deliberate firing and have once won the timed fire match at Camp Perry with the longer barrel I naturally favor it for such work.

In the matter of sights the S. & W. revolvers are better equipped than the Colts. Changes of elevation are made on the front sight of the latter and there is only a limited adjustment possible, whereas the adjustable rear sight of the S. & W. target guns permits a much higher elevation. For use with my Colt Officer's Model I have had special high rear sights made for two and three hundred yard shooting and these used with the adjustable front sight give a wide range of sight settings.

Chapter XX

HINTS ON
USING THE SERVICE AUTOMATIC

THE Colt automatic pistol, caliber .45, known in the army as the "Model of 1911" and designated in the catalog of the Colt's Patent Fire Arms Manufacturing Co. as the "Government Model," is here referred to as the Service Pistol because it is the official side arm of the Army, Navy, and Marine Corps. This title is also given to this weapon in the program of the National Rifle and Pistol Matches and frequently in other pistol competitions. Referring to the program for 1928 we find the following: "THE SERVICE PISTOL. Colt automatic pistol, caliber .45, model 1911, as issued except that the front and rear sights may be of commercial manufacture similar in design to the issue sights, though different in dimensions. Not less than four-pound trigger pull." This paragraph defines the pistol that may be used in matches restricted to the service weapon. There is a further restriction in that the ammunition used in these matches must be: "Full-charge ball cartridge ammunition manufactured for or by the Government and issued by the Ordnance Department for use in the service arms." In competitions other than those conducted by the War Department the service pistol may, in some cases, be used not as issued and this permits the owner to "doll up" his gun as he sees fit. Alterations that aid in holding may consist of specially made grips to fit the hand of the shooter and any kind of open sights he may prefer. In regard to the latter, however, it is well to stick to the same design as now issued by the manufacturer as these have proven to be very satisfactory.

Since its adoption by our Ordnance Department in 1911 and especially during and since the World War, many thousands of our citizens have used the Service pistol and there are great numbers of these automatics now in their hands in addition to those in use by the Army and Navy. With this in mind it was thought advisable to offer to its many possessors a few hints on the use of this particular gun, which like many of its contemporaries has certain peculiarities of its own and a knowledge of these will work to the advantage of the user.

Let us consider first the safety devices. This particular automatic is equipped with four means of preventing accidental discharges. They are: The half-cock notch, the safety lock, the grip safety and the disconnector.

The half-cock notch when engaged with the sear prevents the pistol being fired even though the trigger be firmly squeezed. It also serves the purpose of catching the hammer should the latter slip while being cocked. It should be frequently tested when the gun is empty and if the half-cock fails to function the defective parts should be replaced.

The safety lock will, if in proper order, prevent the hammer from falling when cocked and locked. To test this device the hammer should be cocked, the safety lock engaged, the grip safety pressed down and the trigger firmly squeezed. If the hammer is released the safety lock is not functioning properly and should be released or repaired.

The disconnector is for the purpose of preventing the release of the hammer until the slide and barrel are safely locked in the forward position, and also prevents one squeeze of the trigger firing more than one shot. To test the disconnector draw the slide to the rear about a quarter of an inch, press the trigger firmly to the rear at the same time letting go of the slide. The hammer should not fall. Now release the pressure on the trigger, squeeze again and the hammer should fall. A further test of the disconnector is to draw the slide fully to the rear and engage the slide stop. Then press the trigger, at the same time releasing the slide. The hammer should remain cocked. On releasing the trigger and squeezing it again the hammer should fall. Were it not for the disconnector the pistol would become an automatic in the strict sense of the word.

The grip safety prevents the pistol from being fired until it has been depressed. This occurs without conscious effort when the butt is gripped in a normal manner by the shooting hand. In testing this safety the pistol should be cocked and the trigger pressed without depressing the grip safety. The device is defective if the hammer falls.

In spite of its safety devices, this pistol is not foolproof and great care should be taken in its use at all times. There are a few rules almost universally found on well regulated ranges which it is well to keep in mind. They are: (a) Do not load a pistol until on the firing line ready to fire. (b) Do not snap a pistol behind the firing line. (c) Unload your pistol before leaving the line. (d) Keep the slide of your automatic drawn back except when ready to fire. (e) Always keep the muzzle of a pistol pointing in a safe direction.

An automatic is different from a revolver in that the cartridges it contains are concealed. For this reason the first step in an inspection of a pistol should be to remove the magazine and then draw back the slide. This will extract a cartridge in the barrel and will prevent another from being fed into the chamber when the slide is released. The service automatic may be carried loaded with a full magazine and an additional cartridge in the chamber. It is perfectly safe to carry this pistol so charged with the hammer down, and is safer than to carry the gun with a cartridge in the chamber and the hammer cocked and locked. An inspection of the pistol will show that the firing pin is shorter than the breech block in which it operates and that when its rear end is flush with the firing pin stop, as it would be when the hammer is down, the point cannot project or rest on the primer of the cartridge. The firing pin base projects to the rear when the hammer is cocked and is held there by a coil spring so that it is necessary for the hammer to hit it a sharp blow in order to drive the point against the primer.

During a field inspection of the 107th Co. C.A.C. in 1914 a lieutenant approached the Captain with his automatic in hand and remarked that he did not seem to be able to make the safety function. The captain explained that the gun must be cocked before the safety could be engaged. He cocked the pistol by drawing the slide to the rear and then engaged the safety. After showing this to the lieutenant he shoved the safety off and pressed the trigger. An explosion followed and a small boy some distance away was hit in the eye with the .45 bullet from the pistol.

This accident illustrates what may happen when safety precautions are violated, especially those fundamental rules which are so simple and yet so vital to the safe use of firearms. A gun should be kept loaded only when necessity dictates such a course. Every gun we handle should be considered as loaded and we should make it a paramount rule never to manipulate one until we have assured ourselves by personal inspection that it is empty or until we have unloaded it. As an added precaution we should always develop the habit of elevating the muzzle well before snapping a hammer out-of-doors. Special care should be taken when snapping practice is held and I have personal knowledge of two cases of careless men shooting through the walls of their rooms when snapping at targets with pistols they thought they had unloaded.

The chance of the hammer being drawn to the rear and then falling on the firing pin so as to discharge the piece is very small and the danger much less than there is when the gun is carried cocked and locked. It is an easy matter to shove the safety off by the pressure of the clothing or of the holster while carrying the gun or drawing it in a hurry. To lower the hammer with a cartridge in the chamber hold the pistol in the right hand, place the right thumb on the hammer spur and press it back until the grip safety is forced forward. Then while holding the hammer securely, press the trig-

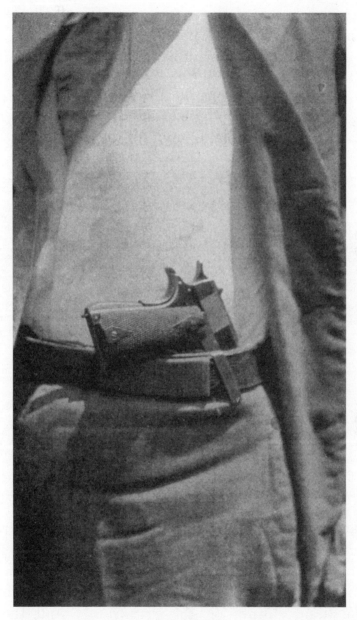

A good way to "pack" the Service automatic. This device was made for the author by a former Deputy U. S. Marshal of Oklahoma

ger so as to prevent the sear from entering the hammer notches, and lower the hammer slowly.

A few years ago the author used this pistol quite extensively for aerial shooting and found that by using an open holster tied low on the thigh he could toss a target in the air with the left hand, draw and cock the gun with the right hand and hit objects as small as

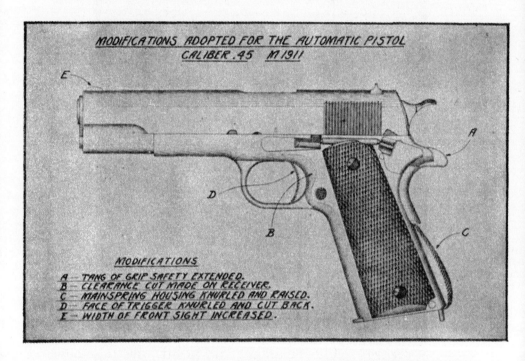

MODIFICATIONS ADOPTED FOR THE AUTOMATIC PISTOL
CALIBER .45   M 1911

MODIFICATIONS

A — TANG OF GRIP SAFETY EXTENDED.
B — CLEARANCE CUT MADE ON RECEIVER.
C — MAINSPRING HOUSING KNURLED AND RAISED.
D — FACE OF TRIGGER KNURLED AND CUT BACK.
E — WIDTH OF FRONT SIGHT INCREASED.

French pennies. Many hundreds of shots were fired in this manner without a single accidental discharge and it is safer than to cock and lock the gun before drawing. If the gun is cocked and locked there is always danger of the hand closing on the grip safety and the gun firing as it is drawn, whereas by cocking as the pistol is drawn the hand will not press the grip safety until the muzzle is clear of the holster.

There are now two models of the service pistol in the hands of the Army and Navy and scattered throughout the country. They may be referred to as the old model and the improved model. Actually they are one and the same weapon except for the substitution of certain parts that have been improved in design and consequently have changed the outline of the old model slightly. A few years' experience with the first model had convinced many users that for the average man this pistol was too much of a handful; that due to the angle between the barrel and the grip the muzzle pointed slightly downward when held in the normal firing position; that the long hammer spur and short grip safety generally pinched a shooter's hand, if his hand was at all fleshy and the gun was held with the proper high grip. In addition to these characteristics it was found difficult for a small hand with a short index finger to reach the trigger so as to squeeze it straight to the rear in firing.

On the improved model the trigger reach has been shortened by cutting away both sides of the receiver just in rear of the trigger face and by shortening the trigger itself. The face of the latter has also been checked so as to present a rough surface for the trigger finger to press in firing. The tendency to point low has been remedied by enlarging the main spring housing so that it is now raised or arched on the rear face. When the butt is gripped this projection causes the muzzle to be raised more than it was with the old style housing. As the arched housing is now checked it aids one in holding the pistol with the same grip for each shot. A grip safety with a longer spur has replaced the old one so there is much less chance for the hand to be injured between the hammer and safety spurs when the slide and hammer are forced back by the regular operations of the automatic mechanism. In the case of a very fleshy hand, however, it is well to get a hammer with a shorter hammer spur or file off a little of the underside of the spur of the hammer issued on the gun. In general, the gun was improved by these changes and its handling and firing was made much simpler for the man with a small hand. A study of a few other characteristics of the pistol, especially of the older model, will aid one in improving his shooting with this popular weapon.

The service automatic should be gripped more firmly than a revolver for the reason that failure to properly seat it in the hand may cause one to ease up on the grip safety in the excitement of a rapid fire match to the extent of putting the gun on "safe" so that it will not fire. This is demoralizing but has been done by men accustomed to maintaining a very light grip on target revolvers or pistols.

If one expects to use the older model in competition or qualification firing he should make a careful analysis of his technique in so far as the shooting hand and arm are concerned. With the arm fully extended and the gun held naturally in the firing position the muzzle will have a tendency to incline downward and the effort to raise it will put a slight strain on the wrist which is generally increased materially by the shock of recoil during firing. This makes the operation of holding more difficult than it would be were it not necessary to bend the wrist and raise the hand while aiming and firing. This little detail is not appreciated by many users of this pistol and while all are not affected by it because of individual peculiarities of technique it does affect many and retards their progress. To illustrate my point I will again take the liberty of using an incident of personal experience. When the .45 automatic was first issued as the service pistol I found great difficulty in consistently making forty out of a possible fifty points on the Army "L" target at fifty yards slow fire, although I had been shooting the revolver and target pistol successfully a long time. This was quite embarrassing and even exasperating and much effort and time was spent on overcoming the difficulty, with apparently little success. One day after an especially discouraging practice I mentioned my troubles to my battery commander who, while not an excellent shot, had some very definite ideas about the game and shot very well. He had me demonstrate just how I fired and the minute I extended my arm fully he criticized me for so doing and all arguments for this manner of shooting went for naught with him although he approved of the rest of my technique.

The next day while practicing it occurred to me to try out the old captain's method. I extended my arm fully as I always had done and then relaxed it slightly so as to have a slight bend at the elbow. To my surprise and pleasure I found that my scores jumped up at once and out of seven strings of five shots fired that day I made better than 40 points on every score but one and that was a 39. By bending the arm slightly at the elbow I had relieved the strain on my wrist and from that time until the improvements were made on the pistol I used that method of firing. Since my discovery I have heard a very fine pistol coach advocate the same procedure in shooting with the older issue service pistol. Another point to be studied in connection with gripping this gun is the effect of the automatic operation on the firing hand. This gun is so different in shape and action from a revolver that the reactions set up in the hand muscles **are** quite astonishing at times. A beginner with this

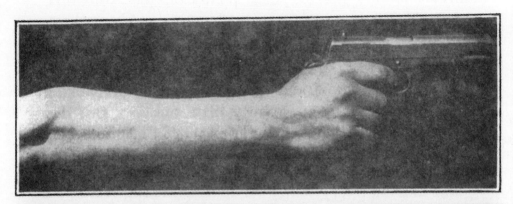

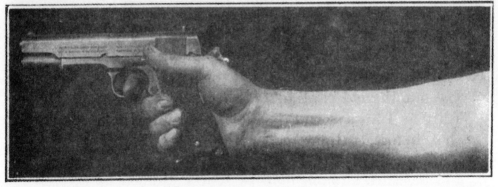

The correct way to grip the service automatic. Note position of the trigger finger, arm and wrist.

weapon will find that his first score is generally his best one and that after firing a few shots he will begin to flinch and his hand will tremble very noticeably. Even experienced revolver shots find when using this pistol that they develop unsteadiness in holding much quicker than they do when using the six shooter. When we remember that this is among the most powerful hand guns made and that there is normally a strong recoil from the cartridge used, we must expect to get considerable shock during firing. If we fire rapidly the repeated shock of recoil quite naturally causes tremors in the hand

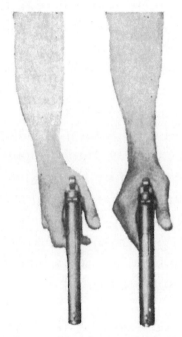

Left—The wrong way to grip the service automatic. Pistol not in prolongation of the arm. Right—The correct way to grip the service automatic.

which in turn cause unsteadiness in holding. The shock from a revolver comes mainly against the fleshy part of the hand between the thumb and first finger and if firing is continued this part of the hand will become sensitive and may cause flinching. When using the automatic there is of course less recoil felt but the effect of the vibrations of the slide and its adjoining mechanism as it is driven to the rear and then forward again by the counter recoil action is even worse than the effect from the recoil in its tendency to set up tremors in the shooting hand. Let a beginner fire a few scores rapidly with the service pistol and he will soon find his hand quivering from the reactions of the mechanism which has been working back and forth above it. If this condition is properly appreciated the marksman will welcome every opportunity to shoot slowly with this particular gun and to take enough time between strings of rapid fire to prevent his hand from reaching the quivering point or, if it does develop tremors, to rest it long enough to quiet them. In the use of any pistol it is generally considered good practice to extend the thumb along the side of the piece if the conformation of the weapon will permit it. With the service gun there are several reasons why this is advisable. The large butt causes many persons to grip it more on the right side than is correct. This results in greater pressure on that side and a tendency to shoot left caused by the pressure of the hand and of the index finger when squeezing and firing. If this weapon is properly seated in the hand so that the barrel is parallel to the center line of the forearm it can be held more uniformly with the thumb along the side at about the same height as the third joint of the index finger. To secure uniformity of pressure with the thumb try this method: When the pistol has been well seated in the hand with the grip safety pressed in properly let the right thumb fall naturally on top of the second finger and then roll it up until it is parallel to the bottom of the slide and slightly below it. This should be done for each shot fired deliberately and for each string of rapid

fire until it becomes natural and one does it uncon-
sciously.

Due to the fact that the service weapons were turned
out in great quantities during the recent war and that
the parts were made interchangeable without fitting,
there is apt to be more looseness in many assembled pistols than is desirable in a target gun. As a result many
of them do not seem to give the accuracy that can be
expected of a good gun of this model. The most noticeable defects of this kind are the loose fit between the
slide and the receiver and the play between the barrel and
the barrel bushing and between the latter and the slide.
Too much play between the slide and the receiver can be
reduced by removing the slide, laying it on a firm support and tapping it along the lower edge with a small
lead or bronze hammer. This must be done carefully
by working from rear to front and trying the slide on
the receiver frequently. The object should be to take
up the looseness without making the parts bind at any
points. The play between the barrel bushing, slide, and
barrel can be overcome by substituting a thicker bushing
if one has access to spare parts.

The kind and condition of the barrel will have more to
do with the shooting qualities of the pistol than any other
parts. There have been several changes made in the ammunition and the diameter of the barrel in recent years
and one should assure himself that he has the latest size
barrel and match ammunition, if he expects to get the
most out of his pistol. The Colt's company sells special
match barrels which are greatly superior to those issued
by the Ordnance Department. Their cost is relatively

low and the satisfaction of having one more than pays for its expense.

Occasionally one gets a gun that jams during the extraction and ejection of the empty shells. This may be due to having a recoil spring that is too stiff and it can be improved by cutting off a few of its coils. If a jam occurs during the reloading or feeding of the shells into the chamber it is usually the fault of the magazines which become defective by much use and abuse. When jams occur test the gun first by using a good magazine and then if the trouble continues look for it in the gun itself.

The older service automatics were issued with rear sights with circular tops whereas those of more recent issue have the more satisfactory rectangular rear sight bars. The older front sights were low, thin and quite pointed when seen from the rear. It has now become the practice to mount broad front sights on the service pistols selected for the National Matches and is permissible under the rules. These can be put on the slides of all pistols except certain lots that were made by Springfield Armory. The sights on these Springfield slides were made integral with the slide and cannot be removed and replaced. The disadvantage of the old pointed sights, in addition to the difficulty of aligning them accurately, was the effect of heat waves on their appearance. On very hot sunny days while firing rapid fire, heat waves from the barrel will play across the sight and make it very difficult to see clearly and with a corresponding bad effect on one's score. The use of the broad front sight largely eliminates this trouble.

The trigger action of the service pistol is different

from that of a revolver and should be given special study by persons unaccustomed to its characteristics. The first pressure on the trigger does not affect the hammer but merely takes up "slack" and brings the disconnector against the sear whereas in a revolver any pressure on the trigger affects the hammer. There is no danger of firing the pistol if the slack is properly taken up and the trigger pull is what it should be. With all straight pull weapons the pull seems less than the same amount does on a revolver or pistol that receives an angular pressure. For this reason a heavier pull can be used on this weapon to advantage. The rules for all army competitions require that the trigger pull be not less than four pounds tested with the barrel held vertically. A clean five-pound pull can be used very satisfactorily unless one is accustomed to the very light ones allowed on target pistols. If one attempts to reduce the pull below four pounds he will find that he is unable to use it for any but single shots. The jar caused by the heavy slide springing forward after the previous shot has been fired and the shell ejected, is so great that it will release the sear from the hammer and the latter will follow the slide forward. This may occur with a pull of four pounds although the author has used a pistol for several years with a pull slightly over that amount and it has never failed to function properly in this respect.

There is little doubt that obtaining a suitable trigger pull is among the first problems that a marksman meets when he begins using the average service gun. All pistols issued to the services have unusually heavy pulls unless they have been specially selected for the National Matches or other competitions and even then they are apt to be heavier than an experienced shot desires. This is a wise precaution for it is dangerous to issue guns with light pulls to recruits or novices, especially if they are mounted and expect to fire from the saddle. For a while the minimum trigger pull allowed in the army competitions was 6 pounds, but this has now been reduced. It would not be so bad if the heavy pulls were smooth and clean so that when the sear released the hammer it did so with a clean break. This is usually the exception in issue guns, for in addition to being heavy the trigger action is rough, creepy and uncertain. There is also frequently found on service pistols what is known as a spongy trigger pull which is almost as bad as creep. It is due to the sear trying to raise the hammer by a camming effect before it can release itself from the notch.

When the trigger is pressed it in turn presses against the lower end of the disconnector and the center prong of the sear spur. The disconnector then presses the lowest end of the sear and this pressure tends to release the point or nose from the hammer notch. From this long operation it is easy to account for possible creep. The first movement of the trigger to the rear presses back the sear spring until the disconnector is against the sear and any additional pressure then acts on the hammer. Before attempting to lighten the trigger pull an effort should be made to eliminate all the creep caused by rough contacts. This is done by polishing all bearing surfaces and especially those of the sear nose and the hammer notch. After this has been done if there is still creep present and the weight is too great other steps must be taken. Before encouraging anyone to attempt to reduce the pull on the service automatic let me state that I believe that to make this adjustment on this particular gun is the easiest and yet the hardest trigger adjusting job a pistol man can undertake. It is easy because it can be done quickly if one knows the knack or tricks of doing the work. On the contrary to do this job well requires a careful study of the problem and infinite care and patience on the part of an amateur. For eight years to my knowledge the Colt company has sent to the National Matches, one of their factory experts, J. H. FitzGerald, whose duty among others has been to gratuitously assist pistol shooters in every way possible. "Fitz," his table and large umbrella have become a familiar sight back of the pistol firing line. His main occupation has been to adjust pistols, and the ease and skill with which he does this is quite marvelous. As there are hundreds of service automatics present to one revolver he naturally gets more of the former to adjust. It must not be assumed from this that the Model 1911 is always in need of adjustment, for if one buys a new pistol of this model from the factory he will find it is all that could be desired in the way of accuracy, adjustment and workmanship and will not need repairs for years if properly cared for. When we remember that most of these pistols in use today were made under pressure of a great national emergency when the best materials and labor were not available and the usual high standards of workmanship could not possibly be maintained we can understand why there is great need of adjustments for these guns if they are to be required to give satisfaction in target competitions. For four years I have watched "Fitz" adjust the pistols of the team with which I fired, to say nothing of the hours I have spent observing him in action at Camp Perry. From him I have absorbed sufficient knowledge and skill to in turn assist others.

The methods used by FitzGerald on the firing line are necessarily emergency measures for he has hundreds of jobs given him each day and he has to work fast to accomplish the most good. A favorite expedient of his in reducing the trigger pull or the creep therein is to burnish the sear and the notch by pressing hard on the hammer at the same time he presses the trigger. If this does not do the business he quickly dismounts the gun, inspects the parts and either substitutes others or with a few strokes of a quick-cutting, smooth file touches up those that need it. His thorough knowledge of the weapon and his long experience in this particular work enables him to accomplish wonders in a minimum of time, and incidently, these methods are not to be recommended for the amateur. Emergency adjustments usually answer for the emergency but do not as a rule hold up very long, and it is much better to take more time and do the work slowly, carefully and thoroughly.

The following is offered as a safe procedure in working on a service pistol. Study the sketch showing the hammer, sear, disconnector and trigger. Pay particular attention to the way the sear fits the notch, and the angle the two bearing surfaces make with relation to the line from the center of the sear pivot to the innermost point of the sear. In other words, determine first what you want to do without question or in the words of Davy Crockett, "Be sure you're right, then go ahead."

Note that one of the unusual things about the hammer

is that it is split so that the sear rests in two separate notches, one on either side of the cut-out center. You have actually two notches to work on and one sear, which is different from other arms. If the angle of the notch seems to be correct try rubbing down the sear nose first until it fits the bearing surface of the notch. Do this on a hard, smooth surface stone. For years I have used various shapes of Arkansas stones which are not always

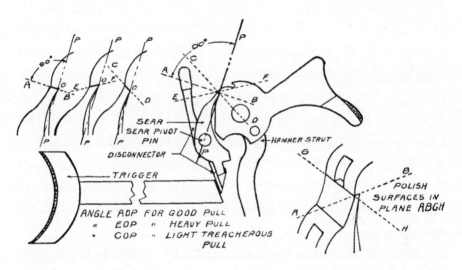

easy to obtain but will give the greatest satisfaction of any of which I know. A good hard razor hone can be used. The Arkansas stone is white, or nearly so, when new and if it has sharp corners or a knife edge shape on one side it should be carefully protected, for it will chip easily. It is not necessary to put oil on the stone if one wants a polishing rather than a cutting surface. Another necessary piece of equipment is a magnifying glass to enable one to see clearly the shape of the small surfaces and angles with which he is working. For this purpose I finally adopted a jeweler's glass with a 3½ inch focus which cost 75 cents. Examine the sides of the hammer and sear around the notches and point respectively and remove any burrs found by laying the parts flat on the stone and polishing them. In polishing the sear nose be careful to keep this small surface flat on the stone to avoid taking off more on the sides and leaving a convex effect in the center. After getting the sear polished satisfactorily try the action of the trigger by assembling it and squeezing it very carefully, at the same time aiming and holding carefully on a small target. If it is still too heavy it will be necessary to work on the notch and sear and grind them off very slowly, trying the action frequently. A trigger weight with a convenient hook to slip on the trigger as the pistol is held vertically is the best means of testing the work. The weight including the hook should be half a pound heavier than the pull desired. This is where the operation becomes tedious and one is inclined to finish the job with a file. If one has an unusually deep notch this procedure may be necessary, but that can be determined by study beforehand. When working on the pistols of soldiers I have frequently resorted to this method and have several small smooth files of different shapes. The one I prefer is a jeweler's square taper file about an eighth of an inch on the side. It is a pillar file and marked "4 Made in Switzerland." It has three cutting surfaces and one smooth or blank face. A few strokes with this file and a little polishing with the stone is all that is frequently needed. One of the dangers of working with service guns is that the case hardening on the hammer and sear is frequently very thin and once this is penetrated the metal is so soft that a good adjustment will not hold unless one can have the parts again hardened.

A little experience in adjusting triggers will convince one that when he has a reasonably good trigger he should leave well enough alone or send the gun to the factory and have the work performed there. It is realized that there are times when it is not convenient to have a factory job done or even to secure the services of a good gun-

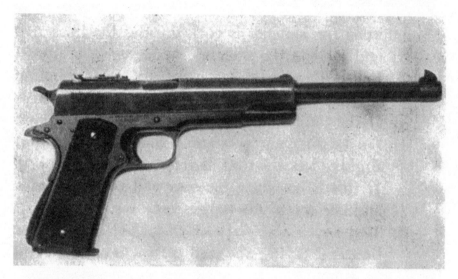

A remodeled Service automatic that became an excellent target pistol.

smith and it is then that knowledge and skill in this work is valuable. The greatest drawback to sending one's gun away is the time it takes to get it back and the loss of practice in the meantime. A real pistol man should be able to make these adjustments and after a little perseverance and patience he can do it quite satisfactorily, but like the other details of the game it requires time and study to master.

To sum up the instructions given here on adjusting

triggers and to clear up any ambiguous statements the following steps are recommended:

1. Polish the bearing surfaces of the hammer notch and the sear nose and remove burrs from the edges.
2. To reduce the pull, grind down the bearing surfaces until they are flat and so that they make a right angle with the line from the center of the sear pivot to the inside point of the sear nose, when the hammer is cocked. See the lines A–B and P–P in the sketch.
3. Polish these surfaces carefully and round off slightly the inside edge of the sear nose.
4. If the pull is still too heavy, bevel very slightly the bearing surfaces until they make an angle slightly less than 90 degrees with the line P–P. If this is overdone the sear will not hold safely and accidental discharges may result.
5. Test your work frequently by assembling the action and trying the pull with a trigger weight.

Chapter XXI

HOLSTERS FOR SHOOTING

HOLSTERS are the most important accessories to practical pistol practice. Without suitable ones all forms of pistol work that serve useful purposes would be done less efficiently than would be the case if properly designed and serviceable types were used. Poorly constructed holsters are an abomination, and yet I know of no other single accessory to pistol work of which one can find more unsatisfactory examples today, than of these necessary adjuncts. There are on the American market holsters of every conceivable shape, size and material. They are made of cloth, leather, metal, fiber, wood, rubber and what not. They are constructed with flaps, straps, thongs, and springs to keep the pistol in place. They are designed to be worn on the thigh, in the pockets, on the waist belt, below the arm pit, on a saddle, attached to the steering wheel of a motor car or carried in handbags or similar receptacles. Every pistol "crank" has taken a turn at designing or attempting to improve the design of holsters, to the end that he may improve his practical shooting, or provide a more compact or protective carrier for his pet gun. Aside from the matter of protection for a gun and efficient service in connection with its use many gun lovers take a great pride in having handsome appearing holsters and belts that are practical and not merely ornamental. Beautiful workmanship whether it be on the gun or accessory is always appreciated by the real pistol lover.

The design of military holsters and the method of carrying them have undergone many changes, some of which have been due to the change in guns and some to the

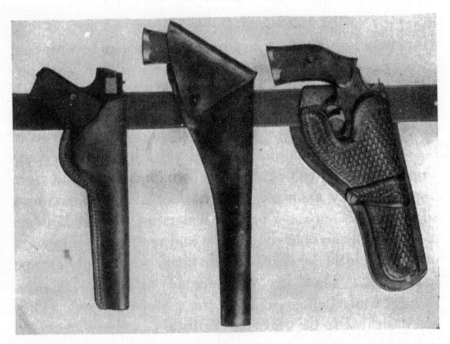

Three small bore pistol holsters of different designs. The one on the left is a substantial, convenient and well fitted holster for the .22 Colt's Woodsman Automatic. That in the center is a cheap, flimsy and poorly made holster for the S. & W. .22 target pistol and the model on the right is a well made and hung Mexican type holster for the S. & W. 22-32 H.F. target revolver.

change in size and location of the soldier's personal equipment or pack. Police officers have switched from carrying their guns in the hip pockets in leather or rubber holsters to the more convenient belt or shoulder types. The target shot varies the practice of carrying his guns in a case with other accessories to packing it in a holster when he does not wish to be burdened with too much equipment. The mounted man, due to the fact that weight of equipment is not such an important factor to him, is apt to encase his weapon in heavier material for better protection against hard service and frequent bumps and falls. The man whose hobby is defensive shooting is continually seeking for the fastest quick-draw holster and some of the designs advocated by these specialists are unique to say the least. Unfortunately most of the leather workers who cut the patterns for holsters are not pistol shots, and apparently have little or no idea of the qualification of good holsters but merely try to design some form of covering for the gun in which it will fit reasonably well, receive some protection and present a neat appearance. To design a holster for protection is one thing, to design it for practical service is quite another, and it is in the latter mission that most leather workers fail. The search for suitable holsters for practical purposes has occupied many spare hours of the writer's time and he has purchased models in Maine and Southern California, in Washington and Texas and in many of the intervening states. The discussion here is the result of his study and experimenting in the designing, making and using of holsters.

What are the qualifications of a good holster? That is the question that arises in one's mind when he considers the purchase of one for carrying his pistol. The question cannot be answered completely until the purpose of the holster is known. If it is merely to protect the gun and afford a means of carrying it on one's person so as to shield the pistol against the weather, or rough service incident to hunting, fishing or camping trips it is sufficient that the holster be made of good leather, that it fit the gun reasonably well, is provided with a flap, contains no surplus material, and has a convenient means for attaching it to the belt or other personal apparel.

If the holster is desired for defensive work in emergencies and is to be carried on the body so that it may be readily accessible to the shooting hand then it must possess other qualifications and the greatest care must be taken in its design and construction. For police officers either in uniform or plain clothes the requirements of rapid drawing are not so essential but nevertheless holsters for their use must possess many of the same attributes as the defensive type.

Consider first this "quick-draw" type of holster. It should be made of good firm ten ounce saddle skirting leather, cut out of the back or shoulder of the hide or, if a lined holster is desired with a smooth interior for greater ease in drawing, the outer leather should be six ounce and the lining four ounce glued together. In no case should a lined holster be made with buckskin, chamois or similar leathers inside, as they are unserviceable and absorb moisture too readily. Good quality saddle skirting leather can be easily shaped, if properly cased, and is firm enough to retain its form after once fitted to a gun. Other kinds of leather are not nearly as satisfactory for the purpose as they stretch more easily and frequently get flabby and useless.

The second qualification is that the holster fit the particular gun for which it is intended. The test for fit is to hold the holster upside down with the gun in it and if the pistol stays in place the fit is not too loose. On the other hand the holster should not be a bit tighter than necessary to accomplish the above test. It should be so shaped and fitted as to hold the gun by pressure on the top of the frame and around the trigger guard. There should be no binding in any other place especially around the front sight or barrel. To accomplish this it

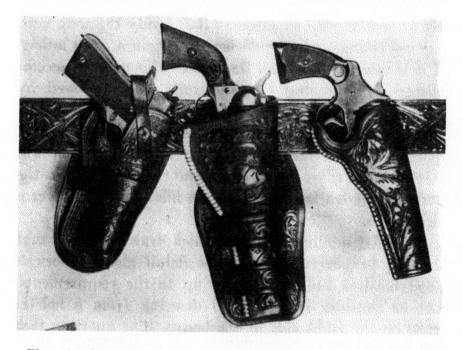

Three handsome holsters hung on the same belt to show the difference in pitch of the barrels. They are, from left to right, the Montford Military Holster, the Hardy Quick Draw Holster and the quick draw holster designed by the author and made by Hardy.

is desirable that the maker actually use a gun or model form on which to fit the holster. The latter may be fitted to a gun as follows: Sponge the leather with warm water until it becomes pliable but not so wet that water can be squeezed from it. Lay it aside for an hour and then place the pistol or revolver in the holster and fit it to the profile of the frame and trigger guard by pressure of the fingers or of a wooden knob. When properly shaped withdraw the gun carefully and let the holster dry slowly at ordinary room temperature. Do not let the holster dry with the gun in it or it will be too large when dry, and do not dry it in the sun. When thoroughly dried the leather may be given a good dressing of saddle soap to preserve it. Apply the soap with a damp sponge, using sufficient to obtain a good lather. If it is desired to darken the leather this may be accomplished by sponging it with oxalic acid, followed by Neatsfoot oil containing a few drops of kerosene. A holster sponged with oxalic acid, oiled, and then rubbed thoroughly and frequently with tragacanth gum will take on a fine gloss finish. The acid cleans and opens the pores of the leather and the gum fills them and gives a rich polish.

The next qualification of a quick draw holster is that it hang properly. In this one detail many otherwise good holsters fail to measure up to the requirements. Let us consider right-handed drawing from a holster worn on the right side of the body. The question that has puzzled many pistol men is that of the proper pitch or slope the holster should have with the belt. Should it hang vertically, or should it hang with the barrel ahead of, or behind the butt when the gun is in place? Having long ago formed my own conclusions as to the way a gun should slope when in a holster I have asked this question of holster makers wherever I have been. The answers have varied but in certain sections of the country I found that the slope was generally with the butt to the front and the muzzle to the rear. A leather worker in Wyoming told me he made them that way because he had always done so, and they seemed to satisfy his customers. Another man in Texas said that the western style of shooting is to pull and shoot as the gun comes up to the target and that this can be done quicker with the butt to the front. He then qualified his statement by saying that for a "hip-shot" the gun should be vertical or with the butt to the rear. Personally, I believe there is a sounder reason for pitching a gun with the muzzle to the rear when worn on the right hip. It is because a revolver or pistol can be carried much more comfortably in this manner than otherwise and that it is not a question of rapid drawing at all. It is also quite noticeable that the leather workers who specialize in quick draw holsters make these models to hang either vertically or with the muzzle ahead of the butt. This is especially true of those intended to be worn in front of the body either to the right or left of the belt buckle. The finest holster for the service .45 automatic that I have ever seen is one that was made for me by J. R. Montford of El Paso, Texas, in 1913. It is patented and so constructed and reinforced on the inside and under the trigger guard that the gun fits it perfectly, the butt is thrown out, and the magazine catch is so well protected that there is no chance of it being pressed in and the magazine lost from the gun as sometimes occurs in using other military holsters. It is the Mexican type and can be easily slipped on the Sam Browne or any other kind of belt. This favorite holster has been in use for fifteen years, including service on the Mexican border and in France and is as good today as it ever was. It is pitched so that when worn on the belt or slightly in rear of the right hip, the barrel is to the rear and except for the weight one does not know it is there. It is shown in the illustrations. This is not intended for a quick draw holster but nevertheless I have done much aerial shooting from it by wearing it on a sagging belt and tying it to my leg with the buckskin thong that was part of it and which I have since re-

The Montford Military Holster on a Sam Browne belt. An excellent design for its purpose.

moved. For quick drawing, holsters hung from a belt low on the right thigh should be designed so that the barrel is either vertical or slightly inclined to the front. Those worn on a tight belt about the waist should be hung so that the barrel inclines always to the left and the angle between the barrel and belt should be about thirty degrees. To maintain a proper balance care must be taken to see that the gun is not hung too high on the belt. Any holster which causes the wrist to be bent at a sharp and uncomfortable angle when drawing, is not hung correctly. This is the acid test for a quick draw holster.

There should be no unnecessary leather used in holsters. The day of the old Mexican type is past. That style had a few advantages and was intended primarily for mounted men. It was simple to make and could be worn on any width of belt but the surplus leather in the wide skirt added materially to its weight and bulk. It was picturesque when worn with a fine carved belt, fancy pistol, and in company with a beautifully made saddle.

The belt loop of the quick draw holster should be formed by bending back the extension of the back of the holster the full width of its upper part and sewing it firmly in the rear. This loop should exactly fit the belt on which the holster is to be worn and for best results this belt should not be less than two inches in width and of good weight. If it is worn tight about the waist there should be no necessity for tying down the holster to facilitate smooth, rapid drawing.

Holsters intended for the use of motorcycle officers, for military or other service that may subject the pistol to rough usage in inclement weather, in windy, sandy country, or in any place where it is necessary to pay particular attention to keeping the mechanism free from dirt should be substantially made and possess a flap. They should be made to fit the gun more snugly than the defensive type so as not to permit the weapon to jump around. Covered holsters should also be closed at the muzzle end, but open ones, worn in all kinds of weather, should be left open at the bottom to prevent water from

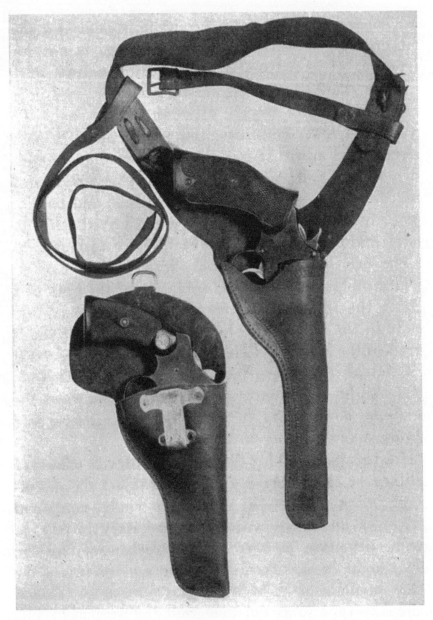

A soft leather shoulder holster of the pouch type suitable for carrying conveniently a small bore revolver. Lower: A serviceable suspender holster for wear inside the trouser band and designed for a pocket revolver.

collecting in them. Open holsters which many prefer for general service may be profitably made with straps or thongs attached with which to secure the pistol in-

The Hardy Quick Draw Shoulder Holster.

stead of a flap. Securing straps or thongs to tie a holster down have no place on a quick draw holster.

If other pistol enthusiasts have experienced as much difficulty in securing good holsters as the author, they will appreciate information of reliable leather workers who turn out well made and correctly designed models. J. R. Montford of El Paso, Texas, and Captain A. H. Hardy of Beverly Hills, California, formerly of Denver, Colorado, are both real experts in leather working and have been making excellent holsters for many years. The latter has been a pistol shot of national prominence as well, and his skill and dexterity with the revolver has given him a real appreciation of the requisite qualifications for holsters for all purposes.

Chapter XXII

AMMUNITION HINTS

ACCURATE pistol shooting is largely dependent on good ammunition. Obviously it is very poor policy to spend considerable time and effort on learning the technique of shooting and then sacrifice one's success by using poor shooting equipment and inaccurate ammunition. The inaccuracy of a cartridge may be due to being unbalanced ballistically or to defects caused by deterioration in powder resulting from old age, or improper storage.

In the great variety of pistol ammunition available today we find cartridges intended for military purposes, for police work, for use in guns made for self protection, and some that is suitable for accurate target work. There are many obsolescent cartridges still being manufactured to meet the demands of owners of weapons of "ancient vintage." This will continue no doubt for many years, for some men will still practice with their old models rather than buy more modern and up-to-date weapons. Granted that there are a few old revolvers that are still great favorites of many members of the pistol shooting fraternity because of their balance, grip, caliber or some other desirable feature, there are a few that should be discarded primarily because of the ammunition for which they are chambered, which is neither accurate, adequate nor effective as judged by modern standards.

To find an ideal all-around pistol cartridge is much like trying to find an ideal all-around pistol, and we must expect to sacrifice something when we are selecting either of these articles.   If we desire a cartridge with maximum accuracy, that is pleasant to shoot and is suitable for indoor use because of the absence of excessive noise and recoil we must go to the smaller and medium bores, but if we want something that has stopping or shocking power we must use the large calibers.   If we wish to find a cartridge to use in either rifle or revolver as our pioneers did, we can still select the same ones they used if we are satisfied with them.   The 32–20 or .32 Winchester, the 38–40 or .38 Winchester and the 44–40 or .44 Winchester cartridges were originally rifle cartridges loaded with black powder, and made for use in Winchester rifles.   As such they proved quite successful, especially the two larger calibers and several of the old model six shooters were chambered for these cartridges in order to simplify the ammunition supply of our early western settlers, who found it advisable and necessary to possess both rifles and revolvers.   They were formerly loaded with 20 and 40 grains of black powder, respectively, from which they derived their common designation.   After the invention of smokeless powder the loads were materially changed and the results in general not so good, especially in revolvers.   Within very recent years these cartridges have been put in the high velocity class as a result of loading them with a more powerful powder charge.   These new loads are not safe for use in revolvers or pistols and great care should be taken when buying any of them to see that only the low velocity kind are purchased.   Realizing the danger

of using the high velocity type in revolvers the ammunition companies have carefully labeled the boxes with
the precaution, "Not for use in revolvers" or similar
warning. The low power loads can still be obtained and
these cartridges are popular with many pistolmen, especially the 44–40 with its 200 grain blunt nose bullet and
effective shocking power. The popularity of this cartridge may also be due to some extent to the fact that
the old favorite, Colt Single Action revolver, known as
the Frontier Model, was originally chambered for it and
the Single Action as sold by the Colt firm today is chambered for any of the three cartridges as well as for several others.

The selection of the most effective cartridge of heavy
caliber involves the question of accuracy, and of stopping or shocking power. Accuracy of high degree is not
so essential in a weapon intended for military or police
use, but the power to stop or instantly disable an enemy,
even though it may be temporary, is what is desired.
The wound from a small caliber bullet may eventually
prove fatal but the paralyzing shock from a heavy, large
sized bullet is much more effective at the critical time
of an emergency. The factors of weight, diameter, velocity, shape, construction and composition of a bullet
all affect its stopping power and these combined with the
place and nature of the impact on a body make it impossible to state absolutely which cartridges and bullets
are the best for the purpose. Jacketed bullets with
round or sharp points and having great penetration are
not as effective as a general thing as blunt nosed, lead
bullets with low, rather than high velocity.

It is not the author's intention in this book on pistol

shooting to fill the pages with discussions on the killing or shocking power of bullets about which much has already been written, but rather to offer such suggestions as his experience and study has taught to be of value to the shooter. It is believed that the .45 Colt cartridge with its 255 grain, blunt nosed bullet, as loaded by most of the cartridge companies, or with the 250 grain bullet as loaded by the Remington Arms Co. is the best "man stopper" made. There is, however, sufficient stopping power in the 38–40, the .44 Special, and the 44–40 and the .45 Automatic pistol and revolver cartridges to answer the purpose and no one will go wrong if he selects any of these for use in a good weapon. If one wants to get the most accurate large caliber cartridges he should by all means select the .44 S. & W. Special and next to that the Service Automatic cartridge with the 230 grain bullet as made by Frankford Arsenal since 1924.

In the selection of ammunition for target practice one must consider the class of shooting in which he is to engage, and then study the ammunition question, keeping in mind that there is no need of trying to secure cartridges that will shoot closer than the best shots can hold. Due to the targets used, the ranges at which firing is done and the time factor in the firing, military and police practice is not expected to be as accurate as very deliberate shooting at the Standard American target at fifty yards or as free pistol shooting at the International target at fifty meters. It is in the latter style of shooting that the greatest care should be taken in choosing ammunition, for a defective cartridge or bullet can certainly ruin a good score very easily when firing is done at the 2 inch center and closely spaced rings of the International target. For this work the .22 caliber single shot target pistols are used and the .22 long rifle cartridge. This particular cartridge has been developed to such an extent in the last ten years that it is recognized as the finest for the purpose and is universally used. The two inch ten ring is about the limit in accuracy that one should expect when using the most accurately made target pistol at the 50 meter range. Of course the best target pistols with high grade ammunition will shoot closer than this when fired from a machine rest, but most shooters are far from human machine rests. Inasmuch as this form of shooting is the most highly refined, it behooves the marksman to make every possible improvement in his shooting and if he uses the best pistol he can secure then the only other thing he can do is to use the most accurate ammunition available. This usually gets down to the question of which brand to use, and therein the matter of psychology enters to no small degree. There are five American makes of .22 long rifle cartridges that are suitable for pistol work, and any of them will give excellent results. With many marksmen the use of a particular make of cartridge is a good deal like voting. They have been taught that one make was the best and so they stick to that kind as they stick to their political party regardless of the fact that occasionally there are poor lots of ammunition just as there is poor material among the candidates for election. Our ammunition firms have had to put their best efforts into the development of .22 long rifle ammunition as the demand for this cartridge is much greater than for any other and the super-excellent shooting that is done now-a-days with our best small arms makes it necessary for the ammunition to keep pace with the guns.   Up to about ten years ago this cartridge was used for short range work entirely and its accuracy was not nearly what it is today, but about that time the U. S. Cartridge Co. brought out what they called the .22 N.R.A. long range cartridge good for rifle work up to two hundred yards.   Since then the other manufacturers have specialized on similar ones so that we now have a most excellent assortment of accurate small caliber cartridges from which to select.

There are now available two classes of .22 long rifle cartridges.   One is the ordinary garden variety known as the regular .22 long rifle ammunition and the other is the .22 match ammunition, which is put out by each firm under a special trade name.   If one goes to a sporting goods store and asks for .22 long rifle ammunition the chances are he will be given the regular kind unless he specifies the match cartridges.   The former is cheaper and for short range work is quite satisfactory, in fact it frequently shoots quite as well as the match stuff, but there is not the uniformity to be found in it that there is in the other grade.   Another reason for using the match cartridge is that there is quite a difference between the muzzle velocities of the two.   Take Remington for example,—the regular cartridge has 930 foot seconds velocity and the "Palma" cartridge has 1070.   One who can hold well and can call his shots very accurately with the pistol will probably detect the difference in accuracy between the regular and the "Palma" cartridge, but to do this he must be able to see exactly where his sights are aligned at the instant the pistol fires.   The difference in cost between the two is three dollars a thousand and is made necessary by the additional handling required in its manufacture. The Palma cartridge is accurate for any range up to 200 yards. The United States Cartridge Co. call their match cartridge the .22 N.R.A. "Marksman" is the title used by the Western Cartridge Co. The Peters Cartridge Co. have two match cartridges both called "Tackhole," but one is designated as the Indoor and the other as the Outdoor cartridge with a difference of 120 foot seconds in muzzle velocity. "Tackhole" Outdoors is credited with 1065 f. s. "Precision 75" and "Precision 200" are the terms used by Winchester in designating their short and long range match cartridges, the former meaning feet and the latter yards. The muzzle velocities claimed for these two cartridges are about 1000 and 1100 foot seconds respectively. Some recent accuracy tests made for me by Winchester's ballistic engineer indicate that slightly better accuracy was obtained with "Precision 200" than with "Precision 75" when used in a S. & W. target pistol, and a Colt revolver. Western claims 1115 foot seconds for "Marksman" cartridges. All the above match cartridges are loaded with Lesmok powder except Peters, which uses a Semi-smokeless charge. Any of these cartridges will shoot closer than any pistol shot can hold provided they are used in an accurate target pistol. Experts of long experience have their favorites, and their choice is usually based on sound reasoning, good results and some psychology. There are variations in the diameter of different makes of cartridges of the same caliber and there are variations in the chambering of pistols and revolvers for the same cartridges. Both of these details affect the grouping or accuracy of the weapon and ammunition. With a pistol or revolver it is more difficult to test the accuracy of ammunition than it is with a rifle, but by using a muzzle and forearm rest or for some pistols a six point rest, we can determine whether the ammunition is shooting as well as we can hold. We can also compare the accuracy of different makes in the same pistol. There is no doubt that some weapons will do better work with a certain make of ammunition and if we can determine which this is we will then have a logical reason for using that particular brand. And once we feel confident that one kind suits our pistol better than any other we should stick to it until we find it is failing to group properly. It is safe to assume, however, that the average pistol shot can accept any of the standard match cartridges and know that they are as accurate as need be for his practice. When he gets to the point where he can shoot above 90% on the Standard American target it will be time enough for him to worry about super-accuracy and refinements.

In spite of everything that is done to make ammunition uniform in every way there is a variation in different lots of the same cartridges. Sometimes this variation is great enough to show material inaccuracy. This is likely to happen in any brand. In one indoor season a team I was associated with fired about 50,000 rounds of one kind of .22 long rifle ammunition without evidence of a single erratic shot, such as a keyhole or flier, to indicate defective ammunition and less than a half dozen misfires occurred to mar the season's record. Yet, the following fall at Camp Perry (1923) this same make grouped so poorly that a number of its users had to switch to another brand. In the case of the ammunition that seemed to suit my target pistols the best and in which I have always had the greatest confidence I have found only one lot that seemed to be below standard in accuracy over a period of nearly fifteen years. At times I was influenced to try other brands, but in each case went back to my old favorite because of getting some unfortunate fliers that affected my scores most adversely. Other marksmen swear by their favorites as strongly as I do mine so we are all happy when we can get the brand we want, and the chances are we shoot better with it than we would with one in which we have less confidence. If the time ever comes when you lose faith in your ammunition do not condemn it for its poor groups until you try it out thoroughly with a rest. Frequent hang fires, keyholes and fliers are sure evidence of poor stuff and are sufficient cause to drop any lot of ammunition.

The latest improvements in long rifle cartridges are to load them with a non-rusting priming mixture which prevents the rusting and corrosion of the barrel. If this is accomplished—the "if" is inserted because all of the new priming mixtures are not entirely successful yet— it will be, from the shooter's standpoint, one of the most profitable developments ever made in small arms ammunition. The Remington Arms Co. was the first to bring out a new cartridge with the non-rust priming mixture and they gave it the name of Kleanbore. Its adoption makes it possible to use smokeless powder in small bore arms which in the past was not considered good practice if one thought anything of his guns. If the new combination proves as accurate as the old Lesmok cartridges there will be several advantages in its use in addition to the big one of eliminating work and worry over the care of the bore of the pistol.   It will improve indoor shooting conditions by preventing the accumulation of smoke in the range, an occurrence that can be quite unpleasant at times and which has a material effect on the appearance of the bull's-eye in the course of an evening's practice on a crowded range.   The cartridges available at this time with non-rusting priming mixtures are:

>   Remington Kleanbore.
>   Peters Rustless.
>   Western Non-corrosive.
>   U. S. Self Cleaning.
>   Winchester Staynless.

All are loaded with smokeless except Peters, which are charged with semi-smokeless.

In the realm of medium calibers, the most accurate revolver cartridge is the .38 S. & W. Special, in fact there is little doubt that it is second only to the .22 Long Rifle match cartridge, for any kind of target work.   The full factory loads when used in a good target revolver are very pleasant to fire, though they are a little noisy for indoor work.   For the latter purpose there are several mid-range cartridges that can be used in lieu of the full loads and they will give good accuracy up to 20 yards.   For competition work in which revolvers of greater than .22 caliber are prescribed the .38 S. & W. special cartridge is one's best bet, for it will be found that the most accurate target revolvers are made to take this cartridge and its contemporary, the .38 Colt Special. The latter has the same ballistics except for its blunt nose, which probably gives it greater stopping power.

No discussion of ammunition problems, however sketchy, would be complete without a few paragraphs on that all important item of shooting expense, and ways and means of securing all the practice we can for the funds we have available. There are many pistol men who prefer big bore shooting to small caliber practice and to do much of this kind of work involves considerable expense. There are two solutions to the problem. The first is to substitute small caliber for big gun practice and the other is to reload one's ammunition. Obviously the "gun bug" who is addicted to the use of the heavy artillery of pistol work will scoff at the idea of giving it up and using small bore pistols. The only other legitimate means of getting the practice he desires is to join a National Guard unit armed with the pistol and take advantage of the opportunities to use government ammunition or to buy a set of reloading tools, a good book of instructions on how to use them and spend his spare time making his own gun fodder. Reloading is a very practical solution to the problem of getting a maximum amount of shooting for a minimum expenditure of money, but it is not the easy get-rich-quick method that one is led to believe when listening to an enthusiastic advocate of reloading talk about its strong points. Its greatest advantages are to the rifleman who uses high powered ammunition that costs from nine to twelve cents a shot when purchased from commercial manufacturers. It has been stated by persons who should know, that the ammunition bill can be reduced to half or one third that of commercial make. This is the big argument in favor of reloading, altho there are others of more or less import. The reloading game is

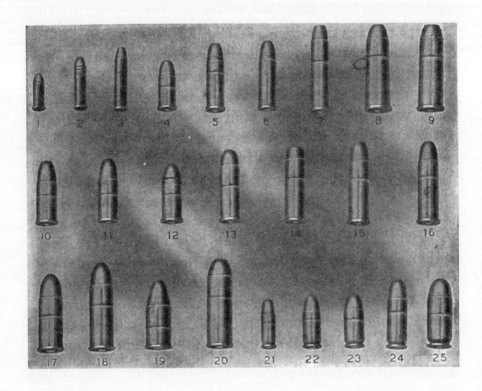

This illustration shows the cartridges adapted to Colt pistols and revolvers. (Courtesy Colt Pat. Fire Arms Mfg. Co.)

No. 1—.22 Short
" 2—.22 Long Rifle
" 3—.22 W. R. F.
" 4—.32 S. & W. (Short)
" 5—.32 Colt Police Positive
" 6—.32 S. & W. Long
" 7—.32-20 (Winchester)
" 8—.38-40 (Winchester)
" 9—.44-40 (Winchester)
" 10—.38 Colt Police Positive
" 11—.38 S. & W.
" 12—.38 Short Colt
" 13—.38 Long Colt

No. 14—.38 S. & W. Special, Mid Range
" 15—.38 Colt Special
" 16—.38 S. & W. Special
" 17—.44 Russian
" 18—.44 S. & W. Special
" 19—.455 Eley
" 20—.45 Colt
" 21—.25 Automatic
" 22—.32 Automatic
" 23—.380 Automatic
" 24—.38 Automatic
" 25—.45 Automatic

very interesting to those with an experimental bent who wish to study its problems and gain a knowledge of the use of powders, bullets and loads for various purposes. It is not for the careless man who thinks he can load a shell approximately correct and get away with it. The factors of safety are so small when it comes to loading revolver ammunition that the addition of a few grains in weight over a full load may result in extremely dangerous pressures and the probable bursting of the cylinder and the damage of other parts of the weapon. In order to avoid dangerous pressures factory ammunition has a factor of safety such that the loads do not always give the maximum power or accuracy that it is possible to get out of a particular gun or cartridge, and in certain calibers an improvement can be made by a skilled reloader. This is true of the .38 and .44 Special cartridges. When these are desired for such purposes as long range target practice, they can, by careful hand loading, be made to give better results than are forthcoming from factory loads, provided always that the loader knows what he is doing.

For him who has a hankering to play with the reloading game, and who does not at some time in his shooting career, it is well to mention a few of its disadvantages or we would not be playing fairly with the uninitiated novice. To begin with, the cost of a suitable set of reloading tools will be more than that of a good revolver and to use poor ones courts failure and even disaster. To learn the game to the extent of getting really good results requires a lot of time, study and patience which might in many cases be used to better advantage in shooting practice. It has been my experience that the men who have gone the farthest in the pistol shooting game are those who put the time they have for the sport into shooting and not into side lines that develop men into cranks rather than shots. The country is full of pistol fans who like to play with all the accessories of the game and who get a lot of real pleasure out of them, but when it comes down to shooting they are only in the average class. If they would put half the energy they spend on side issues, into studying the technique of shooting and in actual practice they would be of much more value to the sport as coaches and instructors and would find greater rewards and benefits for themselves than they do by becoming authorities on the side issues of pistol practice. My advice to shooters is to get all the practice they can from the funds they can afford to expend and if it is a case of spending only a nominal amount on ammunition then spend that on small bore cartridges until the time comes when the personal budget will permit greater appropriations to be made for big bore shooting. Large caliber enthusiasts should know that members of the National Rifle Association can buy service .45 caliber pistol ammunition at government prices from the Director of Civilian Marksmanship.

For a further comparison and study of the ballistics of pistol cartridges the reader is referred to the ballistic tables published by the several cartridge companies.

Chapter XXIII

ACCESSORIES

SHOOTING accessories are the spice of the pistol game. They add zest and interest to the sport not only when one is actively engaged in it but also during those periods of anticipation when preparations for practice take the place of actual firing. They comprise numerous articles more or less important to one's comfort and convenience, the securing and assembling of which give much pleasure.

The care and preservation of one's shooting equipment is an important factor of success in target practice as well as in all forms of practical shooting. Pistols that are not properly cleaned, oiled and protected from the weather, and from unnecessary wear and abuse will not give the efficient service of which they are capable any more than will any other instruments of precision. If they are given the attention to which they are entitled they will last a lifetime barring minor repairs due to fair wear and tear. With this thought and its close relationship to shooting in mind the author will discuss a few of the more important accessories in addition to that of holsters which has already been covered.

CLEANING MATERIALS

Pistol shooting neither demands nor requires expensive or elaborate cleaning apparatus and instead of such articles simple and sensible materials will give most satisfactory service. Compared with rifles a pistol or revolver barrel is easier to care for because of its shorter length and the fact that the ammunition to which it is adapted is less injurious to its bore. The extreme pressures in high power rifles using heavy charges of smokeless powder of either the nitrocellulose or nitroglycerine compounds cause considerable erosion in time, and the accuracy life of such weapons is comparatively limited, whereas the lower pressures and smaller charges of less harmful powder permit of longer service from hand guns. Pistols using lead bullets are easier to care for than those in which the so-called "metal cased" bullets are fired. Those using black, semi-smokeless or Lesmok cartridges can be cleaned with water or any simple solution that will aid in removing the residue from the burned powder. They can then be oiled and put away without fear of further harmful effects due to the chemical reactions that took place in the bore. When smokeless powder is used in high power rifles this is not a safe rule to follow. Nor is it advisable to trust to one cleaning, a pistol that uses metal cased bullets and smokeless powder. This is especially true of the Service automatic pistol, which to my mind is the most difficult of all hand guns to keep in A–1 shape inside the barrel. Fortunately new barrels do not cost much. Black powder when used soon accumulates a residue in the bore that will affect the accuracy if not frequently removed by wiping, but beyond this tendency it will not react on the metal in a harmful manner. Semi-smokeless or Lesmok powder is several degrees better than black powder in this regard, as it leaves less residue in the bore. Smokeless is of course the cleanest of all and many rounds can be fired without affecting the accuracy of the practice, but it is well to examine the bore about twenty-four hours after cleaning it the first time to see if there are any effects noticeable from the acid reaction of the primer compound. If this is neglected in the case of pistols using metal cased bullets, especially the Service automatic, one will soon find the grooves of his barrel filled with a rough corrosion very difficult to remove and in time very detrimental to accuracy. For the care of this type of pistol I have found it advisable to keep on hand one or more wire and bristle brushes with which to scrub the inside of the barrel while first cleaning it and thereafter whenever it shows signs of needing it. For pistols in general it is well after firing to swab them out with a reliable nitro solvent solution or with plain hot water. The bore is cleaned thoroughly and quickly by using water and seldom needs further attention provided it is properly dried and then oiled with a good gun oil. In swabbing out the bore use the solution or the water to get out the residue that has accumulated there and then by passing clean patches through the barrel, on the end of a tight fitting rod, clean it until there is no evident discoloration on the patches. This is the one and only proof that the bore is clean. To run a few patches through the barrel and then say it is clean because it looks so when examined with the eye is the method of the lazy simpleton. For .38 or larger caliber pistols it is advisable to have a cleaning rod of hard wood slightly smaller in diameter than the bore and with a suitable tip over which can be placed a cleaning patch that will tightly fill the grooves when pushed through the bore. For .22 caliber pistols it is well to use a rod made of polished tool steel 3/16 inches in diameter and fitted with a small wooden knob for a handle. One of this type will be much more satisfactory than one made of any other material, especially wood or brass. For removing lead or rust from a barrel it is well to have a rod, to the end of which can be screwed a brass wire brush. For ordinary swabbing of the barrel a round bristle brush may be used. Good patches of Canton flannel cut to uniform size are much more satisfactory to use than miscellaneous ones made of any old cloth, and will save time and trouble in the end. It is quite annoying to have a cleaning rod puncture a patch while in the bore and get stuck for it is not the easiest thing to remove. A piece of Canton flannel about a foot square well impregnated with sperm oil or any good gun oil, with which to wipe off the entire pistol before putting it away after firing or handling is excellent for preventing rust forming on the outside of the frame or barrel. In the case of revolvers care should be taken to clean the inside of the frame where the escaping powder gases come in contact with the metal.

PISTOL CASES

Whenever one starts from home for an afternoon at the range or an evening at the pistol club the matter of carrying his equipment comes first into consideration. He must have some means of packing his guns, ammunition, and the accessories he expects to use and the more convenient this is, the better will be his comfort and peace of mind. A casual inspection of the various means used by pistol men for getting their equipment from place to place will show that everything from pockets, boxes, and holsters to "Boston" bags, miniature suitcases and specially made gun cases are usually in evidence. Many assemble their stuff in a small bag of some kind and when they need anything therefrom it is necessary "to paw over" everything else to locate it.

The design of a good case gives plenty of opportunity for one to exercise his inventive ingenuity and many an attractive article of this kind can be found among shooters. If one limits himself to but one form of practice his problem is simplified, for only a small case is needed in which to transport one pistol, ammunition, cleaning materials, spotting telescope and scorebook. But if one wishes to indulge in several forms of shooting and intends to go some distance for a day on the range he needs more space and yet a convenient means of carrying his equipment. If the case finally adopted is of convenient size and one does not need many accessories on any particular occasion it is a simple matter to leave them out and lighten the load. It is well to carry high grade target pistols having adjustable sights and high finish, so that they will not rub and knock against other articles, if we would care for them properly. A holster on a pistol affords some protection and can be carried in the case with less danger of damage to the gun. However, it is very bad practice to leave a gun in a holster because of the latter's tendency to absorb moisture. A better way to arrange one's case is to have racks or pockets made to fit the pistols and keep them in place. The same plan should be followed for other accessories and then they can be readily seen, and taken from their places without disturbing the others. After going through several years of hit and miss methods of carrying equipment the author designed the case which is illustrated herein. It is shown for the purpose of offering suggestions to others in solving the problem. It is of suitcase type and was originally designed for the .22 S. & W. target pistol with 10 inch barrel, the .38 Colt Officers' model revolver with 7½ inch barrel, the .45 Service automatic, a 12 power spotting telescope, a pair of shooting glasses, cleaning materials, and additional space for ammunition, score book, stop watch and one or more smaller revolvers or pistols. It is 10½ inches high, 17¾ inches wide and four inches thick, all outside dimensions. It was made by a trunk maker, is of good leather over a wooden frame, and cost $25.00. It is compact, adequate and convenient to carry and use. Its ca-

Three views of the Author's pistol case, showing the closed case and
each compartment with contents.

pacity can be judged better by studying the cuts. The cost is perhaps higher than most marksmen feel like paying, but the work required in making it and the high grade materials used in its construction make it worth the money it cost. It is advisable to line the case with felt or velvet to protect the guns from scratches. The felt is serviceable but the velvet makes a handsome case. There are many ways of constructing cases and not a few shooters prefer a compact wooden box in which to fit their guns and accessories. These can be made to any size and shape and for any number of guns and while not always as handy to carry or transport as the suitcase type they are quite convenient to use on the range. For pistols of the European type with their large hand grips and long barrels, it is almost necessary to have a special individual carrying case made to hold them. This seemed to be the practice in Europe and shooters attending the matches are frequently seen with these slung across their backs while they carry their accessories in a small bag.

PISTOL CABINETS

For the protection of one's "arsenal" at home, for convenience in inspecting its components and for the sake of having one's equipment where it can be seen, and perhaps admired, it is a good plan to keep it in some form of cabinet where it will be secured against dust, changing atmospheric conditions and molestation. Pistols that are left lying around the house always come to some bad end either through breakage or loss, to say nothing about the trouble they may cause other members of the family by being in the way. Unlike rifles or shotguns, they do not require much space. If one is a shooter of the other weapons and has a cabinet for them he can easily find space in it where a few pistols can be hung or placed. In certain climates it is very difficult to keep guns in proper shape especially as regards their bores and any parts devoid of bluing. I have found it most advantageous to have an electric light fixture on the inside of my cabinet by means of which I can keep the air dry. A cabinet made with space for holding guns, with a few drawers or a small closet in which to keep the balance of one's shooting equipment is one of the most useful and convenient articles a shooter can possess, for it enables him to have a place in which to chuck his stuff when he comes in from the range, a receptacle in which to keep ammunition, spare parts, and the many adjuncts essential to keeping one's pistols in good adjustment. With such a piece of furniture one can be assured of knowing where to find what he wants instead of searching through a dozen drawers, closets or tool chests. The advantage of having all of his equipment in one place is always appreciated most by the marksman when he wants to assemble it preparatory to a visit to the range. A small work bench in conjunction with the cabinet or nearby is also a very useful thing to own, for there are always periods when one must make adjustments, change sights, or perform numerous operations on his pet guns. A small vise with cork jaws in which to hold a pistol for cleaning purposes adds greatly to the convenience of that duty. It goes without saying that a small set of necessary tools should complete the equipment of the work bench.

INCIDENTALS

Among the numerous small things that a pistol shot will find useful is a suitable spotting telescope or binocular with which to observe the location of hits on paper targets. For firing under artificial light on indoor ranges it is customary to have the firing point provided with some form of bracket in which a telescope can be placed or fastened. By means of this the marksman can observe the location of bullet holes in his target without going to the butts or bringing the target back to the firing point. A few years ago on the completion of the construction of an indoor range for one of our large universities it was necessary to select suitable telescopes to complete the equipment. Several kinds were tried out, varying in power from 5 to 33, and after a series of tests to determine which was the most satisfactory for use in artificial light at from 50 to 75 feet we selected one of 12 power which gave the best results for a reasonable expenditure of money. This one was better for the purpose than one of 20 power. Such a scope is also quite suitable for outdoor use at pistol ranges when mounted on a tripod or in some convenient place where it can be used without holding it in the hands. A good pair of eight power binoculars are also satisfactory for this work, but they of course cost considerable more than the small telescope. When using big calibers at the ordinary pistol ranges of fifteen or twenty-five yards it is frequently unnecessary to use a glass to see the holes in the target, as they are of such a size as to be visible to the naked eye, especially if there is a sky background behind them.

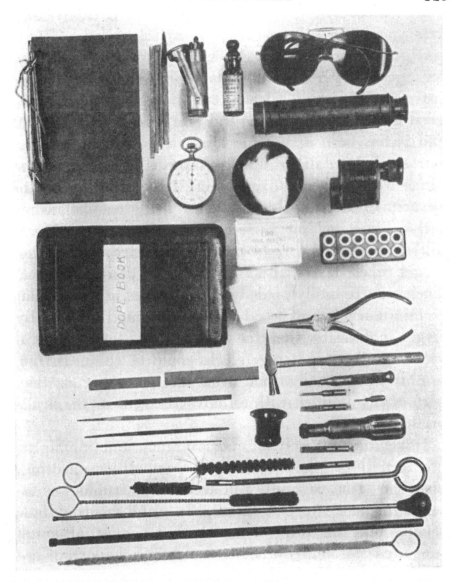

This group of tools and accessories has proven to be very useful and quite essential at times in connection with pistol practice. It consists of: Scorebook, pitch pine sticks, matches, sight black, Riflelite shooting glasses, stop watch, friction tape, cotton, spotting telescope, monocular field glass, Dope book, thumb tacks, cartridge block, canton flannel patches, long pointed pliers, Arkansas oil stones, files, jeweler's hammer and magnifying glass, assorted screwdrivers, cleaning rods and brushes.

For those pistolmen who believe in rapid and timed firing, a stop watch is a desirable article to have. This need not be of the very expensive kind but one with a nickel case of the kind used by track coaches for timing foot races is suitable I have one, purchased in an army goods store just after the war, for which I paid $8.00 and it has been in use for nine years without repairs. For small bore deliberate fire, especially on an indoor range with darkened firing point, it is advantageous to use a small cartridge block. When firing ten-shot scores such a block, holding the required number of cartridges will often save one from putting an extra shot on the target when it is neither needed nor desired. These blocks can be easily made by boring holes in a small flat rectangular piece of wood with a brace and bit slightly larger in diameter than the caliber of the shell. Several years ago these cartridge blocks could be obtained from several of the ammunition firms for the asking, as they were neatly painted with an advertisement of the firm's products.

Depending entirely on perseverance and intelligent practice, those who specialize in competition shooting, sooner or later, certainly will accumulate trophies as rewards for their efforts and skill. In pistol shooting these usually take the form of medals and badges, although cups are occasionally offered for the more important national events. The athlete usually decorates the mantelpiece or some other prominent piece of furniture with his cups or similar trophies, but the shooter as a rule tosses his medals in a cigar box or other receptacle and forgets them until he wants to exhibit a particular one to a friend. Then he has to comb the house to locate it, and is lucky if he finds it at all. A number of years ago a friend of mine on the Seattle Revolver Club designed a neat cabinet for his medals and after inspecting it, during an evening visit to his home, I followed his example

The Author's cabinet for medals showing the top raised. It is hung from a picture molding.

and had one made to preserve my limited collection. It has proved to be most useful and also a constant and pleasant reminder of the days when I was most active in the sport and not in the class of the "has beens." The only advice I have to offer in regard to this accessory is that one should not be too modest when making his first display cabinet, for it is surprising how rapidly medals accumulate once one gets into competition in earnest. The cabinet can be finished to match the furniture of the particular room or den in which it is to be hung and should be lined with a harmonious colored felt or velvet cloth. Dark green is an excellent color for the lining, and makes a good background for medals.

As theory and practice both play important rôles in any art or science the student of pistol shooting should not be content to learn by practice alone. He will wish to round out his experience and further his education by taking advantage of the knowledge of others as found in printed publications. Books, pamphlets, and articles such as may be found in the better sporting and firearms magazines should be studied with the idea of sifting out the good points and ignoring the impractical. A reference library on the subject is therefore believed to be quite an important accessory to the game. The literature on the subject is comparatively limited and most of the books on it cover the field in a general, rather than specific manner, many of them being devoted to the material rather than the technique of shooting. The author has derived much pleasure and benefit from the volumes and pamphlets in the following list, which includes a variety of information, and from many short articles in magazines which are of course too numerous to mention. If any of these books cannot be obtained from the usual sources they may be found in the library of older pistol enthusiasts. They are listed in the order of their issue, the date of the first copyright being 1901.

The Art of Revolver Shooting, Walter Winans.

Firearms in American History, Charles Winthrop Sawyer.

Pistol and Revolver Shooting, A. L. A. Himmelwright.

The Long Shooters, Wm. Brent Altsheler.

The Book of the Pistol, Capt. Hugh B. C. Pollard.

Pistols and Revolvers, Maj. J. S. Hatcher.

Pamphlets

Instructions in Learning Accurate Pistol Shooting, Gunnery Sgt. J. M. Thomas.

Pistol and Revolver Training Course, Col. A. J. MacNab.

Training Regulations No. 150–20 & 320–15, War Department.

The last item I will mention is one that has proved not only useful to me but of great interest as well, and it will increase in interest with time. It is what I term my "Dope Book." This is a loose leaf volume of convenient size in which a record is kept of items of interest concerning my pistols, guns and shooting. It is not a scorebook as we know such articles but is more of a book of useful information. It contains reminder lists of things to be assembled for a trip to the range, so they may be quickly gathered up and none omitted. There are found the results of tests, notes on observations made of celebrated shots in important competitions, and all manner of data concerning arms and accessories. The future may demand a knowledge of the number, date and place of the purchase of a pistol or one may wish a ready reference as to the weight of a gun, the approximate number of rounds it has fired, the sight settings for different ranges and loads, and many other details, concerning similar data. A comprehensive dope book on pistols and pistol shooting will be found to be not only valuable for reference but, to the student of the game, it affords a most interesting pastime to maintain.

Chapter XXIV

A FEW DON'TS

Don't think that you must possess unusual natural talents to make a success of pistol shooting. Any person of average physique and intelligence can learn to shoot a pistol well.

Don't begin pistol practice until you know what to do and how to go about doing it. Learn these fundamentals from a good instructor or text on pistol shooting. Unintelligent practice is of little value.

Don't expect too much at first. It takes time to train the mind, nerves and muscles. Patience and perseverance are important factors in one's progress.

Don't do too much firing. A little is better than a lot.

Don't neglect "dry shooting." Shooting exercises, especially trigger-squeeze and rapid fire, are very essential at all times.

Don't neglect details. Many a match has been lost by one point.

Don't get into a rut. Practice rapid as well as slow fire.

Don't be a potterer. "He who hesitates (to shoot) is lost."

Don't indulge in snap-shooting while training for standard target competitions.

Don't be a fair-weather shot, or a lone-shooter.

Shoulder to shoulder competitions are the life of the sport.

Don't change pistols just prior to or during a match.

Don't shoot on the wrong target. This mistake cost a world championship in 1924.

Don't point pistols at persons—unless you intend to shoot them.

Don't fail to "Hold 'em, squeeze 'em and call 'em."